Napoleon's Line Infantry –
From the Battle of Jena
to the Invasion of Iberia

To Vincent Bourgeot and fond memories

Napoleon's Line Infantry – From the Battle of Jena to the Invasion of Iberia

Uniforms and Equipment

Paul L. Dawson

FRONTLINE BOOKS

First published in Great Britain in 2025 by
Frontline Books
An imprint of Pen & Sword Books Limited
Yorkshire – Philadelphia

Copyright © Paul L. Dawson 2025

ISBN 978 1 52678 399 8

The right of Paul L. Dawson to be identified as
Author of this Work has been asserted by him in accordance
with the Copyright, Designs and Patents Act 1988.

A CIP catalogue record for this book is
available from the British Library.

All rights reserved. No part of this book may be reproduced, transmitted, downloaded, decompiled or reverse engineered in any form or by any means, electronic or mechanical including photocopying, recording or by any information storage and retrieval system, without permission from the Publisher in writing. NO AI TRAINING: Without in any way limiting the Author's and Publisher's exclusive rights under copyright, any use of this publication to 'train' generative artificial intelligence (AI) technologies to generate text is expressly prohibited. The Author and Publisher reserve all rights to license uses of this work for generative AI training and development of machine learning language models.

Typeset by Mac Style

The Publisher's authorised representative in the EU for product safety is Authorised Rep Compliance Ltd., Ground Floor, 71 Lower Baggot Street, Dublin D02 P593, Ireland.
www.arccompliance.com

For a complete list of Pen & Sword titles please contact

PEN & SWORD BOOKS LIMITED
47 Church Street, Barnsley, South Yorkshire, S70 2AS, England
E-mail: enquiries@pen-and-sword.co.uk
Website: www.pen-and-sword.co.uk
or
PEN AND SWORD BOOKS
1950 Lawrence Road, Havertown, PA 19083, USA
E-mail: uspen-and-sword@casematepublishers.com
Website: www.penandswordbooks.com

Contents

Acknowledgements		vi
Chapter 1	The Line Infantry	1
Chapter 2	Paying for it All	9
Chapter 3	Making it All	12
Chapter 4	Dress of the Soldier	20
Chapter 5	Grenadiers and *Voltigeurs*	27
Chapter 6	Drums and Trumpets	36
Chapter 7	All Change	48
Chapter 8	Change and Change Again	63
Chapter 9	Regulations in Practice	77
Chapter 10	Conclusions	198
Notes		241
Bibliography		256

Acknowledgements

This book sets out to describe what the various regiments of light infantry, National Guard and support troops wore during the course of the 1ᵉ Empire. The data set used can be found in the archive boxes preserved in the French Army Archives. These sources provide potentially bias-free empirical data – it is based on personal judgement, thus is not error free – from which we can reconstruct the life story of a regiment, its officers and above all its clothing. Empirical data as defined by the Annales School[1] is obtained from records concerned with data capturing in a quantifiable way, which in this study comprises:

- Regimental accounts
- Inspection returns
- Purchase accounts for clothing from the various regimental 'masses' discussed below.

We bolster these records through a critical analysis of period iconography, as well as extant items of clothing and equipment. This approach will leave gaps, and no doubt in the gaps will be some readers most cherished regiments at a certain point in time. The scale of a project to analyse tens of thousands of documents is a task beyond a single person. To that end I am indebted to my friends, who have supported a 20-year obsession.

More than 20 years ago I made my first visit to the Château de Vincennes, the home of the French Army Archives, in the course of 2002. It is a place I have come to know intimately in that time, and the 'holy grail' it keeps within its walls of millions of documents from the 1ᵉ Empire. My two or three annual pilgrimages to 'worship at the shrine of archive research' came to a juddering halt in March 2020. My writing stopped and this book hit 'the buffers'. Yves Martin's unfailing support and friendship with his most generous assistance in the provision of research material and illustrations was invaluable during the Covid 19 lockdown. Without Yves this book would not exist.

I am also indebted to Sally Fairweather. She has accompanied me willingly on my pilgrimage to Paris more than twenty times, and spent hours and hours photographing archives and developing 'Vincennes Back' from standing for hours at a time photographing records. Without her help, friendship and dedication, this book would have taken years longer to write.

Martin Lancaster, Ben Townsend and Robert Cooper must be heartily thanked for their encouragement of this book and my research: their support and critical input to my thinking have kept this projecting progressing for the last seven years. I hope, gentlemen, that the finished thesis lives up to your expectations and the thousands spent on flights, hotels and dedicated patronage of Le Drapeau at Vincennes has been worth it.

The staff at Service Historique de la Défense Armée de Térre in Paris need to be thanked for answering questions and locating items of research that have made this book possible.

Paris, 5 May 2025

George David, grenadier of the 4th battalion 61ᵉ de la Ligne. This dated portrait shows a grenadier in society dress. He has silvered shoe buckles, and wears his regulation pantalons less gaiters. We see by the middle years of the empire how short cut the veste was under the habit. The habit has no cuff flaps: these officially were not re-introduced till Bardin in 1813. His bearskin has no plate, but carries a grenade device.

Chapter 1

The Line Infantry

During the peace of Amiens, Napoleon had time to rebuild the French army in the form he envisioned for it.

The line infantry that Napoleon inherited upon becoming Consul had been established on 1 January 1791 when regimental titles and the infantry were reorganised into 104 line regiments and 12 *chasseur* battalions that were ostensibly light infantry. Each battalion was composed of eight companies of fusiliers and one of grenadiers; each comprised one captain, one lieutenant, one *sous-lieutenant*, one sergeant major, two sergeants, one *fourrier* – company clerk ranking midway between corporal and sergeant – four corporals, four chosen men (termed *appointes*, they were men selected for aptitude and potential to be NCO's), one drummer and 40 grenadiers or fusiliers. A few months later, on 22 July 1791, the formation of 185 battalions of *Gardes Nationaux Voluntaries* was ordered.

The next major change occurred with the decree of 21 February 1793 when *demi-brigade de bataille* were formed. In order to combine the discipline of the old regulars with the revolutionary zeal of volunteers, one regular infantry battalion and two volunteer battalions were formed into *demi-brigades de bataille*. A grenadier company comprised one captain, one lieutenant, one *sous-lieutenant*, one sergeant major, two sergeants, one *fourrier* four corporals, four chosen men, 48 grenadiers and two drummers. Fusilier companies had an additional one sergeant, two corporals, two chosen men and 19 fusiliers. On 22 November 1793 grenadier companies were made the same strength as fusilier companies, each company now mustering 104 men. The rank of chosen man was removed. These two decrees were not enacted until 8 January 1794. Each battalion comprised eight companies, one of which was the elite grenadier company. Attached to each *demi-brigade* was a company of artillery manning six 4-pdr field guns. The number of guns was reduced to three in 1795.

Demi-brigades d'infanterie de Ligne were formed in 1796 (by the decree of 1 February) from *demi-brigades de bataille* and these gave a much larger formation. The 238 *demi-brigades de bataille* became 110 *demi-brigade d'infanterie de Ligne*. In a *demi-brigade*, each fusilier company comprised a captain, a lieutenant, a *sous-lieutenant*, one sergeant major, five sergeants, one fourrier, eight corporals, two drummers and 104 fusiliers. A grenadier company differed by the virtue of it having four sergeants and just 64 grenadiers. A *demi-brigade* in theory mustered 96 officers and 3,300 men. Under Bernadotte as minister for war, a comprehensive review of what the soldier wore was carried out during 1798. The resulting regulation of An 7 was the basic building block for what the French army wore until 1812. For details on this regulation see the author's work *Uniforms and Equipment of the French Revolutionary Army*, also available from Frontline.

2 Napoleon's Line Infantry – From the Battle of Jena to the Invasion of Iberia

This Austrian engraving captures the look of the French *Ligne* infantry during the Jena campaign. In the foreground is an officer of fusiliers, behind a grenadier and on the right a fusilier wearing a *chapeau*. Both grenadier and fusilier carry *capotes* strapped on their *havresac*.

On 27 August 1800 demi-brigades were reduced to two war battalions and a third forming the *dépôt*. On 26 October 1801, the First Consul reissued Bernadotte's An 7 regulation. In doing so, Bonaparte had realised Bernadotte's reforms had not been fully implemented and with peace sought to bring some semblance of order to the army now

A coloured rendering of a line engraving showing how the *ligne* infantry looked on campaign. Baggy linen overalls worn over linen gaiters. The scarlet epaulettes mark out a grenadier: since 1791 grenadiers had both a bearskin and *chapeau*, the latter to be worn on campaign.

it was for the first time in nearly a decade on a peacetime footing, and in thorough need of a shake down in organisation. As we noted earlier, a soldier had his uniform issued on a regulated basis. In order to bring some semblance of order to the army after the chaotic revolutionary years, two new regulations were issued in quick succession: October 1801 for equipment, February 1802 for clothing. The decree of 22 February 1802 laid out the dress of the line and light infantry as follows:

Line and Light Infantry.	
Items of clothing or equipment	duration (years)
Cloth *habit*:	2
Cloth *veste*:	2
Tricot *culottes*:	1
Chapeau:	2
White buff leather waist belts or shoulder belts:	20
Giberne:	20
White buff leather *Giberne* belt:	20
Musket sling:	20
Drum and drum carriage:	20
Sapeurs apron:	20

IV. *Sous-officiers* and soldiers will be required to provide *bonnets de police* at their expense.

V. *Sous-officiers* and soldiers will not be able to dispose of the *culottes* from the previous issue until after the end of the year, so that each soldier always has two pairs.

VI. The *habits* and *vestes* that will be replaced in year X will belong to the regiment; the best will be kept for the clothing of the new soldiers, for the guard house, the prison and the discipline room.

VII. *Sous-officiers* and soldiers will be allowed to provide white linen *pantalons* for the summer, while complying with the provisions of the instruction which will be written and addressed to each regiment by the Minister of War.

VIII. The boards of directors will take steps to procure for each ordinary or barrack room, a number of canvas smocks for the men to wear on fatigues.[1]

On 24 September 1803 the *demi-brigades* were re-christened as regiments, and the regimental artillery was done away with until 1809.[2] It reappeared in 1811 and lasted until 1814. In February 1808, each infantry company was reduced to six companies (four fusilier, one *voltigeur*, one grenadier) each of the same strength. The cadre from the disbanded fusilier companies were to form the nucleus of the new third war battalion. Some regiments already had four battalions by this date, and formed a fifth.

A Soldier's Clothing

In theory a French 'squaddie' under the terms of a decree of February 1802, was issued a hat (*chapeau*), undress cap (*bonnets de police*) a coat (*habit*), a short jacket with sleeves (*veste manches*), a pair of breeches (*culottes*), a pair of linen overalls (*pantalons de toile*, also known as *pantalons de route*) and two pairs of gaiters, one pair made from black

The Line Infantry

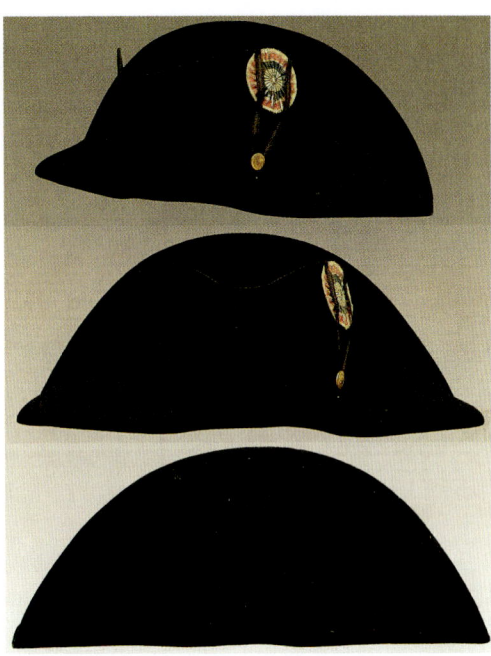

The felt *chapeau* had been the headdress of the French soldiery since the eighteenth century. On campaign, these items quickly deformed, and offered very little head protection. Despite this, it remained the standard headdress of the army until spring 1808.

twill with leather or horn buttons, and a pair made from linen, with horn buttons. In wet weather and on the march, he was issued a top coat (*capote*) and his coat was to be carried in his backpack (*havresac* or *sac de peau*: both terms are used in the period for the same object). He wore at his neck a black stock (*col noir*) with two spare lengths of white piping (*rabats*) and on parade a white stock (*col blanc*). He also had three shirts (*chemise*) and a pair of underwear (*caleçons*) as well as a long pair of woollen stockings and two pairs of linen ankle socks, and last but not least three pairs of shoes. Since 1802 in summer a squaddie could buy at his own expense a white linen waistcoat (*gilet sans manches*)

This soldiers' *habit* accords to the 1799 regulation. The cuff lacks cuff flaps – an innovation primarily of the 1806 regulation. It is characteristic of thousands of items in use during the early part of the Empire. (*Musee de l'Armée*)

6 Napoleon's Line Infantry – From the Battle of Jena to the Invasion of Iberia

Under the *habit*, soldiers wore an underjacket, called a *veste*. This garment, made to the 1810 or 1812 regulations, is broadly similar to the garments worn earlier, except that the collar was much lower, the pockets had flaps and the front had a V notch. *Voltigeurs* had chamois or yellow collars to their vestes, fusiliers blue and grenadiers had scarlet collar and cuffs, at least in theory. (*Private collection Switzerland*)

to be worn in lieu of his broadcloth *veste*, which also provided an extra layer for warmth in the winter. He would also have alongside his *havresac*, ammunition box (*giberne*) and if a member of an elite company his sword (*sabre briquet*) and belt (*baudrier*). Every man had a firearm, even drummers, as well as a bayonet. The bayonet was carried on the *giberne* belt (*porte-giberne*) or for grenadiers and NCOs (*sous-officiers* ranking corporal and above) from the *baudrier*.

As fashion changed during the early nineteenth century, the use of *culottes* began to be gradually abandoned. Pantalons or trousers became increasingly common place. Linen overall trousers for fatigue and marching dress were authorised from 8 December 1802 if

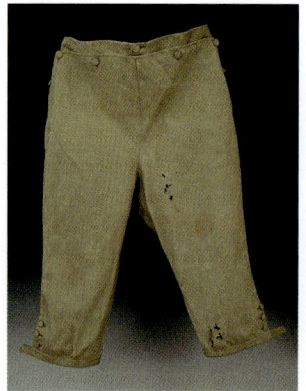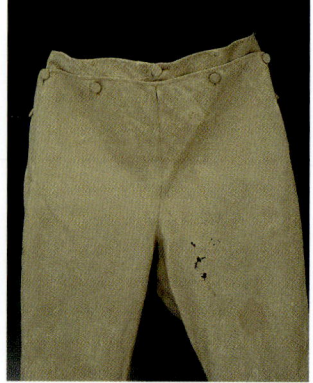

Soldiers wore breeches (*culottes*) made from tricot in most orders of dress. This pair gives a very good idea of how these garments looked. (*Photograph and Collection of Bertrand Malvaux*)

the regiment's funds could afford to have the garments made. They were cut broad/loose and the bottom of the leg was to be hemmed 110mm from ground. They were worn over the linen or black tricot gaiters and in cold weather the *culottes*. These were service, campaign and often combat trousers. They were to be paid for with the abandonment of white parade gaiters allowed for under the An 7 regulations. A circular of 27 September 1803 authorised all regiments destined for the invasion of Britain to have linen *pantalons*.[3]

The tradition of wearing white gaiters on parades was abandoned for the line with the circular of 20 December 1805, the tradition being maintained by the grenadiers and *chasseurs* of the Garde Impériale alone.[4]

Everything Else

The soldier received items of *petit monture*. The *trousse* contained the *petit monture*, which included according to regulations:

Enshrined as part of the 1802 regulations, soldiers were allowed linen overalls (*pantalons*) for use on fatigues, on the march and on campaign.

> Art 8. Objects of clothing and *Petite Monture*
> 189. The objects of *petit Monture* will comprise items for cleaning and carrying out necessary repairs, and will comprise a *trousse*, a brush for cleaning copper, a *vergette* for the *habit* and a shoe brush, needles and a box of grease.
>
> 190. The *trousse* and items of clothing.
> The *trousse* will contain linen thread for sewing, material for mending uniforms, a pair of scissors in a case, needs, an awl, two sets of gaiter foot straps, spare buttons for the gaiters, *habits* and breeches, a spare needle file for the *epinglette*, a piece of leather to protect the leg, two *rabats* for the stock, a button stick, a comb a razor.
>
> 191. *Petit Monture*
> A pay book contained in a white metal case, *giberne* cover in waxed linen, a cover for the *schako* made from oil cloth [funded by the clothing fund at the same time as the *schako*], a musket worm [provided by the magazines of the empire], a screwdriver, a piece of grease, lead to hold the flint, a wooden flint, a bottle of oil for the musket, every corporal will have these objects as well as a spring clamp for his squad.[5]

The case for the pay book appears to have been cylindrical, and carried from a cord. For personal hygiene, the soldier would have some soap, and a linen towel and a comb (*peigne*).

He would be shaved by the company barber twice a week.[6] He also had his canteen (*petit bidon*). This was made from white metal, kidney shaped in plan and regulated to hold a pint. The neck was to be stopped by a cork. It was carried from a leather shoulder strap, 25mm wide, which was adjustable by means of a buckle. By summer 1814 wicker-covered bottles (*bouteilles clisse*) had become the regulation item. A report from autumn 1803 tells us that for immediate needs 6,851 *marmites* were needed, along with 3,352 *gamelles*, 9,721 *grand bidons*, 62,756 *petit bidons* and 33,724 leather *banderoles de petit bidons*.[7] In new year 1807, 32,984 white metal *petit bidons* were issued to replace lost items.[8]

Chapter 2

Paying for it All

The men of the Grande Armée were paid professionals. They were paid, in theory, weekly, according to rank and status. In all cases, the pay was subject to a number of deductions for communal funds (*masses*), which left very little actual pay. The purpose of the pay was actually not to give the soldier pocket money to spend on wine, women and gambling but so he could pay for fines, pay repair bills for his clothing and equipment, purchase soap and cleaning equipment and if needed buy new items of clothing. All of their clothing and equipment was provided by the state out of the man's pay, the *messe générale* or general fund, and all the other items like stocks, shirts, cleaning kit etc from a fund called the 1st Issue (1ᵉ *Messe*). Shoes and equipment, as well as replacement shirts, were provided from additional funds.[1]

The decree of 25 April 1806 established the *masse d'habillement* – literally, clothing fund – and set this fund at 48fr 29 centimes per man per year in the line infantry, and some 49fr 53 centimes for a soldier in a light infantry regiment. From this fund, the regimental Council of Administration drew its necessary funds to buy raw materials, equipment, headdress as well as to pay the regimental workmen. It also covered sundry items such as the epaulettes of the *adjutant-sous-officiers*, lace for rank stripes, service chevrons, musicians and drummers' lace, plumes and pompoms. The fund was to provide a soldier with his full issue of uniform and equipment.[2]

Linen and Shoe Fund

A soldier, in addition to his basic issue, needed more than a single shirt, stock and pair of shoes. This was paid for with more stoppages from his pay being sent to the Linen and Shoe Fund. The fund was paid for at the rate of 12 centimes a day for *sous-officiers* and 7 *centimes* for other ranks. Prior to 25 April 1806 this had allowed for a pair of white parade gaiters. The cost of these was carried over to pay for a pair of linen overalls. Some regiments ignored this, as the accounts of the 84ᵉ *de Ligne* signed off 1 January 1807 reports:[3]

Pairs of Gaiters
70 pairs *de Toile Grise* at 2fr 60 each, total 182fr
479 pairs black twill or broadcloth at 5fr 50 each, total 2,634fr 50
335 pairs white linen gaiters at 3fr 50 each, total 1,172fr 50
330 metres linen 5/4 for gaiters 330fr
112 metres linen 4/4 for linen black gaiters, total 58fr 50
434 metres black twill for gaiters, total 1,294fr 81

It seems colonels were relatively free to 'pick and choose' which aspects of the regulation to which they chose to adhere. The fund also covered the cost of providing a soldier with three shirts, two white stocks, two pairs of cotton or linen socks, one pair of woollen stockings, two pairs of shoes, and a set of four buckles: stock, knee buckles, *culottes* back buckle, shoe buckles, in addition to those issued upon joining their unit.[4] Again, returning to the accounts of the 84ᵉ *de Ligne* we note:[5]

> 60 shirts of 2nd quality, 5fr 50 each, total 3,330fr
> 25 shirts at 3rd quality, at 4fr each, total 100fr
> 273 black stocks at 1fr each, total 2,736fr
> 699 white stocks at 50 centimes, total 349fr
> 292 pairs cotton stocking at 2fr 60 a pair, total 759fr 20
> 12 pairs of linen socks, at 1fr 75 each, total 71fr
> 570 pairs of shoes at 6fr 15, total 3,505fr 50
> 286 pairs of knee buckles, at 50 centimes, total 143fr
> 801 stock buckles at 40 centimes each, total 320fr
> 132 *culotte* waistbelt buckles, at 40 centimes each, total 52fr 80

The records cited here are typical for every regiment in the Army at this period, and all show variation in what was purchased.

The Ordinary

Once the conscript had given over most of his pay to buy his uniform, most of what money the soldier had left was retained by his unit to pay for his daily ration, the 'ordinary' (*Masse Ordinaire*). At the start of the epoch, 14 to 16 men in the same company were grouped into an ordinary, which was not necessarily the same group as the squad. The company captain would appoint a *chef d'ordinaire*, literally a 'chief', who was often a corporal, who was required to be literate and understand the new metric system of weights and measures. Each ordinary possessed a register (the French army adored paperwork. Lots of little men running around with lots of bits of paper, even on campaign, made the army either a bureaucratic nightmare or dream depending on one's viewpoint!). In the register the 'chief' was to record all expenses from the purchase of groceries to laundry expenses. Each man was to contribute the value of one shirt per week to the fund. The chief would write the expenses in the register and sign it, recording the names of the men in the ordinary, and the name of those who accompanied him on his chores. The numerous 'chiefs' were paid by the *caporal-fourrier* (the sergeant major's clerk in essence). Every fifteen days the captain inspected the books to ensure fair play, that the men were not be defrauded out of food and the chef was not spending the money on drink. To ensure food was being purchased, the company sergeant major visited the butchers, grocers and bakers recorded in the register to double check the accuracy of the records, to ensure the records were accurate and to satisfy himself the ordinary was not in debt.

The regulation amount of food was established on 12 March 1806 and stated that each day a soldier was to receive three ounces of bread for thickening the soup; half a pound of meat and vegetables. The fund was set at 17½ centimes a day for each member of the ordinary.[6]

Repairing it all

All repairs were carried out under the auspices of the *caporal-fourrier*. Minor repairs were to be carried out to clothing and equipment by the soldier; for more major repairs, the *caporal-fourrier* took the soldier and his damaged items to the captain clothing officer, who authorised the regimental workmen to undertake the repair. If the repair was judged to be the fault of negligence of the soldier he had to pay for the work or a replacement item from his pay.[7]

The definition of negligence and clothing simply falling to bits because it was badly made was a fine line.

A glimpse of how the process worked comes from the Livret of MAT No. 8101 Jean Spee. Born on 12 June 1791, the son of Theodore Spee and Catherine Vangelez at Meer, he stood 1m 64cm tall and was a clerk by profession, being conscripted on 18 April 1811. He arrived with his unit, the 37ᵉ *de Ligne*, on 10 May 1811 and was placed in 1ᵉ company, 6ᵉ battalion. He passed to 1ᵉ company 2ᵉ battalion on 15 August 1811. He was granted a year's leave on 1 January 1813 and never seen again.[8] His pay book records he was issued:[9]

> 1 *sac de peau*, 2 pairs of shoes, 3 shirts, 1 pair of grey linen gaiters, 1 pair of black twill gaiters, 2 pair of cotton socks, 1 pair of woollen stockings, 1 black stock, 3 white stocks, 1 *sac à distribution*, 2 cockades, 1 set of buckles comprising *culottes* knee and stock buckles, one vent prick and screwdriver and his small kit.

He also received one *habit*, one *veste*, one pair of *culotte en tricot*, one pair of *pantalons de route*, one *schako*, one *bonnet de police*, one *capote*, one *giberne* and belt, and one musket and bayonet. His pay book further records the following costs and items he had to buy from his pay or meagre savings as he had damaged or misplaced his original items:[10]

> 11 May: 1 *sac de peau* 8fr, 1 screwdriver 30 centimes, 1 pair of stockings 1fr 30, 1 pair of shoes 5fr.

> 21 May: 1 vent prick 10 centimes, 1 set of buckles 90 centimes, 1 black stock 40 centimes, 2 white stocks 60 centimes, 1 pair black gaiters 3fr 70, 1 pair grey gaiters 2fr.

> 30 July: 1 pair of shoes 5fr 50, 1 pair of shoes 5fr 55.
> 15 September: 1 pair of shoes, 5fr 50, 1 *sac à distribution* 5fr 75

Either he was extremely careless in looking after his kit, or on arriving with his unit he had to buy items he had not been issued to make up for shortcomings at the *dépôt*. After being reported in Magdeburg in January 1812, Spee drops out of history.[11] What the pay book does show is that it was extremely difficult to not have to pay for the privilege of being in the army.

Chapter 3

Making it All

Providing the kit and paying for it was just one aspect of the functions of the regimental *dépôt*. It was here that the bulk of the clothing was made. Clothing was issued on a regulated basis, and each item had a specified duration period. A *habit* had to last two years, for example. Every year a regiment would be inspected on 1 October, and the condition of the clothing assessed. A return of all the clothing to be struck off/disposed of was made, and the appropriate number of new items ordered. Clothing and equipment needing repairs was also logged, as was how many items had been repaired since the last inspection. From this data, the clothing officer was able to report the total number of items needing to be replaced or repaired. Every year a third of the regiment's cloth work was replaced, so every 36 months a soldier received a new *habit*. It was very much 'make do and mend' by the time the cloth items of equipment were coming to the end of their service life.[1]

The regiment's clothing and equipment was overseen by the unit's clothing officer and he had to oversee the purchase of all items of equipment and clothing for the *sous-officiers* and men. He was a member of the regiment's Administrative Council that ran the unit. Officers provided their own uniforms and equipment. The clothing officer also had to ensure that all regimental property held in the regimental magazines at the *dépôt* were in good condition and all accounted for. The clothing and equipment of men in hospital was also the responsibility of the clothing officer, who had to ensure it was stored in good condition while the soldier was hospitalised. Each company commander had to keep a report of the items of clothing and equipment issued to their company, and note what items needed repairing, what was beyond use, and what items were new. These reports were submitted to the clothing officer, who then collated the information. The magazines and regiment were to be inspected every year by a Commissioner for War to ensure that the paperwork of the regiment matched reality, and to agree to the disposal of worn-out clothing and equipment.[2]

Clothing was made in two ways: in regimental workshops or via direct purchase. Each regiment had up to six master workmen. Their workshops were located in the regimental *dépôt*. Each workman would take on at least two of the regiment's children as apprentices. The workmen included:[3]

> Master tailor. He ranked as a sergeant and was responsible for manufacturing uniforms for his regiment, as well as making repairs to the uniforms.
> Master cordwainer. This shoe maker ranked as a corporal and was responsible for manufacture and repair of shoes and boots.

Master gaiter-maker. The gaiters of a regiment had prior to 9 September 1799 been made by the master tailor; after that date the duties were passed to the gaiter-maker.

The master workmen ran their own workshops: by and large from 1812 the contracts for work were 'put out' as 'piece work' to the seamstresses, cobblers, leather cutters and other artisans around the *dépôt*, and their work overseen directly by the master craftsmen because the workshop staff simply lacked the capacity to reclothe the army. Workshop staff tended to come from the lame, the old and crippled of the '*compagnies des hors rang*'. Regimental children were often apprenticed to the master workmen, and we find children as young as four at work.

Uniforms came in three standard sizes. This standardisation in size made production far easier logistically. The regiment bought materials locally, as cheaply as possible, seldom with recourse to army standards, out of necessity. In most cases the master tailor would cut material out for the required number of *habits, gilets, pantalons* etc and then would engage x number of people who came in to the *dépôt* to collect 'kits' to sew into garments at home. They then handed the finished items back to the master craftsmen and only when the contract was completed and items approved as being of acceptable quality were they paid, roughly three months later. These 'kits' appear very frequently in regimental records. We know external tailors, seamstresses and cobblers were used out of necessity on campaign, particularly in Spain, Germany between Essling and Wagram, and in 1813 for the men who were billeted in Prussia and had survived the Russian campaign. The survivors of the campaign were issued funds from their regiments, in real terms promissory notes of credit that were never paid, to get their new kit made up where they were living, using whatever kit they had with them that had survived the campaign as examples to copy. Due to demand, it was often the case that the regiment would employ a subcontractor to make *gibernes, schakos* and shoes as well as uniform items from specialist firms whose trade was to supply the armed forces. These companies operated out of large factories in urban centres like Metz, Strasbourg and Paris. The worker force stitched up 'kits' in the warehouses on a set wage per week or again piece work. In all cases, to standardise clothing and equipment, rather than relying on the written word, one of the innovations of the 1799 regulations was that the War Ministry issued sealed patterns or *effects de modèle* for each item of equipment that was the established model to be copied.[4]

The army used two types of wool cloth:

Broadcloth – a dense plain-woven woollen fabric.
Twill – woven with a pattern of diagonal parallel ribs. This included serge (cadis) and tricot.

The defining characteristic of broadcloth is not its finished width, but the fact that it was woven much wider (typically 50–75 per cent wider than its finished width) and then heavily milled (traditionally the cloth was worked by heavy wooden trip hammers in hot soapy water in order to shrink it) in order to reduce it to the required width. The effect of the milling process is to draw the yarns much closer together than could be achieved in the loom and allow the individual fibres of the wool to bind together in a felting process. This results in a dense, blind, face cloth with a stiff drape that is highly weather resistant, hard wearing and capable of taking a cut edge without the need to be hemmed.[5]

Based on the examination of original *habits* in museums and private collections, we know that these garments required different grades of broadcloth:

1. Body cloth of approx. 560gsm in 1800 reducing to 450gsm by 1812
2. Body cloth of approx. 250gsm for lining and piping
3. Facing cloth for collar of approx. 560gsm reducing to 450gsm by 1808
4. Facing cloth of approx. 200gsm for cuffs
5. Serge to face tails and line the tails and upper body
6. Heavy linen to provide button stands, centre back and interlining the collar. This cloth was also used to reinforce the leadingn edg of the coat.
7. A lightweight linen for pockets

The French War Ministry laid down clear regulations on cloth colour and cloth quality. This was introduced 23 September 1807. Each mill/cloth supplier had to provide to the War Ministry a length of cloth 1 aunes (119cm) wide by 19 aunes (20m) for the cloth quality to be checked and the quality of the dyed colour to be checked over the entire length of the fabric, before the War Ministry would order the cloth. The War Ministry had a list of approved contractors and set prices for cloth type and colour. This was adhered to throughout the Empire. The colours of uniforms were confirmed again with the Bardin regulations of 1812. Some colours were obtained by mixes, notably beige, which was made from brown and white fibres; iron grey from blue and white fibres. Napoleon's famous greatcoat is not grey; it is actually a very fine-quality beige.[6]

Beige in 1810 was not natural wool colour, and came in either grey or brown hues. The shade of the cloth varied as the degree of brown probably varied according to where the cloth was made, and how carefully they selected and sorted their wools. The cloth was made from a mix of natural fleece fibres, and black fibres. The cloth regulations specify the amount of black-dyed fibre for a given quantity of undyed/natural wool. It doesn't specify the amount of brown that was allowed in the quantity of natural fleece. In an area with more improved sheep there would be less brown, thus the cloth would be grey beige, and in an area where they sorted it more there would be less too, hence the contemporary comments on the differences in shade. In areas of unimproved sheep, the natural fleeces would contain a higher proportion or brown and red fleeces, thus the resulting cloth would be of a browner hue. White cloth was obtained by weaving fabric from natural fleeces, or by bleaching the woven cloth. Bleached white broadcloth was reserved for the Garde Impériale, the *ligne* was allowed only ecru or natural fleece-colour white cloth.[7]

Checking cloth quality was the role of the Inspectors of Review and War Commissioners. Colour could vary between batches of dye and mills, but overall, the colour of cloth was very well regulated. With blue cloth and scarlet, the colours dyed in say 1811 are the same in 2023 less dirt. Quality of finish of the cloth, and the selection of wool fibres, and the way in which the cloth was dyed, all affect colour. Therefore, we have a lot of factors to consider when trying to recreate the colours of the period. The colour blue was created by the length of time the cloth or yarn was in the vat and how old the vat of dye was. But the shade of blue an item is now is pretty much the colour it was when new. The majority of the blue colours were indigo derived. At the start of the Imperial period, indigo was the dye of choice. However, from 1808 woad (pastel in French) was mixed with a percentage of indigo, of a ratio of 256g of indigo to 100kg of woad, to provide a cheaper blue dye. Woad contains indigotin, but at a weaker concentration compared to indigo obtained from those plants in the genus *Indigofera*. In Napoleonic France woad was primarily grown around Albi, Turin and Florence, and the dye was sold at 18 to 20fr per kg under a set tariff introduced in 1791. The cost of obtaining indigo dye is why the French army became dressed in undyed cloth uniforms for a period in 1806 and 1807. For red colours, Cochenille, Kermes and Galle were used, while for yellows, gaude wood and sumac fustet. A dye book printed in 1811 says that the rose colour for facings was obtained by mixing sumac fustet and cochenille to make Rose, capucine and aurore.

Cloth was coloured in two ways:

1. In the thread.
2. In the piece.

For high-quality cloth used by the middle and upper classes, generals and the Old Guard, the yarn was dyed to the required colour before the cloth was woven. Cloth woven with dyed thread had a longer production time. This method of production produced a much stronger and more consistent shade through the cloth. It was noticeably far costlier than cloth dyed in the piece, as the clothier had to buy the cloth ready dyed in far longer lengths than the cloth dyed once woven. It was and is easier to buy 1,000m of plain cloth and dye 10m blue, and the rest another colour, than having to buy 1,000m of dyed cloth and only needing 10m initially in the chosen colour. The yarn used in this high-grade fabric contained a percentage of imported Spanish merino wool, mixed with high-quality, French-produced yarn. This high-grade cloth was produced in the Elbeuf region. Dyeing the yarn before weaving gave a better quality of colour, but it meant that a mill had to produce minimum quantities of cloths of different colours.[8]

For the lower classes and the soldiers of the line, the cloth was dyed once it was made. This cloth is known as dyed in the piece. The wool would be made at a mill, and the resulting 'white cloth' sold on to a dye works for the cloth to be dyed. This meant that a clothier could readily supply large lengths of cloth of different colours, and could produce a cheaper product as the looms produced a natural cloth, using yarn that was not as well sorted or selected as the higher-grade fabric. This coarser fabric was known as *Drap de Lodeve*, and was it seems the 'bog standard' army cloth. The better-quality yarn and finish on the cloth would also reflect the way in which the dye was taken up into the yarn fibres, so the same dye on a high-grade superfine would look different to the same dye on a much lower-grade and coarser fabric.[9]

Issuing Kit

In the ideal world, once a conscript had joined his regiment, he was measured by the master tailor and the closest 'off the peg' garment would be fitted to him. In time of war, this was not possible, and conscripts got what they were given. A War Ministry circular dated 18 March 1811 tells us that 'Johnny raw recruit' received nothing new:

> 15. Our directing minister is responsible for providing the initial uniform as well as grand and petit equipment for conscripts.
>
> Consequently, when a levee is ordered, he will immediately make the appropriate arrangements so that the regiments receive the materials and the funds necessary for the production and the purchase of all the effects which compose the clothing and equipment of the new levee so that conscripts can be dressed and equipped from head to toe upon their arrival at the *dépôt*.

For this purpose, each conscript will be allocated:

> 16. He will use the effects of grand equipment that the regiment may have available, and the directing minister will only supply those necessary items to complete the clothing and equipment of conscripts in each regiment.
>
> He authorises that the regiments will only deliver new clothing to those conscripts who appear capable of maintaining it, and to give to former soldiers who are used to maintaining the clothing and equipment and of a good behaviour, those new items intended for the conscripts who would not be in condition to look after the items.
>
> The corps will provide, at the end of each year, to our directing minister, a general account of the receipts and expenses which they will have made, for the clothing and the equipment of the men of new levee.[10]

Thus, conscripts in essence were issued the old and battered items of kit in the *dépôt* and their allocated brand-new clothing was given to existing men with a proven track record of caring for kit, and one who had also learned the habit of 'staying alive' on campaign. It takes time for a soldier to learn to care for their kit, so it made perfect sense to foster on to the 'newbies' the kit scheduled to be binned for them to learn to look after, and once they were shown as capable of looking after their kit, and survived, they would get new kit issued. We wonder how many 'veterans' forced their old worn-out clothing on new 'wet behind the ears' conscripts! The decree also gave official sanction for using up all the hundreds of items lodged in regimental *dépôts* and government stores before any newly made kit was issued. The Administrative Council also had to quality control the materials that had been purchased. Regimental inspection returns are a fantastic resource for outlining what a regiment actually wore rather than the theory based on the regulations, and the quality of clothing produced. Regimental inspections comment on the clothing worn on the day of the review. Reading the various reviews, we get the feeling that the three sizes of army clothing tended not to actually fit the men and that for cost effectiveness cheap substandard materials had been used to make the 'one size does not fit all' uniforms.

As well as defective tailoring, regiments faced the problems of defective materials being supplied by unscrupulous cloth merchants. For example, when the cloth recently purchased for the 3ᵉ *Régiment Artillerie à Pied* by the *sous-inspecteur aux revues* and the *local commissaire de guerre* on 13 January 1807, they refused to accept 73 bundles of tricot, dispatched from Tours, as it was of too low a quality for use by the army.[11] Similarly, for the 3ᵉ, 4ᵉ, 5ᵉ and 13ᵉ battalions of equipment train, based in Toulouse, between 20 to 27 April 1811 refused 80 per cent of the cloth sent to the battalions to equip the conscripts of 1811. The 3ᵉ battalion refused to accept 205m of *bleu celeste* tricot and 24m of imperial blue tricot, which was the battalion's total cloth allocation. Generally, the textiles were refused because they did not correspond to the samples sent. The reason given by the 3ᵉ battalion for rejecting the cloth was that it was badly dyed and the cloth was simply not strong enough: indeed, the report of the examination of the fabric by the 3ᵉ battalion stipulates, '20 April 1811, that the fabric was stretched at stakes in order to obtain its required length and stretched again, lengthening it beyond all reason'. It was discovered that only the warp resisted whereas the weft of the cloth was broken. In response, the War Ministry on 29 April 1811 rejected all cloth supplied by Jouradan Captier & Co. and they were no longer permitted to be an army supplier.[12]

It is also undeniable that most military suppliers were somewhat corrupt, or at least chased a healthy profit. When the 3ᵉ *de Ligne* was disbanded in November 1815, it had fraud cases on its accounts since 1805. The data gives us a good idea of the number of items needed by a regiment and the huge strain placed on the regiment's budget by unscrupulous contractors:[13]

Year	Month and Day	Item	Amount	Contracted price	Delivery price	Difference	Total cost increase
1805	20 November	Scarlet broadcloth	100m	14fr 75	15fr	.25	25fr
1806	25 September	Lace for chevrons	36m 20	60c	90c	30c	10fr 86
1807	18 September	White broadcloth	15m 50	9fr 25	9fr 48	23c	3fr 63
	18 October	White serge	437m 36	1fr 30	1fr 62	32c	139fr 95
	19 November	Lace in wool	81m 23	1fr 60	1fr 70	10c	38fr 22
		Scarlet broadcloth	3m	14fr 75	14fr 80	05c	145fr
	26 December	*Chapeaux*	8	4fr 80	12fr	7fr 20	57fr 60
	30 December	Scarlet broadcloth	5m 95	14fr 75	16fr 09	1fr 34	7fr 97
1808	12 March	Scarlet broadcloth	3m	17fr 58	18fr 50	92c	2fr 76
		Scarlet broadcloth	7m 75	17fr 48	18fr	42c	2fr 41

Year	Month and Day	Item	Amount	Contracted price	Delivery price	Difference	Total cost increase
	20 March	Musket slings	602	1fr	1fr 20	20c	120fr 40
		Schakos	322	10fr 25	12fr 50	2fr 25	724fr 50
		Schakos	360	10fr 25	11fr	74c	270fr
		Chapeaux	1	5fr	22fr 50	17fr 50	17fr 50
		Grenadiers' pompoms	160	1fr	1fr 50	50c	80fr
	19 April	Drums, carriages, slings and aprons	8	48fr 35	60fr 74	12fr 39	99fr 12
	24 April	*Schakos*	25	10fr 25	11fr	75c	18fr 75
	29 April	Chamois broadcloth	2m 17	10fr 64	12fr	1fr 36	2fr 95
	25 June	Scarlet broadcloth	2m 75	17fr 58	21fr 50	3fr 92	10fr 78
	18 July	Scarlet broadcloth	1m 35	17fr 58	23fr 60	6fr 02	8fr 12
		Linen for lining	19m 57	1fr 35	1fr 55	20c	3fr 97
	27 July	Drummers' aprons	15	2fr 60	5fr 55	2fr 95	44fr 25
		Drumsticks	9	2fr 60	8fr 32		74fr 88
	30 July	*Sapeurs'* axes	5	27fr 08	55fr 50	28fr 42	142fr 10
		Axe cases	4	6fr 25	27fr 75	21fr 50	86fr
		Sapeurs' baudriers	4	4fr 40	8fr 01	3fr 61	14fr 44
		Sapeurs' aprons	4	4fr	17fr 26	13fr 26	53fr 04
		Sapeurs' gauntlets	4 pairs	3fr	7fr 40	4fr 40	17fr 60
		Lace for corporals' stripes	27m	60c	80c	20c	5fr 40
		Voltigeurs' houpettes	52	60c	1fr 38	78c	40fr 36
	23 September	Scarlet broadcloth	1m 02	17fr 58	27fr	9fr 42	9fr 50
	27 September	Blue broadcloth	1m 53	11fr 60	13fr 61	2fr 01	3fr 07
		White serge	3fr 06	1fr 25	3fr 02	1fr 97	5fr 04
	28 October	Adjutants' epaulettes	6	25fr	30fr 31	5fr 21	31fr 26
		Scarlet broadcloth	1	17fr 58	18fr 50	92c	92c
1809	21 January	Scarlet broadcloth	2fr 4	17fr 58	19fr	1fr 19	2fr 66
	23 January	White serge	14	1fr 40	1fr 85	45c	6fr 30
	25 January	Lace for service chevrons	115m 48	60c	1fr 20	60c	69fr 23
	1 March	Grenadiers' *Schakos*	130	10fr 25	12fr 50	2fr 25	292fr 50
		Grenadiers' pompoms	130	1fr	1fr 50	50c	65fr
		Grenadiers' epaulettes	296 pairs	3fr 50	4fr	50c	148fr
		Voltigeur houpettes	130	60c	1fr 20	60c	78fr
	2 June	White cadis	450m	1fr 40	1fr 50	10c	45fr

Year	Month and Day	Item	Amount	Contracted price	Delivery price	Difference	Total cost increase
	20 June	*Gibernes* and belts	98	9fr 20	12fr	9fr 80	274fr 40
		Schakos	12	10fr 25	13fr	2fr 75	33fr
	24 June	Grenadiers' pompoms	90	1fr	3fr	2fr	180fr
		Voltigeurs' houpettes	85	60c	1fr 33	73c	625fr 05
		Fusiliers' *houpettes*	640	60c	80c	20c	128fr
		Grenadiers' epaulettes	81	3fr 50	7fr 50	4fr	324fr
		Voltigeurs' epaulettes	44	3fr 50	5fr 55	2fr 02	242fr
		Lace for corporal stripes	20m	60c	1fr	40c	8fr
	26 June	*Capotes*	80	24fr 65	27fr	2fr 35	188fr
	28 August	*Gibernes* and belts	130	9fr 20	12fr	2fr 80	364fr
	7 September	Grenadiers' pompoms	60	1fr	2fr 50	1fr 50	90fr
		Voltigeurs' houpettes	60	60c	1fr 83	1fr 23	73fr 80
		Lace for service chevrons	47m 20	60c	1fr	40c	18fr 88
	21 September	*Capotes*	43	24fr 65	27fr	2fr 35	101fr 05
	28 October	Musket slings	80	1fr	1fr 20	20c	16fr
TOTAL							5,003fr 98

What the table shows is the constant year-on-year price increase and that different suppliers all seem to have been adding an additional cost to increase their own profit. The War Ministry helped create this problem: rather than allow market forces to dictate prices, they issued a fix price list of what items were to cost. This offered contractors incentives to 'cut corners' by using lower-grade materials to ensure profits, or to provide goods of different dimensions to regulation; to make 100 *schakos* from the material, which officially would only make 90. We see this 'cutting corners' when we measure original items: most original *schakos* and *gibernes* are all slightly under regulation size. With only a limited number of suppliers providing military goods, being purchased by both the state and individual regiments, it is very easy to see how this competition drove up prices.

All this system did was to drive down quality. With published prices for items, and the same price was set across the Empire, in order to make profits, as we have seen with cloth supply, contractors simply skimped on materials to meet the set price, or as we have seen ramped the prices up at point of delivery.

Chapter 4

Dress of the Soldier

What the soldier wore and when was governed by War Ministry regulations, bolstered by regimental-level standing orders. About the dress of the soldier, the 1808 regulations stated:

Art. 1. The uniform prescribed by the clothing regulations will be exactly observed by the officers, non-commissioned officers and soldiers; and they will comply, in the different circumstances, with the rules of dress detailed below.

The superior officers will be personally responsible for the dress of the officers of the regiment which they command, and those of that of the non-commissioned officers and soldiers of their company.

From the Dress of Sous-officiers and Soldiers.

8. Only grenadiers will wear moustaches. It is forbidden to wax them and put any chemicals or greasy matter in them, the use being unclean and unhealthy.

9. The hair of non-commissioned officers and soldiers will be tied near the head, and tied in a queue, bound with a ribbon of black wool, which will be simply stopped by a pin and without rosette; they hair will be cut short on the head; the side beards will be in the manner called for *'front-guard'*, and should not extend below the depth of the ear lobe; the queue cannot exceed the length of eight pouce, and the ends of the hair cannot exceed the ribbon by more than one pouce.

10. *Sous-officiers* and soldiers will have their *chapeau*, bearskin or *schako* as their headgear, as they are assigned to their particular uniform. The *chapeau* will be placed over the right eyebrow, the front horn placed above the left eyebrow, which will be uncovered the thickness of half an inch; it will be in conformity with the model sent, and no changes can be made to it. The bearskin cap and the *schako* will be placed straight on the head, so that the centre of the peak is above the nose. The *schako* plate and trim will be always cleaned; the bearskin will be well brushed.

11. *Sous-officiers* and soldiers will habitually wear the black stock, conforming to the model which will be prescribed; they will wear the white stock only on days of grand parade: the collar of the shirt will always be covered so it is not seen.

12. *Sous-officiers* and soldiers will always wear the *habit*, *veste* and *culottes* assigned to their regiment. The first two hooks on the chest will always be fastened as will the turnbacks. The sleeves will be pulled low enough so that the cuffs of the shirt cannot be seen. The *veste* will be buttoned in all its length, and well pulled down, so that it fits hips. The *culottes* will be pulled up as far as possible, the waistbelt of

which will be secured above the hips, by means of a buckle; it will be fastened below the knee by the knee buckles.

During the summer, when *sous-officiers* and soldiers are not on duty, they may wear a white linen *veste manches* and *pantalons*; but they should always be fashioned like those cut from broadcloth or tricot.

13. *Sous-officiers* and soldiers will wear the uniform buckles conforming to the model.

14. The *sous-officiers* and soldiers on duty will be in black gaiters; on the march, they will wear gaiters of grey canvas.

15. The *sous-officiers*, grenadiers, drums and musicians will always be armed with their sabres; they will wear it over the shoulder.

16. All parts of the clothing will be beaten and brushed, and kept in the greatest state of cleanliness. The spots of dirt will be removed, either with soap, or with pipe clay, used with very clean water, which will be left to dry naturally, and which will be removed by rubbing the fabric lightly against itself. It is expressly forbidden to wash clothes, this method being detrimental to the preservation of fabrics. To maintain the cleanliness of the clothing, without harming its solidity, when it is in white cloth, we will only use the beater, and as little as possible; the use of any pipe clay or chalk, recognised as caustic and corrosive, is strictly prohibited. The buttons and the buckles, as well as the sabre mounts and the copper fittings, will be cleaned with diluted Spanish white, of which a liquid paste will be formed with which they will be rubbed; and, so that this mixture does not spoil clothes and jackets, we will enshrine the buttons in a piece of wood made on purpose, whose shape is known in regiments, and by means of which, the fabric being covered, the buttons can be rubbed without inconvenience.

17. All parts of the equipment which are in white buff will be bleached; the use of varnish to make them shiny is forbidden. The *gibernes* will be waxed, even on the sides; we will use a boxwood polisher to rub well in the wax.

18. The weapons will be maintained cleanly, inside and outside, without being polished; screws and nuts kept in good condition.

19. The sergeants and the corporals will be responsible, in their section and squad, for the exact observation of what is prescribed above, relative to the behaviour and cleanliness of all the effects of clothing, equipment and armament.

The sergeants will particularly take care that the corporals carefully teach the recruits the means to maintain their effects, and above all to dismantle and reassemble the different parts of their armament.

20. The *sous-officiers* and soldiers will observe, in their marches, the same accuracy in their dress, and the same cleanliness as in garrison.[1]

How the theory was acted upon at battalion and regimental level can only be learned from regimental orders and inspections. For the 1804 to 1805 era, the regimental orders of the 64ᵉ *de Ligne* provide very useful details:

29 October 1804. Divisional marches. The men will wear *petit-tenue*; their *capotes* will be attached to the *havresacs* in a manner of a *port-manteau*. The cooks will wear smocks and not carry arms, but carry their utensils; the pelotons will be formed from the left.

13 January 1805 […] the company chiefs will ensure that the *sous-officiers* and soldiers have their smocks and *capotes*.

31 January. The defaulters that form the work party in town will wear when away from camp their *habit* and *chapeau*, and carry with them their smock and *bonnet de police*.

19 February. For the inspection tomorrow the men will wear *grande tenue*, their *capotes* and smocks will be folded on their *havresac*. The officers will be in *petit tenue* [elsewhere described as blue *frac*, blue *culottes*, épée with white sword knot – ed].

3 March. For the visit to the corps by Marshal Soult the officers will be dressed in *petit-tenue*, *gorget* and *baudrier*, sword knot in gold.

4 March. […] the officers will wear *petit tenue*, the *sous-officiers* and soldiers in grey gaiters and black stocks.

10 March. For the great parade, the officers will wear *grande tenue*, without their *gorgets*, but with the *baudrier* and gold sword knot, they will carry épée.

11 March. The minister remarked that the grenadiers when under arms were wearing gloves. The general of division allowed gloves to be worn when under arms.

17 March […] For the parade the officers will wear *petit tenue* and white linen sword knots. It has been noted some men on guard duty wear large kerchiefs in lieu of the stock. After this date they will wear a stock.

19 March … inspection by the Minister of War … all ranks will be in *grande tenue*, therefore black gaiters and black stocks.

20 March. The captains will take from the magazine for their men the *culottes*, cockades, *epinglettes*, stock buckles, knee buckles and stock buckles. Tomorrow there will be delivered pompoms for *chapeaux* for all companies.

21 March […] for the grand parade the men will wear white stocks and grey gaiters.

1 April. For arms drill the men will be dressed in *grande tenue*, the officers in *petit tenue* with *baudrier*, *gorget*, white sword knot. The *chapeaux* of the *fourriers* will have yellow wool lace, the same as on the sleeve of their *habits* conforming to the clothing of the regiment; no other lace is permitted to be worn on the *chapeau*.

3 April. In the morning for exercise the companies will be dressed in their *vestes* and *capotes*, smocks and *bonnets de police*. There are many *giberne* covers made from linen in use that [sentence cut short. We assume the comment refers to illegal embellishment of the covers rather than their existence – ed], henceforth they will be decorated solely with the regimental number.

9 April. The Marshal notes many *sous-officiers* on guard duty without a musket or *giberne*. This is strictly forbidden.

20 April. Enquire of the master gaiter maker about the progress in the production of white gaiters.

3 May [...] for the drill evolutions, the men will be in *grande tenue*, black gaiters and black stocks will be worn. The officers will wear boots. The drummers, musicians and fifres will carry arms. The drum majors and the band will march in order. The *capotes* of the men will be folded like a *port-manteau* and carried on the *havresac*, and the *havresac* will be worn at such a height as not to encumber the *giberne*. The men will wear the pompom and cockades in the *chapeau*.

17 May. The conscripts that have joined the regiment are to be armed and equipped, the master gaiter maker was to measure the men to ensure the gaiters fitted perfectly. There will be delivered to the conscripts the pompoms of the colour of their company as they are entered into the 3e battalion.

21 May. The men departing from the *dépôt* will carry away with them their arms and *giberne*s. Their *capotes*, smocks, and linen *pantalons* will be retained.

29 and 30 May [...] the *bonnets de police* are to be uniformly rolled [...]

4 June. The escort to the colour will comprise 8 sergeants or corporal-fourriers.

13 June [...] For arms drill the officers and men will be dressed in their regulation clothing, grey gaiters and white stocks.

17 June. The *sous-officiers* and *corporal-fourriers* are henceforth not allowed to wear in their *chapeau* a small *ganse* in gold lace the same as the officers made from bullion. The *sous-officiers* and *corporal-fourriers* will instead wear a wide *ganse* made from gold lace 6 *lignes* wide with a large gilt button of No. 64.

22 June. The body of the drums will be decorated with a large eagle as soon as practicable, the straps use to carry the drum should be made from buff leather.

23 and 24 June. For the colonel's inspection officers and men will be in *petit tenue*, white stocks and grey gaiters.

4 July [...] the men on guard duty in Boulogne will be dressed in *petit tenue*; *capotes*, grey gaiters and white stocks except on Sundays when they will wear *grande tenue*, with black stocks and black gaiters. Once the hour of retreat has been sounded they are allowed to wear their *bonnets de police* and *pantalons*, and are to wear this ordinary dress (*veste manches, pantalons de route, bonnet de police*) until one hour after the *Diane* is called. The same dispositions for the drummers and band.

13 July. Remind the *sous-officiers* and men that the *epinglettes* are to be only worn from the third button on the *revers* on the right-hand side. Inspect the *petit bidons* and camping equipment, especially the *marmites, gamelles, grand bidons*, hatchets, bill hooks, pickaxes and shovels; all except the *grand bidons* are to be in their covers.

20 July. The colonel has observed that several *sous-officiers* are wearing kerchiefs around their neck when under arms. They must wear the stock like the men.

27 July. The officers are to remove the gold-embroidered No. 64 from the tails of the *surtout* as well as the *habit* and replace them with gold-embroidered stars.

1 August […] for divisional exercises, the officers will be in *petit tenue*, with white stock, *gorget*, *baudrier* and white sword knot. The men will wear white stocks and grey gaiters […]²

For undress it is clear from the pages of the order book of the 64ᵉ *de Ligne*, as well as from the order books of the Grenadiers a Pied of the Imperial Guard, that grey gaiters were worn habitually, black gaiters for full-dress parades in exceptional circumstances and white preserved presumably for parades in front of the Emperor only. The 64ᵉ *de Ligne* hardly ever wore its black gaiters, which were clearly kept for best. We know white gaiters did exist at some stage. The grenadiers wore non-regulation white gloves on parade. We wonder if all the grenadiers in the army packed their bearskins away at the start of the campaign? If this is the case, the only bearskins at Austerlitz may have been those of the Garde Impériale. For the period after Austerlitz, the orders of the 3ᵉ *de Ligne* offer some guidance:

29 August 1806 … the regiment will pass in review for an inspection … the regiment will wear black gaiters … the officers will wear white *vestes* and *culottes* and boots with *retroussis* [i.e. jockey-style boots].

17 March 1807. Guard mounting will be tomorrow at half past 11 in the morning; the men will wear their black gaiters and wear their best dress [i.e. full dress. Full dress in the Royal Navy Reserve was known as 'best dress' or 'full blues'. Seemingly, using an affiliation for the term 'full dress' dates back to the Napoleonic era if not before – ed]. At 2 o'clock the regiment will be assembled under arms for inspection; the men will wear black gaiters; the buff work will be whitened, as will the *vestes* and *culottes*.

17 April. The regiment will before the arrival in Stettin be dressed in their best dress. At the halt, the men will adopt their black gaiters, take their *habits* from the *havresac*, roll their *capotes* and place them on their *havresacs*. The grenadiers will wear their bearskins, taken from the regimental waggons.

17 May. In the morning for the grand revue, the men will wear their black gaiters, the company chiefs are to ensure that the men whiten their buff work, *revers*, *vestes* and *culottes* and that their *chapeaux* are brushed […]

23 May. For the inspection tomorrow by the general of brigade, the regiment will wear black gaiters, the ribbons for the men's queues are to be cleaned, as are the *chapeaux*. The men that have cut their hair and their hair in consequence is not long enough to be tied into a queue are to wear a false queue. The straps on the

men's *havresacs* are to be squared away [in the Royal Navy Reserve, squaring away meant making sure things were done neatly, and identically – the reference here is for the straps that held the *capote* to be rolled tightly and not left to hang – ed] and whitened.

3 December [...] For the inspection tomorrow, the regiment will wear black gaiters [...] the companies in white *habits* will whiten their *habits*, *vestes* and culottes; those in blue will whiten their *revers*, *culottes*, *vestes* and linings. The buff work will be whitened and the *gibernes* will be well blackened and cleaned.

24 January 1808 [...] I remark that the gaiters of the grenadiers are too short; they are also badly cut; the gaiters should not stop at the middle of the calf; they need new ones that are much longer.

2 February. The 5th instant at midday, the regiment will be reviewed by Marshal Soult [...] the men will be in their best dress. The regiment marching to the review will wear grey gaiters, and will exchange these for their black gaiters on arriving at Prenzlow. [This has a very reliable ring of truth to it. In the Royal Navy Reserve, we would often carry our white gaiters in our small pack and only wear them once we had arrived at the parade ground to prevent them from getting dirty – it seems the same pragmatism I encountered in the 1990s transcends time! – ed]

22 February [...] the Colonel observes that most of the gaiters are too short, we need to obtain more twill fabric. The gaiters must pass beyond the top of the calf by at least 4 pouces, so that when the soldier is on bended knee it is guaranteed at all times that the *culottes* are not stained or damaged [i.e., the gaiter was to enclose the knee and so that when on bended knee to fire in three ranks the gaiter was in contact with the ground and not the *culottes* – ed].[3]

Clearly, grey gaiters were worn at all other times bar full dress parades, when black were worn. Men since the days of the *ancien régime* were to wear their hair in a queue. We are lucky that we have found references to the way the men dressed their hair. In the 3e *de Ligne* the colonel ordered:

24 January 1808 ... many of the men's queues are too long, they should be no longer than 5 pouces [13.5cm], the knotted portion is 4 pouces [10.8cm] long and commences from the back of the head, it is covered with ribbon so that the extremity is 1 pouce long. The grenadiers are authorised to wear their queue one pouce [27.07mm] longer.[4]

Inspected in 1805, the inspecting officer noted that the officers' hair in the 15^e *de Ligne* was excessively long and was 'clubbed and queued', i.e., turned back on itself and knotted.[5] In comparison, the regimental standing orders of the 64^e *de Ligne* make this comment:

13 February 1805 […] the battalion commanders of the regiment had remarked that many *sous-officiers* and soldiers have cut their long hair. It is reminded that in the regiment the hair is not to be cut close to the head and with an '*avant garde*' in front of the ears.

26 February 1805. The colonel orders that the officers that had had their hair cut '*a la titus*' will purchase a false queue and will wear this until their hair has grown. The same order is to be enforced rigorously among the *sous-officiers* and men of the regiment.[6]

By this we assume the officers and men had the queue and side beards. We don't find any regulation about the men cutting their hair short until 18 May 1809. Potentially this confirmed what was already then currently in vogue.

Chapter 5

Grenadiers and *Voltigeurs*

Prior to 1808, each battalion comprised one company of grenadiers, and eight of fusiliers. The grenadier company were marked out by their height and length of service, recognised with distinctive uniform.

Enshrined as part of the 1801 regulations, grenadiers were allowed to wear bearskin caps and red-fringed epaulettes. These items appear in inspection reports and regimental accounts. We stress, however, that they seldom do appear, which makes us wonder as to how many regiments actually put the decree into action. Colloquially known as the beehive, the most characteristic feature of the uniform of the grenadiers was the tall *bonnet a poil* (literally fur hats).

The 1801 dress regulations stated that the *bonnet* had a leather carcass, which was to be 352mm tall and 231mm wide. The carcass was covered in bear pelt. A leather sweat band adorned the bottom. At the top rear of the bearskin was the back patch, some 162mm in diameter. It was quartered blue and red and decorated with a white lace cross. In full dress the bearskin was adorned with scarlet worsted cords. The knotted portion of the cords was to be 921mm long, the tassels to be 88mm long, and the raquettes to measure 115mm deep by 74mm wide. At the front of the bearskins was a copper plate. The copper plate was to be embossed with the flaming grenade. The plate measured 137mm tall, 205mm wide at the base and 135mm wide in the middle.[1]

To mark out the status of grenadiers under the 1786 regulations, they were issued with red broadcloth shoulder straps piped white – the same shape and form as the straps for fusiliers. Red epaulettes with red fringes were authorised on

Martinet gives us the theoretical full dress of a grenadier. Very few regiments actually possessed bearskins.

Suhr gives us a wide selection of uniforms c.1808. Of interest for us, is the fusilier wearing his *chapeau* and carrying a regulation white metal canteen (*petit bidon*), a *cornet* of *voltigeurs* with chamois *schako* and collar, and a grenadier. For some reason he is wearing full dress but no plume to his bearskin. Regimental orders of the 3ᵉ, 64ᵉ and 75ᵉ *de Ligne* show bearskin cords were never worn without plumes. Presumably this grenadier has lost his.

1 April 1791. Fusiliers continued to wear simple shoulder straps through to the end of the Empire. A pair of grenadiers' epaulettes preserved in the Borodino Museum in Moscow measures 45mm wide across the strap, but by 1810 the strap measures 60mm wide. Grenadier epaulettes became standardised under Bardin. The trademark of the grenadier was their tall bearskin cap, with cords and plume. But as we have seen earlier, bearskins were very rare things indeed if we rely upon period documentation.

Grenadiers were also allowed red worsted lace sword knots. In 1809 the same fund that paid for epaulettes was to pay for the sword knots. The War Ministry noted 'the sword knots are part of the distinctive marks of the grenadiers, by use and tolerance, but not because of any law, decision or regulation: before the revolution they were not worn'.[2]

This contemporary image by Berka gives a good impression of the rear of a grenadier's uniform. The bearskin had a white lace cross, and he had grenades on the tails of his *habit* and *giberne*. The *sapeur* has a very simple uniform. The belt that carries the axe vase carries a Medusa's head, and he had red crossed axe devices on the upper arm. We also see a *voltigeur* in the background with a green-tipped yellow plume, yellow *schako* cords, epaulettes and collar to the habit. On the right is a fusilier. Oddly our *sapeur* has blue, presumably broadcloth, overalls rather than linen.

Voltigeurs

The major change to the uniform of the infantry had been the introduction of *voltigeur* companies with the decrees of 13 March 1804 and 24 September 1804 in regiments of light infantry only. They were allowed yellow epaulettes with yellow fringes and chamois collars to the *habit*, as well as to carry the sabre, to mark them out as elite soldiers.[3] A decree of 16 September 1805 created *voltigeurs* in the line infantry:

Martinet presents this *sapeur* of grenadiers. It bears close comparison to the image by Berka. In this case the army badges are presumably gold embroidery on red backing. The use of the eagle-headed sabre is recorded by just the 100ᵉ *de Ligne*.

Grenadiers and *Voltigeurs* 31

Voltigeur of the 76ᵉ *de Ligne*. We note his hair is worn in the regulation queue, and his moustache is neatly trimmed again, detailed in army regulations. He had regulation green epaulettes. Yellow only became officially sanctioned from 1812.

Officer of *voltigeur* company c.1808.

Officer of *voltigeurs* wearing the undress *surtout* with a yellow collar. Of interest, he has earrings, traditionally a marker of elite soldiers.

Martinet presents a *voltigeur* wearing, potentially, the regulated full dress. He has white *schako* cords – the War Ministry ordered green or yellow abolished in 1807 – green epaulettes, and yellow collar and cuffs. The regulations said nothing about the colour of cuffs, and judging from contemporary iconography, yellow or chamois cuffs were not unusual. We do not know how widespread this phenomenon was, however. The white gaiters are in fact the knee-length, off-white linen campaign gaiters. How common yellow cuffs were, we know not. Because one image shows their use, should not mean every regiment had this distinction.

Officer of *voltigeurs* wearing the undress *surtout* with a chamois collar. Of interest, he has earrings, and moustache traditionally a marker of elite soldiers, as well as black waistbelt. (*Photograph and Collection of Bertrand Malvaux*)

On the report of our Minister of War,
The Council of State heard, decrees:
Art. 1. There will be, in each battalion of line infantry regiments, a company which will bear the name of company of *voltigeurs*.

This company will always be the third of the battalion, counting that of grenadiers; but as the number of companies in the battalion must not be increased, it will replace the second fusilier company, which will be dissolved and distributed among all the others in the battalion.

2. The company of *voltigeurs* will be composed of well-formed, vigorous and nimble men, but of the smallest size. The non-commissioned officers and soldiers admitted to it may not stand more than one metre five hundred and ninety-eight millimetres (or 4 feet 11 inches); officers over one metre six hundred and twenty-five millimetres (5 feet).

3. It will be constantly maintained on a war footing, and composed as follows:
1 Captain,
1 Lieutenant,
1 Second Lieutenant,
1 Sergeant Major,
4 Sergeants,
1 *Fourrier*,
8 Corporals,
104 *Voltigeurs*,
2 instrumentalists
Total: 123.
Instead of drums, this company will have as military instruments, small hunting horns.

4. The officers, *sous-officiers* and soldiers of these companies will be drawn from the regiment, and appointed to their rank, by the colonel, from among those of the height indicated and who will show the most aptitude for the kind of service that the *voltigeurs* must make.

5. The strength of this company will not increase that of the battalion, which will remain composed, in number of men, as fixed by the organisational decree for the year 12; but to keep the battalion in full complement, each company of line infantry, that of grenadiers excepted, will be reduced by fifteen men.

6. The *voltigeurs* will be armed with an infantry sabre and a very light musket, the dragoon model.
Officers and *sous-officiers* will have a *carabine rayé* instead of a musket.

7. The *voltigeurs* will be dressed as line infantry, and they will bear the distinctive marks of their respective bodies; but the collar of their coat and *veste* will be in chamois.

8. The *voltigeurs* being especially intended to be transported quickly by the troops on horse in the places where their presence will be necessary, they will be exerted to go up quickly, and jump on the rump of a horse behind the rider; to descend with lightness, to move quickly and to follow on foot a rider either walking or trotting. They will also be particularly trained to shoot with promptness and great accuracy.

9. The pay of *voltigeur* companies will be the same as that of the grenadier companies.

10. The Ministers of War and of the Public Treasury, and the Minister-Director of War Administration, are each responsible for the execution of this decree.
IN PARIS, IMPERIAL PRINTING.
29 Fructidor year XIII[4]

However, with the bulk of the army en route to Vienna, forming *voltigeur* companies was not going to 'happen overnight'. It was not until 2 January 1806, after Austerlitz, that the War Ministry reminded colonels to complete the formation of *voltigeur* companies with war battalions on active service.[5] It is extremely likely that very few *voltigeurs* were so designated at Austerlitz and none had distinctive clothing. The *légère* is a different matter.

In going back to the decree, not a word was mentioned about epaulettes or special patterns of plumes and pompoms! This was amended some weeks later when *voltigeurs* were allowed to wear epaulettes from 19 September 1805, which were to be green.[6] Colonels who had purchased yellow epaulettes, no doubt to get 'value for money' from the purchase, and yellow items were tolerated until 27 December 1807, when the War Ministry reminded colonels that yellow epaulettes and *schako* cords were forbidden.[7] The circular of 15 December 1811 allowed green epaulettes for *voltigeurs*, to cost 2fr 50 a pair, while grenadiers were allowed 3fr 50.[8] We also note that *voltigeurs* had lost their symbol of being elite soldiers, the *sabre briquet* used by grenadiers, with the decree of 7 October 1807.[9]

A War Ministry circular of 11 January 1809 forbade the use of government money, i.e., the clothing fund and stoppages from the men's pay, to pay for sword knots and epaulettes for *voltigeurs*. Ergo, if colonels wanted them, the officers' corps had to foot the bill. Oddly, *schako* cords were tolerated.[10] We suppose therefore that colonels made sure they got value for money for items in use, and in most cases epaulettes and sword knots were discontinued. The lack of inspection reports prohibits any conclusive study on the widespread use of epaulettes etc for *voltigeurs* from 1809 to 1814. Regulations stated that regimental funds were not to be spent on 'fripperies' for *voltigeurs* such as plumes and epaulettes. However, if a colonel agreed that they were to be paid for by the officers, the War Minister would tolerate this, as long as the cost was no more than one day's pay per officer. As we don't have the personal expenses of officers – who also paid for the uniform of the regimental band and their instruments – it is impossible to say exactly what was or was not used unless these items appear in inspections. This is where iconography can assist in helping to understand the reality behind the archive paperwork. Yet, we must acknowledge that iconographic sources – like soldiers' letters – occupy a place between fiction and autobiographic recording. Under Bardin, chamois epaulettes were tolerated, as our companion volume explored.

Chapter 6

Drums and Trumpets

Sapeurs had existed in the army since the decree of 1786 authorised each company of infantry to have two 'soldier carpenters'. Yet it was not until 1808 that *sapeurs* became universal, in theory, across the army. The regulations of 26 October 1801 refer to equipment for *sapeurs*, notably the apron, axe case and belt. The *Journal Militaire* for 1804 notes that the company *sapeurs* were to be drawn from the senior mess of the grenadier companies in the infantry and dragoons and that they were to be given instruction in the use of engineering tools and issued with axes, aprons, and also ordered to grow beards, but on a narrow remit as the circular states:

> when the troops are on campaign, 8 grenadiers (sic) chosen on a rotating basis will be given axes and aprons and will perform the duties of a *sapeur*.[1]

Clearly, *sapeurs* existed only on campaign at this date and they were not permanent positions within a regiment. Nothing was said about beards.

A War Ministry circular of 29 August 1804 refers to *sapeurs* being authorised to carry a *mousqueton* and bayonet. They were to be equipped with a *giberne* carried on the waistbelt, known as 'a la corse'. It was to measure 123mm long, 41mm wide, 95mm deep and contained two packets each of ten cartridges. Its waist-strap was of white buff leather, 75mm wide and fastened by means of a copper buckle.[2]

According to a return of requirements of weapons destined for column heads, made in June, 1804, some regiments already had their *sapeurs* armed with *mousquetons*, while others requested axes, *mousquetons* and aprons. This return informs us that there were 8 *sapeurs* in the 43ᵉ *de Ligne*, 9 each in the 19ᵉ and 22ᵉ *de Ligne*, 12 in the 10ᵉ and 64ᵉ *de Ligne*, 13 in the 46ᵉ and 87ᵉ *de Ligne*, 14 in the 28ᵉ *de Ligne*, 16 in the 3ᵉ and 19 in the 14ᵉ and 25ᵉ *de Ligne*. No other regiments at this date had *sapeurs*. Where two squads of *sapeurs* existed, each was commanded by a corporal, the whole commanded by a sergeant.[3] Clearly *sapeurs* were not universal at this stage across the army.

In his Order of the Day of 12 July 1804, Marshal Soult required that the axes of the *sapeurs* were to be well tempered and capable of being used.[4] A few days later, on 17 July, he renewed his request, and added that *sapeurs* when under arms should carry their *mousqueton* on their back with bayonet fixed, and the axe on the right shoulder, the cutting edge carried at the front.[5] A further decree of 25 February 1806 instructed that all axes carried by *sapeurs* were to be of the same model, army issue.[6] The decree of 7 April 1806 created four *sapeurs* per battalion, to be created in the grenadier company from the

Very few images from the epoch exist of drummers. One of the few is this coloured rendering of an 1808 engraving of a drummer, noted to be 63ᵉ *de Ligne*. His *habit* appears to have gold lace to collar and around the *revers*. Rather than a bearskin, this grenadier drummer has a *schako*.

Martinet presents this drummer, identified as the 3ᵉ or 100e *de Ligne*. Again, the *habit* is decorated with a very simple gold lace embellishment.

Presented by Vernet in 1816, this drummer, noted to be 8ᵉ *de Ligne*, has red and gold chevron lace embellishment. We note as a fusilier drummer, he has swallows' nests at the shoulder.

most deserving men who could not be promoted to corporal due to illiteracy, making 12 in total commanded by a corporal.[7]

The decree of 18 February 1808 authorised just two *sapeurs* per company and a corporal *sapeur* to command them, attached to the regimental staff.[8] It seems reasonable that, as with bands, the uniform and equipment of *sapeurs* was owned by the regiment's officers: regimental accounts and inspections only report items of interest to the War Ministry, it does not show the fine nuance of expense, particularly the use of non-regimental funds.

The Otto MS for example shows a number of *sapeurs* who do not appear in regimental accounts. We are left to conclude that either Otto is wrong, or that the *sapeurs*' items did exist but were not paid for via official means. We accept the Otto MS largely postdates March 1808 and may show figures after archive documentation ends in March 1808; but the suspicion remains after assessing the archive of the 3ᵉ and 75ᵉ *de Ligne* that men allocated to the head of column had their clothing paid for by the officers and we will remain ignorant of how these men appeared.

Drummers

Drummers were the voice of their regiment. Their calls regulated daily life in barracks and on campaign. Until October 1791 drummers had worn a blue *habit*, decorated with royal livery – seven chevrons on each arm, lace to the button holes, lace to long pockets on the tails and *retroussis*, collar and cuff.[9] The lace was removed in 1791, and thereafter drummers' *habits* were to be blue and the same as other ranks, at least in theory.[10] However, many regiments still had drummers' lace as late as 1804.[11]

In 1808 something was done officially to regulate drummers' uniforms. Soult complained to the Minister of War on 30 May that:

> On receiving the letter that Your Excellency did me the honour of to write to me on the 18th of this month, I hastened to make known to the regiments of the corps d'Armée that the distinction of the grenade was reserved exclusively for the grenadiers, and that the *voltigeurs* could only wear for distinction a hunting horn on their *habits*. MM. the colonels were also ordered to conform immediately to this decision. Your Excellency, the reason given for this abuse was that this had been done in most of the French army's regiments, since the formation of the *voltigeurs*, and the use of these distinctions has somehow legitimised their use. They will be removed so long as there is no contrary decision.
>
> But there are still several abuses which deserve the attention of the Government from the inconveniences which they entail and very often by the excessive expenditure which they occasion. All regimental colonels, whether cavalry or infantry, think themselves authorised by custom to arbitrarily change the uniform of the drummers, trumpeters, and musicians. There are some who, taking as their rule only their fancy, pass successively from one shade to another, and from a strange form to a ridiculous one. The same reproaches take place with regard to the headdress of the officers, often of that of the troop, and particularly for the plumes, pompons, &c.
>
> The damage is done when the generals perceive it and it is not always possible to remedy it; besides, as this abuse has always reigned, there are chiefs who have thought that it was in some way tolerated.
>
> It is probably useless for me to dwell on the inconveniences which result from it. Your Excellency understands them, and it is sufficient for me to make the observation of it so that it is deemed necessary to take orders from His Majesty on this subject. I have the honour to request it to accept the sentiments of my highest consideration.
> Marshal Soult.[12]

Drums and Trumpets 41

Suhr presents this trio of drummers. The central figure could be a drummer or equally a musician. The unit designation is not known. The *chasseur*-style plume and grenadier epaulettes are an unusual combination.

In reply on 11 June 1808 the Emperor authorised that drummers' *habits* were to be adorned with lace 27mm wide (1 pouce) disposed as per the 1786 regulation. The lace was to be of the pattern – which based on extant items was a close approximation of the 1786 livery – and only the regimental button would indicate the regiment. No distinctive facings were to be tolerated.[13] This reprimand from the Emperor, in theory at least, abolished distinctive colours and facings for drummers and trumpeters. We also need to note that since 29 August 1804 drummers and volitguer cornets once these companies were created, were issued a giberne a la corse worn on a waistbelt. This decree issued drummers, musicians, cornets and sapeurs with a mousqueton, bayonet and giberne a la corse. Thise giberne is never shown in contemporary records. We therefore wonder if these men instead were issues a standard infantry giberne?

Fifer

Fifers, or in French *fifre*, were a throwback to the armies of the eighteenth century; to the days when company drummers were accompanied by either clarinet or *fifre* players before regimental bands were formed. Fifers tended to be drawn from the regiment's children aged a minimum of 14, and accompanied their regiment on campaign. The *fifre* was made from wood and had a range of two octaves. It was carried in a fife case – a brass tube – fixed to a *baudrier*, described in the manual of infantry. Fifers were extremely rare in the French Army, leaving archive traces in the 12^e,[14] 17^{e}[15], 23^e,[16] and 64^e *de Ligne*, the regimental standing orders of which make this comment:

> 21 December 1804. There will be created 18 fifers in the regiment.
>
> 13 March 1805 … two fifers will henceforth rank as corporals in the regiment, in consequence they will wear the stripes of a corporal.
>
> 21 March. In the morning there will be delivered to the drummers and musicians their *gibernes* and *porte-gibernes*. They will be whitened. Tomorrow for the inspection of the Colonel, all ranks will wear *grande tenue* … the soldiers which act as fifers will be minus their muskets and *gibernes*. The muskets will be worn *en banderole* [i.e., slung over the shoulder on the musket sling – ed] in the manner as the *mousqueton* are carried. As this is not a grand parade the men will wear a white stock and grey gaiters.
>
> 1 April … there will be sewn to the collar and cuffs of the fifers yellow worsted lace, placed exactly as on the *habits* of the drummers.
>
> 13 July … on the order of the Marshal, three fifers are to be suppressed; they are to return to their duties as fusiliers in the companies and will be issued a musket, bayonet and sling in lieu of the *mousqueton*. The lace distinction to the collar and cuffs will be removed.[17]

Drums and Trumpets 43

Top left. Musician of the *76ᵉ de Ligne* c.1805. Sky blue was a common facing colour for bands. Top right band with red facings and gold lace, immitating the Imperial Guard. Our middle image again shows a band with sky blue facings, and sky blue trim to the schako. Our bottom image again shows red or scarlet facings. These two colours are the most commonly shown by contemporary iconography.

44 Napoleon's Line Infantry – From the Battle of Jena to the Invasion of Iberia

Presented by Weiland is this drum major of unknown regiment. (*Collection KM*)

Clearly the *fifres*, like the drummers, were issued a sabre and belt, as well as *giberne a la corse* – regulation for all drummers and *fifres* – carried a *fifre* case as well as their light cavalry *mousqueton*. Quite an incumberance. The lace was clearly the self-same lace, i.e., 27mm-wide *galon cul de De*, as used for corporals' and *fourriers'* distinctions. It is clear that fifers did not exist in every regiment, and were atypical.

Musicians

Military bands first appeared during the Seven Years' War. The Royal Ordinance of 17 March 1788 allowed each regiment to employ eight musicians and a band master. Light infantry battalions were allowed to hire four musicians, who had to play the cornet or other brass instruments. The establishment remained the same until 8 December 1802, when all regiments of line and light infantry were allowed eight musicians, to wear the dress of the regiment's drummers and to have the uniform ornamented with a single row of lace 27mm wide at the cuff. From 29 August 1804 musicians were allowed to carry a dragoon musket and bayonet. It was common for colonels to expand the regimental band with hired men, *gagistes* who were professional musicians, who would be offered a contract to last no more than two years.

In the War Ministry circular of 20 November 1807, the inspector informs us that:

> there exist in several infantry corps a large number of musicians which the regulation does not allow. As there should only be eight in number, those in excess of this number may be admitted as soldiers, but in those cases where they have been admitted as 'gagistes' (musicians not on the strength), they should undertake a military engagement, and if they refuse and if the regiment wishes to retain them they will have no right to any allowance or supplies and will be entirely the charge of the officers, provided that the expense the band needs does not exceed one day's allowance of the officers per month.[18]

Because of the way in which bands were funded, it means we are almost totally ignorant of how bands were dressed: it also means we are ignorant of the dress of the drum major and drum master. We have some iconography to help us, but overall, we simply do not know what the majority of the bands (and head of column in general) actually wore. Musicians were officially allowed to wear the same dress as the drummers of a regiment, but the *arête* of 8 December 1802 allowed a single silver braid 27mm wide at collar and cuff. This was confirmed on 5 May 1811 and in February 1815.[19]

Inspection returns add some information about the dress of the bands. Musicians seldom appear in archive sources, given their clothing was private purchase. The best-documented band is that of the 3ᵉ *de Ligne*. Extracted from the standing orders are the following snippets of very useful information:

> 14 September 1806. The *habits* of the musicians ... the *revers*, collars, cuffs and lining will be in red, to be the same as the *sapeurs*.

Martinet presents this drum major wearing sky blue with profuse silver embroidery. The unit designation is not known.

18 November. The *habits* of the 8 musicians will have brandebourgs in lace, and will have the number '3' embroidered in gold.

26 August 1807. Make arrangements to obtain the lace for the musicians who will have lace of the 'system' 8 lines wide.

30 August. Have arrangements been made for the production of the *habits* for the musicians? Further, I also ask if the cloth for the lining and the red broadcloth for the collars, buttons and lace for these uniforms has been delivered? The lace will be the same as for the *état-major*, 12 lines wide but will be of 8 lines. The lace will be applied to the collar, cuffs, the long pockets, trefoils at the shoulder and at the taille; the stars and number '3' will be embroidered in gold on white. Write to me as quickly as possible at Berlin about this matter … 500 *schakos*, 900 *vestes* and also *culottes* and *habits* are needed.[20]

Thus, we see that the band had *bleu celeste habits*, with scarlet collar, revers and cuffs embellished with gold lace. The band instruments, owned by the officers, comprised at the end of the Empire:[21]

4 Clarinets in Bb, in mediocre condition
1 clarinet in E, to be replaced
1 small flute to be replaced
2 horns with spare crucks in good condition.

One of the regiment's band masters was Jean Baptiste Taviot. He was born on 7 March 1774, son of Jean Baptiste Tavio and Jeanne Guiland. He was admitted to the regiment on 5 April 1809 as '*chef de musique*'. He took part in the campaigns of 1806 through to 1814. He was discharged on 1 October 1815.[22] The band master was an honorary *sous-officier*, appointed by the regimental colonel, the role being created in 1788 and confirmed on 9 September 1799. The bandmaster wore the same uniform as the other musicians but with the distinction of silver or gold braid to collar and cuffs, and with the rank stripes of a sergeant major. Tactically, the bandmaster and band came under the orders of the drum major.

Chapter 7
All Change

Cost and image was foremost in what happened next. Equipping tens of thousands of men in 1803 to 1805 placed a huge and unstainable strain on the production of blue broadcloth: obtaining dye was difficult – the supply of indigo primarily came from England – and costly. A cheaper way forward was needed. Field officers at the camp of Boulogne had complained about the lack of winter clothing, and failings around the uniforms then in use, as Napoleon explained to Berthier on 14 August 1804:

> My cousin, it appears the army is asking for a change in uniform. We would like to do away with the *chapeau*, adopt *pantalons*, boots and a *habit-veste*, giving the soldier a *capote* for winter.[1]

Nothing was done immediately. This was the point of genesis for what happened next.

On 27 February 1805 the 4^e and 18^e *de Ligne* were ordered to dress their 3^e battalion in white on experimental purpose, and to take back the facings outlined in the regulation of 1786.[2]

Following the victory at Austerlitz, the army went into cantonments. While busy planning the Confederation of the Rhine, and the future shape of Europe, the Emperor cast his eye over the army. Men had lost clothing, equipment and weapons. In the mud and snow, the army's clothing had not stood up to the hard rigours of campaign.

In 1806 Napoleon embarked on an ambitious scheme to rebrand the army. During the Peace of Amiens, Napoleon had taken the Revolutionary Army and remade it into the form he envisioned for it. Dressed in the national colours of red white and blue and the *chapeau*, these soldiers were democratically at least dressed all the same. The revolution had ended the system of each regiment having its own unique dress and *esprit de corps*: all French soldiers were to be dressed the same: each man looked the same to be part of a national army. Hugely sensibly when it comes to logistics, but it made it impossible to tell which regiment was which from a distance. Since the

An 1806 regulation habit, attributed to the 21e *de Ligne*. (*Musee de l'Armée*)

A French fusilier wearing a *chapeau*, and a grey single-breasted *capote*. These garments were issued from 1803 onwards.

Grenadier wearing a *capote* on campaign by Martinet. Of interest the collar is scarlet, which is not reflected in any regulation, but not impossible.

A grenadier, this time wearing a *schako*, and also his epaulettes on the *capote*. Nothing is said about this in any regulation, so clearly colonels had a high degree of freedom in how these garments appeared.

An 1806-model *schako*, which has been adapted with the fitting of 1810-regulation chinscales and plates. These items had a theoretical lifespan of decades, and as long as they remained serviceable would be kept in use until life expired. (*Collection de l'Office du Tourisme de Pontarlier. Dépôt au Musée municipal de Pontarlier, France*)

 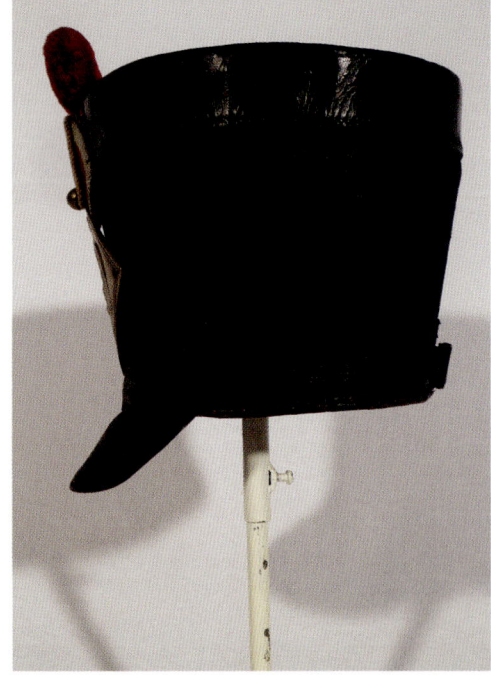

An 1806 *schako* that has not been adapted with the fitting of chinscales, but carried the 1810 *schako* plate. (*Collection de l'Office du Tourisme de Pontarlier. Dépôt au Musée municipal de Pontarlier, France*)

Martinet gives this fusilier wearing full dress, *c.*1807.

54 Napoleon's Line Infantry – From the Battle of Jena to the Invasion of Iberia

Weiland gives this fusilier *c.*1810 in full dress. Oddly, he carries a non-regulation sabre.

coronation Napoleon had sought to brand himself and his regime as 'legitimate' in the eyes of European monarchs. The victory at Austerlitz had cemented both his control over France and supremacy over Austria and Russia: with dynastic thoughts placing his siblings on old – Louis in Holland, Joseph in Naples – and new thrones – Westphalia for example for Jerome – the Revolution had fully embraced the trappings and identity of the régime that the events of 1789 had removed. In this new buoyant world of French hegemony, the French army was to be branded: the politically suspect revolutionary blue uniforms were to be replaced with aristocratic white. Regiments were to adopt distinctive facings that had been abolished in 1793 in seeking to create a national army.

The useless felt *chapeau* was high on the list of items to be consigned to the dustbin of history. The men needed another garment to wear on the march and on campaign – they had only their *habit* and *veste manches*, which had become quickly spoiled in the autumn mud and winter rains. A root and branch reform of how uniforms were funded, made and looked like was instigated, which came into use throughout 1806.

The rebranding project when it reappeared in 1806 was also out of economic necessity: undyed broadcloth was cheap. Indigo blue dye was expensive: with a blockade on English goods – indigo dye – and a hugely increased standing army, costs had to be cut. Swapping to white or undyed broadcloth was the obvious answer. The rebranding also fundamentally changed the silhouette of the French soldier: the decrees of 1806 introduced the *schako*, the *capote*, and a new-pattern *habit* – not cut short nor were *culottes* abolished – as well as a myriad of other changes. The first of these was issued on 18 March:

Art. 1. From October 1, 1806, the first portion of the general fund will be made available to each regiment; it will be paid to them on the basis that will be fixed by us, paid twelve months in advance.

2. The amount of this first portion will be combined with the second, and will form a single fund under the name of general fund.

By means of this decree, the Councils of Administration will be required to provide for the purchase of the objects which according to the provisions of the decree of 17 Frimaire year 11 (8 December 1802), must be supplied to them by order of the War Minister.

3. The War Minister will continue, until 1 January 1808, to agree final contracts and the samples of fabrics suitable for clothing. Deliveries of cloth will still be made to the corps, which must settle the amount within twenty-four hours after receipt.

4. The War Minister will shortly send samples of each type of fabric, and for each main manufacture, at least nine to ten centimetres wide (three and a half inches), and seventeen to eighteen centimetres (six to seven inches) in length, stamped with the stamp of the war administration, with designation of the place of manufacture. The ends of sample pieces will be coated with stamps and seals, and will remain deposited in the offices of the Minister-Director and in that of the Directory of Clothing.

5. The board of directors, immediately after the arrival of the goods supplied to it under the orders of the director-minister, will have them received by one of its members and by the captain in charge of clothing ; and when they have been recognised as good a quality as the samples, he will pay the cash amount within twenty-four hours of their acceptance; and in the absence of this cash payment within twenty-four hours, he will be required to take into account the supplier's interest on his funds.

6. Whenever a Council of Administration believes that it must refuse all or part of the goods supplied to it, it will report to the commissioner of war in the district in which the regiment is located. The war commissioner will immediately draw up in the presence of a delegate of the Council of Administration and the authorised representative of the merchant or manufacturer who will have sent the item, or, failing this, in the presence of the mayor or one of his assistants, a report in which he will note the reasons for the refusal of the Council of Administration, as well as the state, the nature and the quantity of the goods refused. This report will immediately be delivered or sent to the prefecture council of the department, which, after having verified the facts by experts and having heard the supplier or his attorney in his responses, will definitively pronounce the admission or rejection, except the appeal to the Council of State.

The prefecture council will likewise judge all discussions that may arise between the boards of directors and the merchants or manufacturers relating to the execution of contract clauses concerning the clothing and equipment of the troops.

When the Council of Administration believes that it should refuse only part of the shipment, it will immediately settle, within twenty-four hours, as it is said above, the portion that it thought it could accept.

As for the objects which will have been definitively rejected, as soon as the rejection is pronounced, the merchant or manufacturer will be obliged to take them back; and all transport and other costs will remain at his expense. In this case, the body is authorised to enter into over-the-counter contracts, and to obtain replacement fabrics, as it deems appropriate, at the supplier's expense in terms of added value.

7. Line infantry will in future be dressed in white cloth; but, to give the manufacturers time to choose and procure the materials suitable for this manufacture, the regiments (even numbers only) will begin in 1807 to replace part of their blue clothes with white clothes, so that they were completely dressed in the latter colour in 1809.

The regiments (odd numbers) do not begin to replace part of their blue clothes with white clothes until 1808.

Nothing will be innovated, as for the colour and the form, with the clothing of the light infantry, the artillery and the troops of the engineers.

8. The clothing of the line infantry soldier will consist of a white broadcloth *habit* in the proportions of the current clothing; a white broadcloth *veste manches*, which can be worn alone, with small cuffs and a low collar of distinctive colour, a pair of white

tricot *culottes* and a broadcloth capote, to which a shoulder cape that will be attached with buttons, and which the soldier will only use in winter and on the march.

Light infantry, artillery and engineering troops will also have a *capote* with cloth cape.

9. The *habit* will only be given to the soldier on feast days and in barracks and when he requests it to go to town.

10. The *habit* and the *capote* will last four years, the *veste manches* two years, and the *culottes* one year.

11. Our ministers of war and of the administration of war will present to us for the renewal of 1807 a draft decree relating to the fixing of the uniform of each body.

12. Our Minister-Director of War Administration is authorised to have the corps draw up and send the instructions and regulations necessary for the execution of this decree.

13. Our ministers of war, of war administration and of the public treasury, are responsible, each in so far as it is concerned, for the execution of this decree.

IN PARIS, IMPERIAL PRINTING.
March 18, 1806.[3]

The decree concerning the appearance of the *habit* was the first officially regulated change since 1786. The new regulation stated the tails of the *habits* were no longer to be hooked back, but were to be sewn down. Rather than blue, they were to be white. A soldier hence forth had a *chapeau* and *bonnet de police* as headgear, a *habit*, *veste manches* and *capote*. Leg wear comprised a pair of tricot *culottes*, a pair of linen overalls, a pair of over the knee grey gaiters made from linen and a pair of long black gaiters made from twill. White gaiters were abolished. Fusiliers had a *giberne* and cross belt with bayonet frog. Grenadiers and *voltigeurs* carried the *sabre briquet*, *giberne* and belt. All ranks had a *havresac*. Each man in theory had a black stock, two pairs of socks, a minimum of two pairs of shoes, two shirts and his items *of petit monture*. Grenadiers had scarlet-fringed epaulettes, and we assume continued to wear bearskins. Regiments were to be identified by the colour of the collar, cuffs, piping and facings and the direction of the pockets on the tails:[4]

	Regiment number														Buttons	Pockets	Revers	Cuffs	Collar
1	1	9	17	25	33	41	49	57	65	73	81	89	97	105	Copper	Horizontal	C	C	C
2	2	10	18	26	34	42	50	58	66	74	82	90	98	106			C	C	
3	3	11	19	27	35	43	51	59	67	75	83	91	99	107			C		C
4	4	12	20	28	36	44	52	60	68	76	84	92	100	108				C	C
5	5	13	21	29	37	45	53	61	69	77	85	93	101	109	White metal	Vertical	C	C	C
6	6	14	22	30	38	46	54	62	70	78	86	94	102	110			C	C	
7	7	15	23	31	39	47	55	63	71	79	87	95	103	111			C		C
8	8	16	24	32	40	48	56	64	72	80	88	96	104	112				C	C
	Green	Black	Scarlet	Capucine	Violet	Celestial blue	Rose	Aurore	Dark blue	Yellow	Light green	Garance	Crimson	Iron Grey					

The distribution of the new regulation began for depot companies: the war battalions then participating in the Jena campaign, and many miles from home base, did not receive new clothing until new year 1807. The decree of 15 January issued to regiments on service in Germany a total of 53,248 brand-new *habits*, over 90,000 *vestes* and in excess of 100,000 pairs of *culottes*. It is exceedingly likely that these garments were all made to the most recent regulations: therefore, a huge number of white *habits* were issued in the field, to supplement those made in regimental depots. Far more regiments were issued white *habits* than heretofore believed. As far as rebranding the army into a new image, by the time Friedland was fought in summer 1807, most French line infantry were wearing a white *habit*.[5] We must remember that uniforms were expected to last for a minimum length of time: replacement items, regardless or not of being made to a new regulation, were issued in a staggered manner. The roll-out of a new design of *habit* or new piece of clothing or equipment would take several years to complete. To introduce a new regulation with the army on campaign, with battalions scattered between France and the Polish border, was never going to be a simple process. Despite the regulation ordering *capotes* and *schakos*, the adoption of these items was not complete before 1809.

Greatcoats

During the eighteenth century, the *veste manches* was the everyday jacket of the soldier. The *habit* formed the soldier's top coat, being cut so that the tails, which were normally hooked together, could be opened out, and the *revers* (lapels) could be buttoned over, giving the soldier a bad-weather garment. In general, the *revers* were normally folded back to show the facing colour, as were the skirts of the *habit*. As fashion changed, the *habit* became ever more tight fitting, and in the old guard at least, the *veste* lost its sleeves, and the *habit* transitioned into an everyday jacket. With the adoption of white uniforms – easily spoiled by mud – the need arose for an additional top coat, the *capote* or *redingote*.

The *capote* was an item of clothing that was not in general issue during the eighteenth century. Under the terms of the 1753 dress regulation, the *capote* was issued to men on sentry duty in bad weather or at night. Thus, the *capote* was part of the equipment of the guard house. *Capotes* for everyday use had been introduced for service on 25 April 1767 for troops stationed in colder regions during the winter. Their use before 1806 was ad hoc, but did occur.[6] We note in 1799 the Army of the Rhine had thousands of *capotes* in store.[7] As part of the planning process for the invasion of England, General Daru was ordered to make 60,000 *capotes* on 29 May 1803 as a strategic reserve.[8] Days later, on 14 June, Bonaparte ordered all troops at the Channel coast to be issued *capotes*, and General Dejean was ordered to procure 80,000 and 120,000 pairs of shoes by September of that year. For all regiments at the Camp of Boulogne or on service in north Italy that had not yet received *capotes*, corps commands were reminded on 29 June 1804 to complete the production and issue of these garments.[9] These orders have been overlooked in the last 200 years of study of Napoleonic French uniforms.

Regarding both the 1804 and 1806 model *capote*, no colour was specified, although archive documents suggest grey. The presence of a shoulder cape on the 1806 model makes us think immediately of a British greatcoat from the period. We ask, when did the cape disappear from the *capote*? We also note that from examination of regimental orders and original garments, these garments were designed to be worn *over* the soldier's equipment and under it. The pockets in the rear of the garment allowed access to the sabre and/or *giberne*, and the half belt allowed it to be adjusted to be worn over the equipment, or fastened closed and worn under the equipment.

On 22 September 1806 Napoleon ordered regimental depots to begin production of *capotes* to clothe the 3ᵉ battalions before they were sent to Germany as reinforcements. Almost a month later, an order written from Berlin on 28 October, instructed Comte Daru to obtain cloth to produce 100,000 *capotes*. In early November, to make up losses for the Jena campaign, Napoleon gave orders that:

> To speed up training and the departure of these battalions it will not be necessary for the conscripts to be trained, it will suffice that they have eight days of instruction, that they be armed, are given a *veste*, *culottes*, gaiters, a *chapeau* and a *capote*. You must not wait till they have a *habit*.[10]

From practical experience, a *habit* is slow to make, so sending off barely trained conscripts in a *capote*, which was cheaper and quicker to make, made a lot of common sense.

Schakos

Ten days after the decree formalising the *capote* and white *habits*, the decree of 27 March 1806 introduced the *schako* to the line infantry:

> The body of the *schako* is to be made from felt, 176mm in height, the waxed cow hide top to be 230mm in diameter. The folded down portion of the top is 41mm in depth. Around the bottom of the felt is to be a band of leather, 27mm broad, fastening behind by a copper buckle. The peak is to be 60mm deep. A buckle 20mm square appeared at the rear of the *schako* to adjust it to fit. On the side of the *schako* appear two leather chevrons, 18mm wide and 110mm long.[11]

Analysis of handling dozens of original items reveals that rather than felt, *schako* were made from stiff card, covered in felt, as were the 1810 and Bardin types. Indeed, not one of the 100 or so examples the author has handled correlate exactly to the regulation dimensions.

Due to the rigours of campaign, the felt *chapeau* remained the main item of headdress and from October 1806 a huge number of captured Prussian *chapeaux* were pressed into service: 3,000 went to 1ᵉ Corps, 1,000 to 5ᵉ Corps, 1,000 to 2ᵉ Corps and 1,000 to 4ᵉ Corps.[12] We also note 3,014 Prussian *schakos* were issued to the French army: some 9,769 being requisitioned from Berlin, 4,089 remaining in French stores in April 1808, while

1,200 were obtained from Spandau and not issued. From Hanau came 1,650 *chapeaux*, all being issued, and 300 grenadier bearskins, from Stettin Daru obtained 3,951 *chapeaux* and ordered the white lace edging removed before being issued, similar orders being passed regarding the 3,452 *chapeaux* found in stores at Custrin. A further 1,746 came from Posen, 812 from Glogau: Daru reports that just over 28,000 Prussian *chapeaux* found their way into the French Army, along with 22,377 Prussian *gibernes*, 2,649 Prussian *giberne* belts and 3,084 Prussian *havresacs*.[13]

The adoption of the *schako*, and the lack of mention of bearskins for grenadiers, meant that most regiments abolished bearskins at this time, if they ever had them. Indeed, according to the standing orders of the 64ᵉ *de Ligne*, '20 August 1805. By order of the Emperor the bearskins of the grenadiers are to be withdrawn.'[14] This implies these items had been abandoned long before the *schako* was conceived of as headdress, at least as an item worn on campaign and in battle. The 1808 regulations stated:

> The bearskin cap of the *sapeurs* must be enclosed in a ticking case, with an opening, a slide and a cord on each end, so that the cap can be inserted through one entrance and removed by the other, without turning the hair back. The cords must be long enough to be used to attach the cap to the soldiers' *havresac*, each of them is knotted around the belt of their *capote*, and by this means, the case of the cap is fixed by two points.
>
> If the grenadiers when wearing their *havresacs* have handed their bearskin caps into the magazine, or for any other reason, then they put the *schako* in the ticking case, as well as the pompom, and place the case as it says above.[15]

It implies that grenadiers had both bearskins for parade and *schakos* for campaign, which certainly was the case in the 3ᵉ *de Ligne*.[16] This has also been the case since 1801 with grenadiers having a bearskin and *chapeau*.

The end of the 1807 campaign marked the end of the white *habit*: the decree of 30 November 1807 formally abandoned its use and ordered the re-adoption of blue *habits*, with white *habits* to be withdrawn or in the process of being withdrawn by 1 January 1808.[17] Re-adopting blue took time, with white *habits* lingering in use throughout 1808. But this was not the end of the return to white.

The cost of uniforms was always a huge issue for the War Ministry. White uniforms were cheap – they were made mostly from undyed cloth and consequently were a lot cheaper to make. Keeping costs down was clearly the reasoning behind an Imperial Decree signed at Bayonne 12 July 1808, in which the Emperor decreed that the colour of the *habits* of the *Garde Imperiale*, *cuirassiers*, *carabiniers*, dragoons, lancers, *chasseurs*, gendarme and artillery would not be altered. Article 2 states that the line and light infantry would have undyed cloth. White cloth production at Lodeve was to be increased to begin production of new white uniforms in 1809, and to commence with the 30ᵉ to 40ᵉ *de Ligne*, which were to be dressed according the decree of 26 June 1806.[18]

A week or so later, on 26 July 1808, a report was passed to the Emperor concerning uniforms, and issues surrounding obtaining indigo to dye broadcloth blue. The report stated it was impossible to obtain sufficient indigo to dye all the cloth the army needed blue. Therefore, white uniforms were considered to be the solution to the problem. Blue was to be reserved for the Garde Impériale, artillery and *cuirassiers*, the line and light infantry were to wear white.[19] At this the paperwork stops dead. We are left wondering if this change happened. Did the 30ᵉ to 40ᵉ *de Ligne* swap into white *habits* in 1809? Without further research we cannot tell.

The rebranding exercise had failed: white uniforms were without shadow of a doubt hugely cheaper, but the political implication of wearing the same white coats as the Austrians – defeated in 1805 and again in 1809 – overshadowed any economic necessity. Blue was the uniform of the French soldier, just like his garance trousers when they were adopted – they were emblematic of not just soldiers but France herself until 1915.

Chapter 8

Change and Change Again

With the return to blue *habits*, the War Ministry issued a series of new regulations concerning clothing. A War Ministry specification of November 1807 tells us the *bonnet de police*, as in 1799, was entirely blue, with scarlet piping to the turban, and rather than a worsted tassel, a piece of 6cm by 12cm was allowed, to make the tassel. No lace or cording for piping was issued.[1] When not worn, the *bonnet de police* was rolled and carried in the straps under the *giberne*. The *flamme* was rolled starting at the tassel. It was rolled along one edge, so as to create a tight spiral, with the tassel projecting out of the centre. When rolled, the *bonnet de police* was not to exceed the width of the *giberne*. When secured under the *giberne*, the tassel was on the left side.[2]

The 1799 regulations had allowed for the standardisation of uniforms into three sizes, enabling civilian contractors to produce clothing and equipment for the army, rather than relying on each regiment to act as the contracting agent. It allowed the state to generate reserve stockpiles of clothing.[3] The text informs us a *habit* required 1m 34 blue broadcloth for the body, 0m 13 scarlet broadcloth for the collar and piping, 0m 17 white broadcloth for *revers* and piping, 3m white serge to line the *habit*, of which 1m 41 was to be deducted to allow for linen to line the sleeves, and 0m 14 linen for pockets and button stands.[4] The amount of blue broadcloth allowed in 1791 was 1m 66, so clearly by the turn of the century, the *habit* was cut much tighter.[5]

Judging by the extant white *habits* from 1806 to 1807, the skirts (*retroussis*) are fully sewn down with no triangle at the base. Many artists and historians date the sewn-down skirts and removal of the triangle to 1812, but clearly this is not the case and it happened much earlier with the adopting of white *habits*. A specification for a *habit* dated November 1807 reports each one needed:

1m 55 blue broadcloth
0m 12 white broadcloth
0m 15 scarlet broadcloth
3m white serge
0m 75 linen
11 large buttons
22 small buttons

The broadcloth was 1m19 wide and the serge 0m 50 wide. The government specification stated that the *bonnet de police* was to be cut from the blue broadcloth allowed for the *habit*, as were the collar and cuffs of the *veste*, hence the large difference in cloth amount

An eagle guard's helmet adopted from December 1811, but better known as part of the Bardin regulation. (*Musee de l'Armée*)

compared to 1799.⁶ From 23 September 1804, the decoration to the tails of the *habit* were to be numbers or eagles: stars and hearts were prohibited.⁷ We note *sous-officiers'* and *officiers' habits* were made from superfine broadcloth and lined in shalloon (superfine serge recorded in the period as Blicourt), and were dark navy blue: visually much darker than for soldiers. We discuss the types of cloth used later.

The *habit* functioned as a 'top coat' and the *veste manches* was the everyday garment. The *veste manches* had a low collar, 2.5cm tall, the front being fastened by a row of small uniform buttons. The collar and cuffs were officially blue for fusiliers and scarlet for grenadiers. The front of the garment was made from broadcloth, the sleeves and back from tricot. The body was lined in serge. The *veste manches* only had the sleeve cap of the arms sewn to the body of the *veste*. This allowed for a better fit under the *habit* and allowed greater freedom of movement in the shoulder.⁸ A War Ministry specification from November 1807 allowed only blue collar, epaulettes and cuffs.⁹

We note that *sous-officiers* wore a sleeveless waistcoat (*veste*) made from broadcloth, with a white collar.

Eagle Guards

In new year 1808, with the army on a peace footing, the line and light infantry regiments were re-organised into five battalions. Grenadiers were no longer the best soldiers in a regiment, but now had to be the tallest men in a regiment – the criteria laid out for the men nominated as grenadiers based on valour, proven courage, good conduct, have served

Change and Change Again 65

Prior to 1808, eagle battalion had an eagle, carried by a sergeant major. Martinet shows one such figure from the 58ᵉ *de Ligne*. The colour belt is made from whitened buff leather, which accords to archive documentation about how these items appeared.

Suhr gives us the senior officers of the 92ᵉ *de Ligne*. Of interest, the colonel (left) has a bearskin plate with an eagle, while the adjutant with his cane of office has a grenade on his plate. The *porte-aigle* has gold *contre-epaulettes*, an officer's *schako*, as well as officer's épée and waistbelt, yet carries the stripes of a *sous-officier*. Clearly colonels had a high degree of latitude in how the *porte-aigle* was dressed.

for two years and stand 1m 73 set in 1788 were done away with. Grenadiers henceforth had to be the tallest men in a regiment, and have served for four years or taken part in two campaigns. The decree of 18 February 1808 introduced the 2ᵉ and 3ᵉ Porte-Aigle or eagle guards:

Sergeant major *porte-aigle* of the 75ᵉ *de Ligne*. He had gold lace to his *schako* and gold fringing and lace to his epaulettes. (A.S.K. Brown collection)

Officer in campaign dress wearing a frac in an image by Weiland from *c*.1812.

Martinet presents this fusilier on campaign. He has blue and white ticking non-regulation *pantalons*.

Period image *c*.1807 of French troops leaving their billets. It correctly shows the use of natural linen *pantalons* on campaign with matching gaiters. Of interest, the grenadier carries the 1767-model sabre, which is entirely plausible.

Change and Change Again 71

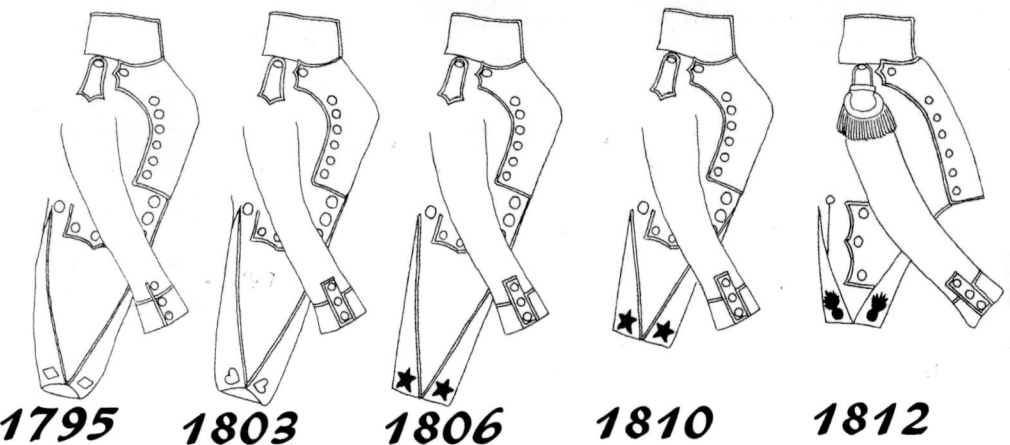

Schematic showing the evolution of the soldier's coat according to official regulations. How well adopted the 1810 model, with its corresponding *schako*, was we cannot tell due to the lack of archive sources.

Article 17
Each regiment shall have an eagle which shall be carried by an eagle-bearer having the rank of lieutenant or second lieutenant and having at least ten years' service, or having made the four campaigns of Ulm, Austerlitz, Jena, and from Friedland. He will enjoy the pay of a first-class lieutenant.

Two brave men taken from among the former uneducated soldiers, who, for this reason, could not obtain advancement, having at least ten years of service, with the title, one of second eagle-bearer and the other of third eagle-bearer, will always be placed next to the eagle. They will rank as sergeant and will receive the pay of a sergeant major. They will carry four chevrons on both arms.

The eagle will always remain where there will be the most battalions together. The eagle-bearers are part of the regimental headquarters. They are all three appointed by us and can only be removed by us.[10]

The circular of 18 September 1809 provided the eagle guards with bearskins, spontoons and pistols:

The Emperor has decreed that the 2ᵉ and 3ᵉ *porte-aigle* of each regiment will in future be armed with a spontoon in the form of a lance, attached to it will be a banner, red for the 2ᵉ *porte-aigle* and white for the 3ᵉ. One side of the banner will be inscribed in gold letters with the name of the emperor, the other the number and indication of the arm of the regiment.

The spontoon will be 6 pied 6 pouce; 5 pied to the bottom of the banner, which will be 8 pouce tall and 28 pouces long and end in a point. The first part of the lance, after it has passed through the banner, is 10 pouces, the horizontal arm will terminate in a rounded blade at one side and a point at the other. To carry the spontoon, the shaft will be from blackened wood, like a bayonet, the red and white banners will serve to mark where the eagle is.

The 2ᵉ and 3ᵉ *porte-aigle*, in addition to the spontoon, will carry a pair of pistols which will be in a case, on the left side of the chest, in the manner of the Orientals.

The case to it can rest against the body and will be flat on the inside and round on the outside; it will be made of strong black patent leather like the *giberne*, the top and bottom will be trimmed with a two-inch serrated trim.

The lower end will be passed and contained in a loop, which is attached to a belt worn on the coat, and will be closed by means of a loop, covered by a square plate, decorated with an N in relief: this plate and the end intended to receive the rounded end of the belt will be polished copper, and the belt black patent leather. The headdress of the 2ᵉ and 3ᵉ *porte-aigle* will be a grenadier's bearskin with a white braid.[11]

The Suhr brothers show this uniform in use in 1813. Did any of this equipment exist prior to 1812? We have no way of telling. Indeed, post-1812 the paper archive strongly argues that a mere handful of regiments ever adopted this uniform. The lack of inspection reports post-1808 means we have no way of knowing if the 1808 or 1809 regulations were carried out. The balance of probability based on evidence from 1813 to 1815 suggests not. The decree of 25 December 1811 confirmed that each battalion was to carry a fanion: white for the 2ᵉ battalion, red for the 3ᵉ, blue for the 4ᵉ, green for the 5ᵉ and yellow for the 6ᵉ. They were to measure 1m square, mounted on a shaft 3m long, topped with an iron lance head, 10cm tall.[12] Such items had been carried since 12 August 1788.[13] No evidence from the epoch supports the existence of company markers carried in musket barrels.

Regimental Artillery

An innovation of the 1809 was the re-adoption of regimental artillery:

Decree 9 June 1809. Artillery pieces attached to the infantry.
Title I, Article I. There shall be attached to each regiment of infantry, line and light, two pieces of artillery, 3 or 4 pounders, three caissons, a field forge, an ambulance caisson, and a caisson to transport the papers of the regiment. These eight waggons always march with the battalion which carries the eagle of the regiment.
2. There shall be attached to each battalion a caisson to carry the infantry cartridges, a caisson for the bread, which, for the four battalions shall make eight caissons.
Title 2, Article 3. The sixteen vehicles are serviced, harnessed, and conducted by a company of cannoneers of the regiment.
The company of cannoneers of the regiment shall be commanded by a lieutenant, a *sous-lieutenant*, three sergeants and three corporals, and shall be divided into three squads.

The first squad shall be composed of a sergeant, a corporal, twenty cannoneers and two craftsmen (*ouvriers*). The corporal has the duty of conductor and magazine-guard of the artillery. He shall have the keys to the caissons, and shall be especially charged with the maintenance the ammunition.

The second squad shall be composed of a sergeant, a corporal and twenty soldiers of the train, which will be charged with harnessing the eight vehicles which march with the battalion to which the eagle of the regiment is allocated.

The third squad shall be composed as for the second, and is charged with the movement and service of the other eight vehicles.

The lieutenant shall be in command of the entire body, but will have overall command of the artillery; the *sous-lieutenant* is charged with commanding the train. Both of these officers shall be mounted.

Our minister of war shall determine the expenses which shall be awarded to the administration councils to put into effect (this decree), to repair and maintain the vehicles (1). See Circular 23rd August 1809, number 175.[14]

The regimental artillery was disbanded once more on 1 April 1810 and was re-formed with the decree of 11 February 1811.[15] We know very little about the clothing of regimental artillery or of its existence from extant paperwork.

2ᵉ de Ligne

A report entitled '*l'artillerie regimentaire du 2eme Ligne*' from 1811 states that the short *habits* – we assume for the drivers – had not yet arrived with the regiment, nor had the *culottes de peau* and boots as required. Instead, the drivers were dressed in infantry uniforms and allocated pantalons made from broadcloth. A second report from 2 January 1812 states that the drivers and gunners were totally equipped as new.[16]

9ᵉ de Ligne

Partial regimental accounts exist from 1812. In preparation for the Russian campaign, 12 new drums and carriages were purchased for the sum of 79fr 20 as well as 44 pairs of boots for the regimental artillery train drivers for the sum of 88fr. An additional 22 pairs of boots were purchased in 1813 for the drivers.[17] This suggests that the regiment kept its guns into the 1813 campaign, and indeed regimental artillery is clearly defined in the Bardin regulation.

21ᵉ de Ligne

The regiment's battalion artillery was equipped with four 3-pdr field guns, six caissons, five infantry munition caissons, one field forge, five stores waggons, one ambulance, and one wagon for rations. The regiment had 36 gunners, 50 drivers and 108 horses. The men were dressed as fusiliers.[18]

24ᵉ de Ligne

The paper archive of the regiment states that on 28 December 1809, 1,069fr was paid by Colonel Chabert personally to reinstate the costs of the artillery to allow it to complete its clothing. Some 280fr was spent the following year, 1810, on equipment and clothing.[19]

48ᵉ de Ligne

Purchased in 1810 were 54 pairs of *culottes de peau* for the artillery drivers, 193m of treillis to line the *port-manteaux* of the artillery drivers, 70m 36 of white worsted lace for artillery drivers' *port-manteaux*, and 54 pairs of boots. The regimental tailor produced 54 *habits vestes*, 54 *gilets* with no sleeves, 54 stable coats, 54 *capotes* made from beige broadcloth, which had cost 5,568fr for 696m, and 54 *bonnets de police* made from 45m 25 of blue broadcloth costing 497fr 75. Some 1,782m of *bleu celeste* broadcloth was purchased, along with 149m of dark blue broadcloth, 80m 46 of dark blue milled serge and 184m 68 of *bleu de roi* tricot.[20] From this we assume the drivers' *habits* were *bleu celeste* with imperial blue collar and *revers*, the tails were lined in *bleu de roi*. The *gilets* were no doubt *bleu celeste*. The men were equipped with standard infantry buff work and *schakos*. We have no details of the dress of the gunners, if they wore anything different to the rank and file infantry.

1810 Regulation

The next major change took place on 19 February 1810. This Imperial Decree established a new specification for uniform of the line infantry:[21]

Item	Cloth	Old Specification	New Specification
Habit	Blue broadcloth	1m 70	1m 34
	White broadcloth	0m 12	0m 12
	Scarlet broadcloth	0m 15	
	Garance broadcloth		0m 15
	White serge	3m 27	2m 06
	Linen for lining	0m 89	1m 09
Veste	White broadcloth for fronts	1m 19	
	Blue broadcloth for collar, cuffs, shoulder straps	Recovered from blue broadcloth for *habit*	
	White tricot for sleeves and back and lining	2m 09	1m 83
	White serge	2m 97	None
	Linen for lining	0m 15	1m 30
Culotte	White tricot	1m 34	1m 44
	Linen for lining	1m 09	1m 15
Capote	Beige broadcloth	2m 50	2m 40
	Linen for lining	1m 17	1m 15

Looking at the changes of cloth allowed for a *habit* shows that the tails became much shorter. The body of the *habit* was formerly lined entirely in serge, henceforth only the tails would be lined this way, the upper body to be totally lined in linen. The *veste manches* was now totally made from tricot, and was entirely lined with linen. The blue collar, epaulettes and cuffs were abolished: presumably also for grenadiers, which had been scarlet since 1793, and we assume *voltigeurs* had entirely white garments. The *culottes* became longer in the leg – as civilian fashion changed and adopted *pantalons* that closed at the ankle, so too did army uniforms. Costly cochenille dyed scarlet broadcloth was now replaced by madder red, which was vastly cheaper. This was a cost-cutting exercise.

On 23 May 1810 the Emperor authorised that henceforth trumpeters, drummers and musicians were to wear green:

1. the *habits* of drummers and trumpeters are to be laced with 2m 70 of lace 27mm wide, to be sewn on to the *habit* conforming to the decree of 1 October 1786.

2. The *habits* of drum majors, trumpet majors and master musicians are to be no longer laced in gold or silver; the drum majors and trumpet majors will not be distinguished, but the master musicians will be by a double row of silver lace 27mm wide at the cuff, and the musicians by a single row in the same place.

The body of the *habit* will be green. The lining of the *habit*, the cuffs, the *revers*, the collar, *veste* or *gilet*, the *culottes* or *pantalons* will retain the colours of their corps and are not to be affected by these changes. No further changes to the remainder of the uniform, such as pompoms, *retroussis* etc are to be made.

However, upon consideration the uniform of the light infantry will change concerning the lining of the *habit veste*, *gilet* and *pantalons*, which are blue. This colour has a disagreeable effect with green, it is therefore decided that that the lining of the *habit-veste*, the *gilet* and *pantalons* are to be green, and also the *habit*, for the drummers and musicians of this arm.[22]

Major Bardin reports that decree was largely ignored in practice writing in 1823, but we must imagine that infantry drummers were to have had green *habits* with white *revers* and tail lining, scarlet cuffs, scarlet collars; that trumpeters of *cuirassiers* had green *habits* with facing colour *revers*, cuffs etc; and that dragoon and light cavalry trumpeters wore the same uniform coat as the other ranks. Given the decree was never published, we doubt it was acted upon.

The next official utterance about drummers was issued almost a year later, on 15 May 1811 when the War Ministry authorised a drummers' *habit* to have wool lace 27mm wide, and required 15m 30 of lace, of a model yet to be determined. A light infantry *habit* required just 11m 50.[23]

The 1810 decree was formally brought into action on 30 December 1811. It was a word for word copy of the earlier 1810 document and said nothing about the proposed new lace.[24] Major Bardin notes that the 1811 decree was not enforced rigorously and that the lace amount and *habit* form was only finally changed with the decree of 19 January 1812.[25] Bardin further notes that new lace was introduced on 17 September 1812.[26]

On 9 November 1810 the *schako*'s dimensions slightly altered to 19cm height and a top of 24.4cm diameter. The former ornamentation of cords and tassels was abolished, chinscales were formally added to the design (brass for line infantry, white metal for light infantry). The *schako* front was ornated by a metal lozenge bearing the regimental number surmounted by a 7cm tricolour cockade. Decorative bands in gold or silver around the top circumference indicated the officer ranks: from a 34mm band with an additional 14mm band located 20mm below (colonel, the only officer with two *schako* bands), 34mm in silver for a major, 27mm for battalion commanders in gold, 20mm again in gold for captains, a single 18mm band in gold (sub-lieutenant or adjutant-*sous-officier*), the latter with a red silk lozenge pattern woven in to it). One novel aspect of the *schako*'s design was an oiled leather neck flap: this was worn folded inside the *schako*, and could be pulled out in wet weather. It tied under the chin with linen tapes, keeping the soldier's neck dry. At the same time, plumes were also abolished, except for the senior officers: white for the colonel, majors white with a red base, battalion commanders red with a white base. Other officers wore pompoms: white for the staff, red for grenadiers, yellow for *voltigeurs*, green for 1st company, light blue for 2nd, aurore for 3rd, violet for 4th. Another decree, dated 21 February 1811, confirmed these changes and added that senior officers' plumes were to be 560mm long in total with at least 300mm of feather. The pompoms were regulated to be made from wool, 55mm in diameter. Officers were allowed a carrot-shaped pompom, termed a *houpette*, 80mm tall, with the narrow part uppermost.[27]

More cost-cutting measures would follow with the proto-Bardin regulations of 1811: on 18 February the War Ministry ordered that newly levied conscripts would use the smaller *tirailleur modèle havresac* issued to the light infantry, 325mm wide – much smaller than the earlier *modèle*. The price difference between the two types was 25 centimes, but when added up across 100,000 items represented a substantial saving in leather and money. The decree was reversed in 24 November 1811, but the light infantry kept the smaller model.[28] In March, the *ligne* was officially ordered to adopt a short-tailed *habit*, worn with light infantry-pattern *pantalons* made from tricot, worn with under the knee gaiters; the new garments to be in production from 1 October 1811.[29]

With planning for the invasion of Russian in full swing and the inextricable increase in the size of the army, in order to ensure that new entrants to regiments were equipped as speedily as was practicable, regimental *dépôts* were ordered on 3 October 1811 to establish a clothing and leather equipment reserve within three months. This reserve was to comprise two hundred complete sets of uniforms and accoutrements for each regiment and a hundred complete sets of uniforms and accoutrements for each foot artillery regiment, all to be of the new model.[30] How far along production of these short *habits* was before the Russian campaign began is impossible to say. The accompanying volumes, also available from Frontline, assess the development and adoption of the Bardin regulation.

Chapter 9

Regulations in Practice

The purpose of a uniform was to turn a civilian into a soldier: the individual became a 'cog in a machine'. The uniform was both a mode of restriction but also of distinction: it set the soldier apart from the civilian, and created a form of collective identity and exclusivity. Uniform was representative of a number of debates in France that linked clothing, appearance and social rank. Uniforms drew directly on contemporary civilian fashions, as a means of fashioning the soldier and officer in line with contemporary ideals of masculinity and taste: dress was a symbol of rank and its relationship and significance in the presentation of self. The dress uniform, the *habit*, was cut to follow contemporary fashions, made in super fine broadcloth for officers. The colour of the uniform reflected the politics of the nation with the adoption of national colours of red white and blue as opposed to the white of the *ancien régime*. Changes in civilian fashion dictated that the looser-fitting clothing of the mid-eighteenth century was replaced with a leaner, tighter-fitting uniform, resulting in a longer and tighter silhouette. This new silhouette resulted in cheaper and more practical uniforms.

Fashion dictated that the mid blue hue of officers' uniforms became almost blue-black. By the later 1790s, sober shades became popular among fashionable men in reaction to the foppish and extravagant dress of the *incroyables* of earlier years. There was nothing in regulations to indicate this change in colour was deliberate policy, yet it is undeniable that original officers' *habits* are strikingly different in colour to that of rank and file soldiers, and surely represented civilian fashion regulating military aesthetics.[1] It would be civilian fashion that drove the Bardin regulation as much as practicality: the dark blue double-breasted tail coat by 1812 was almost a civilian uniform for men from the middle and upper classes.

Being issued a uniform, as we noted, indoctrinated the civilian into the military world. It gave him both a sense of pride and purpose: the cleaning and maintaining of kit is one of the primary occupations of a soldier when not on parade. The life of the soldier as well as his appearance was defined through differing degrees of control, and was contingent on at least the superficial acceptance and adoption of these codes. Furthermore, adherence to the code was theoretically regulated and constructed by an identifiable hierarchy, enforced through differing degrees of punishment. Cleaning kit and taking pride in one's appearance and the discipline this activity gave the soldier, as well as looking and feeling like a soldier, generated *esprit de corps*. In her examination of uniforms held at the *Musée de l'Armée* in Paris, Alison Matthews David noted that French officers often had their uniforms custom made to incorporate discreet interior embellishments such as luxurious silk lining.[2]

This type of modification may never be seen by anyone else but would reinforce one's unique and self-controlled identity, within the communal setting of the army. When we look at inspection returns where the inspectors are looking for regiments infringing regulations, we see colonels allowed discreet changes to regulations as ways of making their regiment not part of the uniform whole. The assumption of visual uniformity ignores the historical, social, and economic contexts in which uniforms actually operate. As our study of regimental inspection has revealed, uniformity in reality compared to theoretical perfection is commonly compromised by miscommunication (for example the misinterpretations of specifications, possibly purposefully to create a regimental uniform rather than that specified by the state), conflicting motivations, multiple manufacturers or channels of command, or material restraints (such as unstable dyes or shortages). Such factors may lead to a variety of effects: substitutions or deficiencies in uniforms, varying levels of strictness from uniform enforcers, necessary adaptations to new contexts, and individualistic alterations. Because of their bureaucratic nature, uniform codes do not always quickly or easily respond to environmental or contextual shifts. Individual wearers, therefore, find ways to adapt uniforms when necessary. The realities of shortages during times of war, and of deterioration on the battlefield, often require creative compensation, which in turn affects uniformity. These caveats all mean that official regulations must be tempered by how regiments responded to them, which is the *raison d'être* of this text.

1e *de Ligne*

The 1e *régiment de la Ligne*, the senior regiment of the line, was inspected at Lille on 28 June 1808. The report lists 5m of green broadcloth used – sufficient for making 25 *habits*. Were these experimental white *habits*, or blue faced in green for drummers? Very likely for the drummers. We also note 1,940m of '*drap blanc ordinaire*' in comparison to 180m of '*drap blanc pour revers*', i.e., the regiment had white cloth of a superior quality for *revers*, and a lot of white cloth for other purposes. Potentially this cloth was used for *culottes* and *vestes*. *Voltigeur habits* had utilised 9m 60 of chamois broadcloth. Every man in both battalions were wearing *schakos*, of which 1,827 were issued. In the 1805 to 1808 period, 87 *habits* had been repaired and 392 brand-new examples were in *dépôt*, along with 96 *vestes*, 138 pairs of *culottes*, and 318 *schakos*, with 205 being repaired since 1805. The *voltigeurs* were armed with standard infantry muskets. No *capotes* existed and nothing for the grenadiers. In the course of spring 1808 the regiment had purchased the following for the 1^e and 2^e battalions:[3]

340 *gibernes* at 8fr 14 each. Total 2,767fr 60
200 *baudriers* at 3fr 30 each. Total 660fr
1,100 musket slings at 88 centimes each. Total 968fr
1,500 bayonet scabbards at 60 centimes each. Total 900fr
9 drum carriages at 5fr 28 each. Total 47fr 52
12 *sapeurs'* aprons at 35fr 30 each. Total 422fr 40

Clearly the war battalions had six *sapeurs* each and were an innovation of the 1808 reorganisation of the line infantry. In total 85, 257fr 68 had been spent reclothing the two battalions as new.⁴

A separate report was made for the 3ᵉ battalion, the clothing of which was mostly in bad condition, 90 men out of 166 present had *chapeaux*, and in terms of material the *dépôt* held:⁵

280m 34 white broadcloth
3,957m 87 blue broadcloth
349m 55 scarlet broadcloth
7,898m 18 white tricot
552m grey tricot
17m 60 grey broadcloth
18,714m 05 white serge
5,528m 57 linen

The grey broadcloth was destined for *sous-officiers' redingotes* and the grey tricot was used to make *capotes* for the other ranks. Stores held stocks of *chapeaux*, 185, and had received in the preceding year some 1,203 *schakos*. The regiment had also had delivered 2,152 *capotes* in 1807.

The next document for the clothing of the regiment is a return from June 1809, listing items lost at the battle of Essling. One of the standout items listed are 63 bearskins for grenadiers: not a single bearskin existed in 1805 or 1808, so clearly these were an innovation of after March 1808 Also lost at Essling were 122 *schakos*, 215 *bonnets de police*, 90 *habits*, 122 *vestes*, 149 pairs of *culottes*, and 215 *capotes*.⁶

2ᵉ *de Ligne*

Inspected on 23 September 1804, the men were all dressed in *chapeaux*, while only grenadiers and *sous-officiers* carried sabres. One surprise is that 94m of drummers' lace had been used over the previous year: alas we do not know how much lace was applied to each garment. We also note 15 light cavalry *gibernes* and belts were in use along with 49 Austrian cavalry *gibernes* and belts, which were taken from use.⁷ A grenadier drummers' *habit* exists in the collections of the *Musee de l'Armée* from this period. It has eight chevrons to each sleeve in 27mm-wide lace, which also adorns the collar and cuff facings. We assume this garment is similar to that worn by the 2ᵉ. By the time of the review dated 25 July 1805, no drummers' lace existed, and no *sapeurs'* equipment or bearskins.⁸ The *voltigeur* company was formed on 28 October 1805.⁹ Presumably the lace had been used making drummers' clothing. Under the terms of the decree of 15 January, the regiment was issued 1813 *capotes*.¹⁰

The regiment was reviewed on 26 November 1807, by which time 19m 20 of chamois broadcloth had been used to make *voltigeurs'* clothing, and 2,876m 77 grey tricot had been used to produce *capotes*. The men had 1,597 *schakos* in use, 1,810 being provided by the regiment, and 1,737 *chapeaux* in use with the 1ᵉ and 2ᵉ battalion. The 3ᵉ battalion and 4ᵉ battalion with the *Grenadiers Réunis* – detached since 1804 – had *schakos*. Issued to the *voltigeurs* on 18 February 1806 were 448 light cavalry *mousquetons* and 34 *carabines rayé*, a further 60 *mousquetons* being issued on 2 April 1807. Remarkably, every man carried a sabre. The inspector ordered fusiliers and *voltigeurs* to hand in their sabres.[11]

A report dated 28 November 1807 tells us that the regiment was in the process of re-equipping with *schakos*. The *dépôt* held 266 brand-new *schakos*, which had been issued to the 3ᵉ battalion in the course of the year, and 706 additional *schakos* had been ordered to complete the equipment of the battalion.[12] Clearly, the 1ᵉ and 2ᵉ battalions were wearing *chapeaux*. In a second document, the inspector reported that in the coming year of 1808 the *dépôt* held for immediate needs 187 *habits*, 197 *vestes*, 219 pairs of *culottes*, 266 *schakos*, and 268 *bonnets de police*. For the year 1808 the regiment needed 1,413 *habits* and *vestes*, 2,826 pairs of *culottes*, a further 706 *schakos*, 137 *gibernes*, 35 *baudriers*, 137 musket slings, 3 drums and carriages.[13]

3ᵉ *de Ligne*

Almost uniquely, the 3ᵉ *de Ligne* has a very rich and complete paper archive. The *dépôt* of the regiment was reviewed on 25 October 1804. The report details that the regiment had 164 new bearskins, 40 needing repairs, and 38 that were to be written off, making 242. Some 46 were scheduled as replacements.[14] Inspected on 6 August 1805, the regiment the grenadiers had 288 bearskins and 2,488 *chapeaux* in service.[15]

The most important of documents relating to the dress of the regiment are the regimental standing orders from 15 July 1806 to June 1808. Extracted from the standing orders are the following snippets of very useful information:[16]

> 15 July 1806. Issue straps to secure *capote* to *havresac*. Fit the new *porte-gibernes* to the men.
>
> 18 July. Colonel reports that the regiment needs 500 cut-out number '3' in copper for the *gibernes*.
>
> 28 July. The new number '3' have arrived in the *dépôt* in Paris along with 60 new bearskins.
>
> 19 August. Copper hunting horns have arrived to be issued for the *gibernes* of the *voltigeurs*.
>
> 25 August. There has arrived at Strasbourg 60 new bearskins, 200 plumes for grenadiers, 1,000 muskets slings, tricot for *culottes*.
>
> 31 August: What are the *habits* of musicians to be like? Do we know when the sabres for *voltigeurs* will arrive? What of the 180 *giberne* plates for grenadiers, the number '3' and the hunting horns for *voltigeurs*? There exist orders to introduce

Sapeur of the 3ᵉ *de Ligne* by Otto, who accurately depicts the uniform recorded in the regiment's archive. (*Collection KM*)

Officer and grenadier of the 3ᵉ *de Ligne* by Otto, who again accurately depicts the dress of the 3ᵉ battalion. The 1ᵉ and 2ᵉ battalion grenadiers had bearskins at the time the artist Otto was working in spring 1808. (*Collection KM*)

the *schako* and replace the *chapeau*. I have ordered from Strasbourg 60 bearskins for grenadiers; these will complete the companies at 80 men strong.

2 September. Enquire about the plumes for the officers of grenadiers.

14 September. The *habits* of the musicians […] the *revers*, collars, cuffs and lining will be in red, to be the same as the *sapeurs*.

20 September. The cords for the *schako* will be white for fusiliers, red for grenadiers and green for *chasseurs* [sic].

Voltigeur officer and private of the 3ᵉ *de Ligne*. Otto again accurately depicts the regiment as it appeared in spring 1808. (*Collection KM*)

30 September. Pass contracts for 400 *capotes*.

10 October. The collars of the *capotes* are to have green piping. We will adopt the *schako* of the model approved. Make arrangements to order 50 plates for the *gibernes* of the grenadiers.

13 October. Make arrangements to purchase 240 pairs of epaulettes, sword knots and pompoms, 200 plumes and 60 bearskins for grenadiers. 330 pairs of epaulettes, pompoms, and sword knots for the *voltigeurs*, 700 *houpettes* for the fusiliers of the 3rd battalions. 1,400 *houpettes* for the first two battalions.

17 October. We have received the first of the new headdress of the definitive model adopted by the regiment which we will commence to wear. It will commence with the *voltigeurs*, who will have green cords.

26 December. For the production of white *habits* for the grenadiers and *voltigeurs*, the cloth had arrived. Sufficient cloth exists for the production of 750 *habits*. Each man will be measured by the master tailor, who must be careful in his work […] I report we have received the 400 *schakos* for *voltigeurs*.

23 May 1807. The men are to wear their black gaiters, the ribbons for the queue are to be cleaned, as are the *chapeaux*. The men are not to get their hair cut and wear false queues. The men's *culottes* are to be whitened.

30 June. Each company chief is to take 6fr from each man for the purchase of linen *pantalons* and short gaiters. The officers are to obtain blue *pantalons* and a pair made in nankeen for uniformity.

14 August. The regiment suffered greatly in the two battles, many men have lost their gaiters and *culottes*; make arrangements to have these made so that they are ready when we arrive in France […] the *habits* and *chapeaux* are in bad condition, make arrangements to produce these items, principally the *schakos*. Shoes: we obtained insufficient numbers for our needs from Berlin … we are missing a number of muskets.

26 August. Make arrangements to obtain the lace for the musicians, who will have lace of the 'system' 8 lines wide.

30 August. Have arrangements been made for the production of the *habits* for the musicians? Further, I also ask if the cloth for the lining and the red broadcloth for the collars, buttons and lace for these uniforms been delivered? The lace will be the same as for the *état-major*, 12 lines wide, but will be of 8 lines. The lace will be applied to the collar, cuffs, the long pockets, trefoils at the shoulder and at the taille; the stars and number '3' will be embroidered in gold on white. Write to me as quickly as possible at Berlin about this matter […] 500 *schako*, 900 *vestes* and also *culottes* and *habits* are needed […]

15 September. Tell me about the 200 copper number '3' and also the stars cut from red cloth for the fusiliers who are dressed in white *habits*.

2 October. The battalion commanders are to make arrangements to fit the hunting horns in copper for the *voltigeurs* and the number '3' for the fusiliers and the grenadiers to their *gibernes*.

1 December. The three companies of *voltigeurs* are to take from the magazine of the regiment their *schakos* to complete the companies […] the sergeant majors of the 7ᵉ and 8ᵉ companies are to draw theirs and make sure they are issued to their company. The *chapeaux* of the 2ᵉ *voltigeurs* and from the 7ᵉ are to be distributed to

the 2ᵉ battalion and the 8ᵉ company distributed to the 1ᵉ battalion. The companies of the 3ᵉ battalion are to obtain sufficient *schakos* for each man to have one […] the grenadiers of the 3ᵉ battalion are to draw *schakos* from the magazine; they will pass their *chapeaux* to the *voltigeurs* of the same the battalion.

3 December. For the inspection tomorrow, the regiment will wear black gaiters … the companies in white *habits* will whiten their *habits*, *vestes* and *culottes*; those in blue will whiten their *revers*, *culottes*, *vestes* and linings. The buff work will be whitened and the *gibernes* will be well blackened and cleaned.

29 December. The soldiers are allowed *pantalons* made from blue broadcloth … they will have buttons made from the same cloth as the *pantalons*.

25 January 1808. The white *habits* and *vestes* worn by the men are to be withdrawn and replaced with blue in their place.

30 January. The officers are to conform with as little delay as possible to change their *frac* or *surtout* to the model now adopted by the regiment, to be as follows: collar and cuffs in scarlet piped with white, piped red on the *frac*, the *retroussis* to be garnished with a no, '3' and star. The wearing of the *frac* will not be tolerated by the *sous-officiers*.

17 February. The white *bonnets de police* that exist with the companies clothed in blue *habits* are to be withdrawn from use and returned to the magazine and replaced with the same number in blue.

3 June. The sabres and *baudriers* are to be withdrawn from the *voltigeurs*. The white *habits* are to be swapped for blue.

The orders have some important information for us. The grenadiers of 1ᵉ and 2ᵉ battalion had bearskins, those of 3ᵉ battalion had *schakos*. They had a cut-out number '3' on the *giberne*, unlike the *voltigeurs*, which had a hunting horn. *Voltigeurs* and grenadiers had epaulettes and sword knots, but grenadiers alone had plumes. The decree of 15 January 1807 issued to the war battalions 1,229 white *habits*, 1,005 *vestes manches*, 1,009 pairs of *culottes*, and 2,237 *capotes* among other items.[17]

Inspected on 1 November 1807, General Schauenburg noted that the drummers and musicians wore *bleu celeste habits* faced in red, confirming the order book and the Otto MS image of a *sapeur*. The regiment was wearing the following clothing:[18]

Item	In Good Repair	In Need of Repair	To be written off	Total	Total made since last inspection	To be replaced
Habits	1,601	422	1,502	3,525	1,611	1,502
Vestes manches	2,047		1,548	3,565	2,017	1,548
Culottes	2,641		924	3,565	2,641	924
Chapeaux			1,765	1,765		1,765
Schakos	1,800			1,800	1,800	

Item	In Good Repair	In Need of Repair	To be written off	Total	Total made since last inspection	To be replaced
Bonnets de police	1,073		2,492	3,565	1,073	2,492
Gibernes	3,475			3,475	2,714	
Porte-gibernes	3,475			3,475	2,944	
Baudriers	1,241			1,241	857	
Musket slings	3,475			3,475	3,475	
Drum carriages	64			64	9	
Drums	64			64	9	
Cornets	8			8	8	

In addition, the *dépôt* held 331 brand-new *vestes* and 51 pairs of *culottes*. The grenadiers' bearskins are notably absent at the time of inspection and not a single *capote* existed in use with the regiment. Sadly, we know nothing else.

4ᵉ *de Ligne*

Inspected on 23 September 1804, the regiment possessed 12 *sapeurs*' aprons, yet the regiment had not a single bearskin for grenadiers or *sapeurs*, at least officially. Regimental accounts report 1,154fr 92 had been spent on distinctions – presumably this includes epaulettes for grenadiers. In addition, 11,360fr had been spent on equipping the regiment with 1,600 *capotes* and *redingotes*, as well as a further 28,800 on buying 1,600 pairs of linen *pantalons de route* and smocks.[19] The regiment was inspected less than a year later on 17 July 1805, when we note destined for drummers were 96 An XI light cavalry carbines that had been delivered since September 1804. In addition, 1,418fr had been spent buying 1,773 pairs of *sabots* and 2,519fr 69 on lace for *sous-officiers* and other distinctions, presumably epaulettes, drummers' lace etc. Again, no mention of bearskins is made.[20]

A document of 23 October 1805 tells us that the major had given orders to disband 2ᵉ company of 1ᵉ battalion, and 2ᵉ company of 2ᵉ battalion and to re-form them as *voltigeurs*.[21] The *voltigeur* companies were not fully organised until 7 July 1806.[22] We know nothing more until 1807. The decree of 15 January 1807 issued to the war battalions 1,163 white *habits*, 2,017 *vestes manches*, 2,016 pairs of *culottes*, and 2,272 *capotes* among other items.[23]

Inspected on 1 November 1807, the regiment had 2,779 *chapeaux* in use and 547 *schakos*. Of the 4,032 *habits* in use, 2,032 needed replacement and 600 needed repairs. The *voltigeurs* had 6 cornets. Looking in depth at the return we see not an inch of chamois cloth was in the *dépôt*. Some 3,508 *capotes* had been obtained, 3,153 had been issued and 372 were in stores. Some 9,902m 16 of cloth for *capotes* had been obtained and 7,727m 80 had been used to make them, with 45m of beige broadcloth in stores, presumably for *sous-officier redingotes*. We find proof positive that at least a battalion was equipped in white. The regiment had employed 149m 35 of green broadcloth, sufficient for the production of 743 *habits* and *vestes manches*. All three battalions must have been so dressed. The inspection return further reveals that regiment had 56 *cornets* and drummers, all of whom were armed with *mousquetons* and sabres as well as issued *gibernes* and belts. Furthermore, the inspection returns reveals that the eight musicians were wearing a sabre from a waistbelt, and also carried *mousquetons* and *gibernes*, as did the drum major and drum master. We note 30 *mousquetons* were issued to *voltigeur sous-officiers*, and every *voltigeur* carried a sabre. All the clothing for the musicians was not army issue and had been provided by stoppages in the officers' pay, hence no instruments or clothing appears in the inspection.[24] It seems entirely plauisble that the green cloth remaining in the *dépôt* in winter 1807 was used to make drummers' clothing.[25] This would therefore confirm what the *Petits Soldats d'Alsace*, a series of post-epoch drawings used by Rousselot, depicts: a blue *habit* with green *revers*, green cuffs and green tail lining with yellow lace to collar, cuffs, *revers* and tails.

5ᵉ *de Ligne*

The regiment was inspected on 23 February 1807, when the regiment's major reported that since 23 July 1805 and 2 January 1807 the unit had processed 3,753 men, of which 936 were killed in action, 672 had deserted, 27 had been 'reformed' i.e., kicked out of the regiment, 6 had been retired, 1 sent to Les Invalides, 10 had been sent to a veteran battalion, and 2 had been sent to a pioneer battalion.[26]

On 18 January 1808 the regiment's clothing and equipment was inspected: 3,162 *chapeaux* were in use, while the *voltigeurs* had 7 cornets. Not a single *capote* existed, nor *schako*. In a letter to the War Ministry dated 20 January 1808, the inspecting officer commented that the regiment had an immediate requirement for 292 *habits*, 375 *vestes*, 898 pairs of *culottes*, 901 *bonnets de police*, and 412 *gibernes* during the course of 1807. The unit had 12 *sapeurs*, all armed with An XI light cavalry *mousquetons*.[27]

We know nothing else about the dress of the regiment until 1814.

6ᵉ *de Ligne*

Based in Italy, detachments of the regiment were stationed on Corfu. Inspected in March 1808, the depot battalion had 93 *chapeaux* in use and 175 *schakos*, with 1,582 in use with the war battalions and a further 260 *chapeaux*. Just 35 *capotes* were with the battalion and 252 in total with the regiment made from grey tricot. For the depot battalion, 3m 50 of chamois broadcloth had been used to make *voltigeur* clothing.[28] Regiment accounts report that in the first quarter of 1811, 24 *sacs à distribution*, 24 canteens (*petit bidons*), 24 water cans (*bidons*) and 48 cooking pots (*gamelles*) were purchased for the sum of 128fr.[29]

7ᵉ *de Ligne*

A letter dated 17 December 1805 sent to the war minister informs us that the regiment was in the process of disbanding two fusilier companies to create *voltigeur* companies in the 1ᵉ and 2ᵉ battalions, then currently on active service. The *voltigeurs* of the 3ᵉ battalion in the *dépôt* were in the process of formation.³⁰ The *voltigeurs* of the 3ᵉ battalion were completely organised on 12 March 1806.³¹ From this document, it is clear that the *voltigeur* companies were not raised until spring 1806, six months after the formation decree. Inspected on 10 November 1807, the first time since summer 1804, the regiment had 1,256 *chapeaux* in use with the war battalions, which the inspector noted were to be replaced with 731 *schakos*, 156 *sous-officier redingotes*, 12 *sapeurs* led by a corporal were under arms and the *voltigeurs* had 6 cornets issued. The 3ᵉ battalion was issued 1,075 *schakos*, stores holding a further 725. We note 21m 95 of chamois broadcloth had been used to make *voltigeurs*' clothing, 1,728m 96 of grey tricot to make *capotes* as well as over 2,000m of black twill for gaiters. Also in use were 354 *houpettes de grenadier*, with 343 grenadier epaulettes and 344 sword knots, and 2,467 pompoms for fusiliers. The regiment had consumed a huge number of items of clothing in three years: 5,677 shirts, 3,387 black stocks, 3,578 pairs of linen socks, 1,360 pairs of wool stockings, 6,222 pairs of shoes, 2,792 pairs of grey linen gaiters, 2,767 pairs of black twill gaiters, 1,080 *sacs à distribution*, 2,658 *havresacs*, 3,800 cockades for *chapeau*, 115m 70 of gold lace for *sous-officiers*' rank stripes, and 3,736m 80 of wool lace, presumably for corporals' stripes, long-service stripes and drummers? We add finally that the band and drum major were issued *carabines rayé*, as were 34 *voltigeur* officers and *sous-officiers*. The *voltigeurs* themselves carried sabres and standard infantry muskets.³²

8ᵉ *de Ligne*

The 8ᵉ Ligne is one of the few regiments that adopted the white uniform where we can tally iconography and archive documents. The Otto MS shows a *sapeur* of the 8ᵉ wearing a white *habit*. The *habit* has a green collar with green piping to the *revers*, so presumably the cuffs matched regulation also. He wears a bearskin with scarlet cords and plume as headdress, and scarlet epaulettes at the shoulder. The upper arm of each sleeve of the *habit* is decorated with cut-out crossed axes in green broadcloth. His apron and gauntlets are oddly shown as chamois rather than white. In 1804 8,053fr 40 was spent on bearskins of unknown number.³³ We know the 8ᵉ had white *habits* as the war battalions were issued 1,502 white *habits* in January 1807 from government stocks.³⁴ Furthermore, the archive of the regiment does list that 108m 35 of green broadcloth had been used to produce 469 *habits* and *vestes manches* and 350m 04 remained unused in the *dépôt*. The regiment's three war battalions were totally dressed in *chapeaux*. Some 519 *schakos* had been issued to men in the *dépôt*. In addition, 1,200m of beige broadcloth and 3,857m of grey tricot had been used to make we assume *capotes* – yet none appear in the inspection return. Not an inch of chamois broadcloth existed for *voltigeurs*. We note 3,683 *chapeaux* were in use, and 6 *voltigeur* cornets.³⁵ Following the inspection, the inspector provided a list of prices for each item of clothing the regiment was authorised to purchase: among that list we find the authorisation to buy green broadcloth at 10fr 85 a metre, *chapeaux* costing 5fr, *schakos* at 9fr 50, black stocks, grey and black gaiters, as well as to pay no more than 1fr 10 to a seamstress to make up *capotes*.³⁶

Regulations in Practice 89

Drum major of the 8ᵉ *de Ligne* in spring 1808. (*Collection KM*)

Sapeur of the 8ᵉ *de Ligne* in spring 1808. He still retains his white *habit*. (*Collection KM*)

Grenadier officer and private of the 8ᵉ *de Ligne* depicted by Otto in spring 1808 accurately reflecting how the regiment was dressed when compared to its archive documents. (*Collection KM*)

Officer of *voltigeurs* of the 8ᵉ *de Ligne* in spring 1808. (*Collection KM*)

Voltigeur and fusilier of the 8ᵉ *de Ligne* in spring 1808. The *voltigeur* had kept his sabre contrary to regulations, but he correctly has green epaulettes and *schako* cords. Our fusilier retains the felt *chapeau*. (*Collection KM*)

Fusilier company officer and private of the 8ᵉ *de Ligne* wearing the November 1807 regulation. (*Collection KM*)

9ᵉ de Ligne

Inspected on 12 September 1805, every man was wearing a *chapeau*, and the inspector noted half the unit's clothing needed repairs or total replacement: 886 *habits* out of 1,758 garments needed repairs and 88 total replacement, for example. In addition, 1,600 *capotes* had been made, with 769 remaining in stores, and 1,600 pairs of linen *pantalons de route* had been made, again 769 pairs remained in stores. The only men issued sabres were drummers and *sous-officiers*.[37]

A report completed on June 1807 notes that in order to clothe the workers making the men's uniform and equipment, each worker had been issued a smock and pair of linen pantalons, costing 18fr 92. Further, 2,400 *schakos* had been purchased from workshops in Lyon, each costing 12fr, which included the copper plate but not shipping. Also purchased were 1,300 pairs of shoes, ordered on 15 March 1807.[38]

On 11 January 1808, the regiment was wearing 2,346 *schakos*, all brand new, 1,746 *capotes* and unlike earlier inspections, grenadiers – as well as *sous-officiers* in fusilier and *voltigeur* companies – carried sabres, and presumably had scarlet epaulettes. Of interest, 25 An XI light cavalry *mousqueton*s were issued to 25 grenadiers: we wonder if these men were *sapeurs*? The *voltigeurs* did not carry sabres, we note. Since 1805, 2,579 *capotes* had been made with 1,475 in service, 1,041 needed immediate replacement, as did 1,493 *habits*: virtually every item of clothing with the war battalions was worn out and needed replacing.[39] Interestingly, the regiment reports that at Essling it lost 5 *sapeurs'* axes and cases, as well as 91 grenadier bearskins: clearly these were all adopted post-January 1808. Other items lost included 12 hatchets, 820 muskets, 856 bayonets, 251 sabres and belts, 820 *gibernes* and belts, 75 *marmites*, 60 *grand bidons*, 96 *gamelles*, 10 drums and 4 cornets.[40]

We know from inspection returns of 1808 that the drummers were dressed in blue *habits* with green *revers*; indeed 262fr was spent in 1810 buying 20m of green cloth for the drummers.[41]

10ᵉ de Ligne

The regiment was reviewed at the end of June 1808. Every man in the war battalions was wearing a *chapeau*, some 2,363 examples. We note 14m 80 of yellow broadcloth had been used in the production of *voltigeurs'* clothing. We also note 1,293m 48 of grey tricot had been used to make an unknown number of *capotes*. Of interest, the report notes that since 1 May 1806, the regiment had purchased 5m 95 of *bleu de ciel* broadcloth, and used 3m 45 in the production of uniforms: likely more of the same already in use. Presumably this was destined for the band or drummers. Ordered on 5 March 1808 were 600 replacement *chapeaux* and 300 *schakos*.[42] The *voltigeurs* of 3ᵉ battalion had no sabres, but were issued 140 An XI light cavalry *mousquetons*, but without distinctive facings. The men of the battalion also had *schakos*, unlike the war battalions, with 434 in use and 66 in stores.[43]

11ᵉ de Ligne

Inspected on 24 October 1803, stores reported black twill, white linen and ecru linen for gaiters, which were fastened in all cases with horn buttons. Stores also reported, but none were held, grenadiers' bearskins, *capotes*, gold lace for musicians, drummers' lace, tricolour feather hackles to be worn in the *chapeau*, 72 *chapeaux*, and 115 pairs of grenadier epaulettes. Drummers' epaulettes are recorded but we are ignorant as to how these differed from grenadiers' examples. Stores did hold 125 fusiliers' pompoms, 1 grenadiers' pompom, and 198 *sous-officier* and grenadier sword knots. Also lodged in stores were 582 black stocks with *rabats* – the removable piping – as well as knee, stock and breeches buckles.[44] Reviewed once more on 23 September 1804, the regiment had 16 *sapeurs*, but officially no bearskins.[45] Inspected again on 21 January 1808, 1,992 grey tricot *capotes* were in use, 3,655 *schakos*, and 8 *voltigeur* cornets, yet not an inch of chamois broadcloth existed to make *voltigeur* clothing. The *voltigeurs* were armed with 496 An XI light cavalry *mousquetons*, we note, but did not carry sabres. However, the *voltigeur* company *sous-officiers* and cornets were issued sabres and also *mousquetons*.[46]

12ᵉ de Ligne

The paper archive for the regiment is remarkable for its coverage of the white uniform. Under the decree of 15 January 1807, the unit received 1,091 white *habits*, 2,002 *vestes manches*, 2,008 pairs of *culottes*, 1,648 ready-made *capotes* with 137 more to be sewn together, 4,763 pairs of shoes and 211 shirts.[47] When it was inspected on 21 March 1808 the regiment had 304 white *habits* in use in good condition, 650 needing repairs and a total of 1,602 had been made. The regiment at the same time possessed 3,201 blue *habits*, 1,398 in good condition, 230 needing repairs and 619 to be written off. A total of 3,964 were made between 1805 and March 1808. Every single white *habit* was scheduled to be replaced in 1808:[48]

Item		Good	Needing repairs	To be written off	Total	Received since last inspection	To be replaced
Habit	Blue	1,398	230	619	3,201	3,964	
	White	304	650			1,602	1,601
Vestes		2,597	453	151	3,201	6,371	1,601
Culottes		2,604		597	3,201	8,791	3,201
Schakos		1,993	307		3,201	3,348	801
Chapeaux				901		2,416	
Bonnets	d'Oursin			275	275		46
	de Police	1,500		315	1,815	2,585	908
Capotes		1,032	434		1,466	1,499	10,67

Suhr shows the 12ᵉ and 13ᵉ *de Ligne* wearing white uniforms sometime in early 1808.

Items processed by the *dépôt* 1805 to 1808 were as follows:[49]

Item		In *dépôt* at last review	Made since last review	Total	Issued	Remaining in *dépôt*
Habit	Blue		4,112	4,112	3,973	139
	White		1,602	1,602	1,602	
Vestes			5,611	5,611	6,371	140
Culottes			8,889	8,889	8,791	108
Schakos			3,675	3,675	3,348	327
Chapeaux		90	2,336	2,336	2,416	
Bonnets	*d'Oursin*					
	de Police	125	2,525	2,650	2,584	76
Capotes		8	1,692	1,700	1,499	201
Smocks		35		35	27	8

In 1807 the regiment had adopted the *schako* to replace the *chapeau*. Some 3,348 *schakos* had been issued since 1807, with 901 *chapeaux* to be written off, being put into the *dépôt* along with 275 grenadier bearskins. This means that the regiment was an early adopter of the *schako*, and that its introduction witnessed the deletion of grenadiers' bearskins as well as *chapeaux* – was this a trend across the army? More than likely, we suspect. We note that 46 new grenadier bearskins were authorised – potentially for *sapeurs* and also drummers as the numbers are too low for a grenadier company as a whole. Looking at the cloth used, 727m 50 beige broadcloth had been used to make *sous-officier redingotes*, 4,889m 42 grey tricot for soldiers' *capotes*, 14m 40 chamois for *voltigeurs*, 150m black broadcloth – gaiters or piping? – and 689m 68 *panne noir*.[50] The regiment in 1807 had spent 1,103fr on new sword knots for *voltigeurs*, in 1808 1,474 *schakos* had been obtained and in 1809 a further 875.[51] A second document tells us that 1,091 white *habits* had been issued from government stocks to the war battalions during the course of 1807.[52]

A portrait exists of Major Raymond Jean-Baptiste Teulet wearing the white *habit*.[53] The *habit* has a black collar piped in white, white *revers* piped in black, black cuff facings, white cuff flaps piped in black, and black piping to the tails. As a mounted officer he carries a sabre, carried off a black waistbelt. The rank chevrons on his *schako* have the points upper most. A second painting of an officer of the regiment, again dressed in white, was sold by Hermann Historica on 9 November 2011 and is identified as Major Francis Marie Cyprien Teulle. Therefore, beyond reasonable doubt the regiment was indeed dressed in the new-regulation uniform.

Reviewed on 1 May 1811, the inspector noted the regiment had 65 officers, 2,388 men and 116 horses. He added that eight officers were needed to bring the regiment up to capacity. He noted 36 drums and carriages were needed and 122 sabres, adding that the men had not been paid since April 1809.[54]

13ᵉ de Ligne

Reviewed in early October 1804, the regiment mustered 1,422 all ranks, of which just 3 were musicians. A staggering 486 men had deserted since June 1802 and 684 men had been sent to the *Grenadiers Réunis*. The inspector ordered 762 *habits* and *vestes* made, 1,532 pairs of *culottes* and 762 *chapeaux*. No bearskins existed.[55] Reviewed on 24 July 1805, only 194 of the new *habits* had been made, but 690 pairs of *culottes* and 460 *chapeaux* had been delivered.[56]

Moving on to 3 December 1807, the regiment's major reported stores held no chamois or red broadcloth, 210 pairs of *culottes* and 80 black stocks.[57] Reviewed on 7 January 1808, 1,990 *redingotes* were in use, 2,177 *schakos* and 144 *chapeaux*. The *redingotes* were made from grey broadcloth for *sous-officiers* and grey tricot for other ranks. Since December, 43m 13 of chamois broadcloth had been employed, and 660 Austrian *vestes* were in use. No bearskins are recorded.[58]

14ᵉ de Ligne

During 1804 we note the regiment had 1,564 *capotes* in service made from 3,808m of broadcloth, 1,600 linen smocks and the same number of *pantalons de route*.[59] In August 1805, the drummers, regimental band and 13 fusiliers were armed with 83 An XI light cavalry carbines.[60]

Moving on a few years, the paper archive of the regiment and contemporary iconography by Suhr agree in showing that the white *habit* was adopted. During January 1807 the regiment received from government stocks 1,000 white *habits*, 2,000 *vestes manches*, 1,765 *capotes* and a further 229 as 'kits'.[61] Furthermore, regimental paperwork says that 2,088m 89 of black broadcloth had been used in the production of 2,210 *habits* and *vestes manches*. The inspector further noted that the regiment needed 1,000 *habits*, 2,000 *vestes manches* and 2,000 pairs of *culottes* because the cloth used was of mediocre quality, and the linings of the *surtouts* – presumably of the officers – were worn out. In addition, the inspector reported that 145 lengths of blue broadcloth and 13 lengths of scarlet broadcloth of Lodeve quality had been returned to the suppliers because it was not of the required quality for army clothing. From this, it seems the regiment had started the process of re-equipping in blue when it was inspected at Sedan on 26 March 1808. Not a single item of equipment existed for *sapeurs* and not an inch of chamois cloth for *voltigeurs*.[62]

Reviewed on 27 January 1809 during the siege of Saragossa, the regiment was in appalling condition: the unit needed 2,344 *habits* and the same number of *vestes manches*, 3,144 pairs of *culottes*, 1,644 *schakos*, 320 bearskins, 2,144 capotes as well as 3,144 smocks. More than 4,000 pairs of shoes were needed, 2,000 pairs of grey or black gaiters, 3,144 black stocks and almost 3,000 *gibernes*, belts and bayonets. What had been a smartly dressed unit nine months earlier was a total shambles.[63]

15ᵉ *de Ligne*

Reviewed on 6 August 1805, the inspection report tells us that the regiment had *habits* of different patterns in use, and ordered the tails to be cropped to the same length. The inspector ordered that the master tailor pay better attention to the regulation and the model items sent from the War Ministry as nothing in service adhered to them. He added that the drummers were to wear the same uniform as the soldiers, and henceforth the red *revers* and cuffs – does he mean cuff flaps? – were to be abandoned. The *sapeurs* were also ordered to remove the offending *revers* and cuffs.[64]

The Bourgeois of Hamburg MS shows in great detail a grenadier of the 15ᵉ *de Ligne*. His *habit* matches the regulation appearance of the *habit*, i.e., black collar, black *revers*, black piping, white cuffs. As a grenadier, he carries scarlet epaulettes and a scarlet sword knot. His *schako* has the 1807 issue plate, and white cords. However, when the regiment was reviewed by General Muller, not an inch of black broadcloth was listed in the *dépôt* on 13 February 1808. It also shows that for 4,644 men under arms, 2,289 *chapeaux* were in service with the war battalions and 2,750 *schakos* with the depot battalion. We also observe that 13m 88 of chamois broadcloth had been used to make *voltigeurs*' clothing, 735m of blue broadcloth and 4,037m 52 of white broadcloth to produce 2,759 *habits* and repair 1,628 examples. The huge use of white broadcloth hints at white *habit* production. We also note the *voltigeurs* had no sabres, 485 An XI light cavalry carbines were in use and 36 *carabines rayé* by officers and *sous-officiers* of *voltigeur* companies. The regimental band had five musicians

Grenadier of the 15ᵉ *de Ligne* in white *habit* by Martinet. The regiment officially had no bearskins.

Regulations in Practice 101

Presumably a voltigeur of the 15ᵉ *de Ligne* sometime in 1807–08 by Martinet.

An alternative print of a *voltigeur* of the 15ᵉ *de Ligne* by Martinet, reflecting the 1807 decree about the colour of epaulettes and *schako* cords, allowing green but forbidding yellow. Despite this, he carried a non-regulation sabre.

of African origin who were sent to the *Bataillon des Pionniers Noirs*. We are ignorant of the band's uniform.[65] Perhaps conforming the Hamburg image, the regiment only received 21 *habits* from government stocks during 1807; presumably they were white and 'more of the same'.[66] An officer of the 63ᵉ *de Ligne* tells us the 15ᵉ *de Ligne* had white *habits*.[67] Further supporting evidence comes from an officer of the 15ᵉ, who tells us among other things how rarely French officers wore full dress uniform during a period of active campaigning: 'I only regret having been obliged to buy new uniforms which resulted in a useless expenditure of 200fr. The Emperor re-instituted the blue habit after only a short time and of the two white uniforms I purchased I wore one only a few times, and the other never.'[68] It seems the 15ᵉ had white. Martinet shows bearskins for the grenadiers, of which none existed in 1805, 1808 or 1811.[69]

16ᵉ *de Ligne*

The regiment is one of the few we can be certain had grenadiers with bearskins: 252 being in use in late summer 1804.[70] The grenadiers of 3ᵉ battalion had 52 bearskins in summer 1805.[71]

Archive documents show that at the time of the regiment's inspection on 22 November 1807, some 930m 67 of black broadcloth had been used to produce 1,238 white *habits* and *vestes*, therefore we can be reasonably sure that the regiment had a single battalion in the white uniform. The inspecting officer noted that 664 *habits* needed total replacement, sufficient white broadcloth existed in the *dépôt* to make *vestes* and revers for the *habits*, and that 1,291 men in the war battalions needed new *habits*. We also note 210 good condition grenadiers' bearskins, with 42 to be

Voltigeur officer of the 16ᵉ *de Ligne*. Of interest, he has a black épée waistbelt. It is of importance to note the *veste* does not extend below the bottom of the revers. Since An11 (1805) the bottom edge of *veste* was stop above navel-quite short indeed. Indeed, so short were the *vestes* they are described as gilets i.e. lacking the skirts (basques) we see in the images by Hoffmann circa 1805.

written off. Accounts show 90 made and issued since 1805. We also note 2,089 *chapeaux* were in use alongside 1,456 *schakos*, while 42m 68 of chamois broadcloth had been used for *voltigeurs'* distinctions – a huge amount of cloth suggesting far more than collars of the *habits* and *vestes* were chamois. Had the cloth been used to make *cornets'* clothing? – 2,142m 89 of beige tricot had been used to make *capotes* and 13 sets of *sapeurs'* equipment were in use. The *voltigeurs* were armed with 372 sabres and the officers of the companies

Regulations in Practice 103

Suhr shows the 16ᵉ *de Ligne* at point of transition from white to blue in summer 1808. The white-coated figure with yellow *schako* cords is presumably a *voltigeur*.

were armed with 27 *carabines rayé*.⁷² Under the January 1807 decree, 140 white *habits* had been issued and 2,158 *capotes*.⁷³

17ᵉ de Ligne

Inspected on 24 October 1803, regimental stores were filled with cloth and clothing. We find 3,366m of black twill for gaiters, 29m 23 of bleached white linen for white gaiters, 25,072 horn buttons for gaiters, 62 *capotes*, 12 copper grenades for grenadiers *gibernes*, 601m of drummers' lace, 56m white worsted lace, 279 tricolour *aigrettes*, 106 fusilier *ganses* for the *chapeaux* and 36 for grenadiers. Stores also held 1,616 pompoms for fusiliers, 31 grenadier pompoms, 38 pairs of grenadier epaulettes, 86 pairs of drummers' epaulettes – how were they different to grenadiers? – 37 grenadiers' sword knots, and 63 for drummers. Stores also held 8 pairs of white gaiters, 20 in natural linen and 80 in black twill. Other items of note are 245 queue pins, 339 black stocks, 343 white stocks with 52 spare buckles and 64 *rabats*. Of note, the regiment's *capotes* were made from green broadcloth, stores holding 128m 29m of this cloth inherited from the 41ᵉ *demi-brigade* and also 24m 59 of green tricot, again to make *capotes*. We assume the 17ᵉ *de Ligne* had green *capotes*.⁷⁴

By the time of the next review, all the drummers' lace seems to have been used. We note the eight-strong band and 36 drummers were issued An XI light cavalry *mousqueton*.⁷⁵

The Bourgeois of Hamburg shows two members of the 17ᵉ *de Ligne*, one wearing a blue *habit*, the other a white *habit*. The regiment's war battalions were issued from government stocks in January 1807, 2,106 white *habits*, 2,827 *vestes manches*, 3,274 pairs of *culottes*, 4,138 ready-made *capotes*, 250 as 'kits', 7,191 pairs of shoes and 2,317 shirts: the regiment was almost clothed as new.⁷⁶ Inspected on 1 January 1808, the regiment had following clothing and equipment in use:⁷⁷

Item	In Good Repair	In Need of Repair	To be written off	Total	Total made since 28 July 1805	To be replaced
Habits	1,830	1,500	3,594	4,594	3,507	2,594
Vestes manches	1,500	1,500	1,594	4,594	4,035	1,594
Culottes	1,000		3,594	4,594	5,626	3,594
Chapeaux			3,040	4,595	3,967	
Schakos	1,554			1,554	1,554	3,040
Bonnets de police	1,591		3,003	4,594	1591	3,040
Capotes	1,228	1,500	1,366	4,594	1,248	1,860
Gibernes	1,144	200	236	4,594	2,190	230
Porte-gibernes	1,144	200	236	4,594	2,190	230
Baudriers	927		50	977	459	50
Musket sling	1,144	200	230	4594	2,640	230
Drum carriage	57		3	60		3
Drums	57		3	60		3
Voltigeur cornets	8			8	8	

Fourrier – corporal-quartermaster – of the 17ᵉ *de Ligne* in summer 1808 from a series of prints by the Suhr brothers.

Sergeant major of a *voltigeur* company of the 17ᵉ *de Ligne* in summer 1808.

Sapeur of the 17ᵉ *de Ligne* still dressed in his white *habit* in summer 1808.

Drummer of the 17ᵉ *de Ligne*, who retains his white *habit* into summer 1808.

Regulations in Practice 107

Grenadier officer of the 17ᵉ *de Ligne* in summer 1808. We also see a corporal (?) of grenadiers of the 17ᵉ depicted by Suhr. He has both a bearskin and *schako*, as well as white crescents to his epaulettes.

Officer of the 17ᵉ *de Ligne* in undress uniform in summer 1808.

The *voltigeur* companies clearly existed by winter 1807 as some 18m 37 chamois broadcloth had been used to make their clothing. Since 1804, 114 An XI light cavalry *mousquetons* were in use with the *voltigeur* company *sous-officiers* and corporals along with sabres, 17 drummers also received these firearms. The *voltigeurs* themselves had 302 dragoon muskets, carried no sabres, and 18 *carabines rayé* were issued to the senior *sous-officiers* and officers of *voltigeurs*. We assume drummers and officers therefore also had *gibernes* and belts. The inspection returns shows that *capotes* were made from a mix of grey tricot – some 2,359m being used to make *capotes* – and beige broadcloth with some 185m 50 being used to produce 1,845 garments. Some 864 *schakos* had been purchased since 1805 and 3,611 *habits* had been made. The entire 3e battalion had been clothed and equipped as new from government issue clothing in Hanover and a company in Stettin – these men must have been dressed in white *habits*.[78]

Reviewed on 1 May 1811, the inspector noted the regiment had 61 officers, 2,060 men and 98 horses. He added 10 officers were needed to bring the regiment up to capacity. Clothing wise, 1,250 *habits* and 2,019 *vestes* needed repairs and 1,992 pairs of *culottes* needed to be replaced, while 167 men had lost their *bonnets de police*. Also needing repairs were 180 bearskins and 741 *capotes*. The campaign equipment was short 97 hatchets, 6 shovels needed repairs and 14 were needed.[79]

18e *de Ligne*

Inspected on 25 September 1804, we note 9,600fr had been spent in the production *capotes*, and a further 11,767fr 15 had been spent buying cloth to make the garments in the year to September 1803. In the year prior to the inspection a further 33,369fr had been spent making *capotes*, *pantalons de route*, smocks and buying 1,600 pairs of shoes. Indeed, we note, 1,600 *capotes* were in service, with 1,588 smocks and 1,264 pairs of *pantalons de route*, and accompanied by 1,547 pairs of linen gaiters.[80] Reviewed again 20 July 1805, we note 1,622 *capotes* were in use, 1,561 linen smocks, 70 grenadiers' pompoms, 1,657 fusiliers' pompoms, 87 pairs of grenadier epaulettes and 52 grenadier sword knots.[81]

Between 20 July 1805 and 4 November 1807, the regiment had used 14m 40 of yellow broadcloth for the collars of *voltigeurs*' *habits*, while also for *voltigeurs* were 543 pompoms, 420 pairs of epaulettes and 360 sword knots. For grenadiers, 290 grenadiers' pompoms, 294 pairs of grenadier epaulettes and 223 sword knots. Fusiliers had 543 pompoms as their distinctions. Nothing explicit was mentioned about the men wearing white *habits*. Nothing is said either about *sapeurs*, so presumably the regiment had none at this date. We also note 3,270 *capotes* were in service – made from beige broadcloth for *sous-officiers* and grey tricot for other ranks – 1,482 *chapeaux*, 857 *schakos* and 31 bearskins. In stores were a further 209 brand-new bearskins waiting to be issued along with 1,143 *schakos*. Armament wise, the *voltigeurs* were armed with 198 An XI light cavalry *mousquetons*, and no sabres.[82] Issued during 1807 from government stocks were 1,005 white *habits*, 2,005 *vestes*, 2,007 pairs of *culottes*, 1,212 ready-made *capotes* and a further 1,407 in 'kit form', 3,329 pairs of shoes and 293 shirts.[83] At least one of the war battalions was therefore dressed in white: further confirmation of white *habits* comes from the fact that 3,*134m* 16 of blue broadcloth had been used since 1805 and 3,776m 65 white broadcloth with 906m 52 of scarlet broadcloth – according to the blue uniform tariff sufficient for 6,000 *habits* – to produce 3,199 garments, of which at least 1,199 were white. We know the broadcloth was not destined for *culottes* and *vestes* as 14,336m of white tricot had been used for this purpose. The blue broadcloth used was sufficient to make just 2,000 garments, therefore more than 1,000 white *habits* had been issued in addition to government-issued items.

19ᵉ *de Ligne*

When inspected on 27 December 1807 there is no indication of cloth used to make white *habits*, but we note 3,257m of white broadcloth and 1,511m of blue broadcloth had been used. Stores reports 3,044 *habits* had been made since 1805: the blue broadcloth used was sufficient for just 940 *habits*, therefore more than 1,000 white *habits* had been made. Confirming the use of white *habits*, the regiment had received under the decree of 18 January 1807, 1,155 *habits*, 2,000 pairs of *culottes* and 2,013 *vestes* that had been supplied directly by the state. Clearly, at this date, with the white uniform being authorised for general use, the *habits* and *vestes* must have been made to the white uniform regulations. Confirming this, 1,184 *habits* out of 2,733 in use had to be replaced as non-regulation. The returns also show that 19m 61 of chamois broadcloth had been used to make collars of *voltigeurs*' *habits* and 2,169m 64 of beige broadcloth had been used to make *redingotes* for *sous-officiers* and 1,924m grey tricot to make *capotes* for other ranks, 1,181 garments of both types being in service, with 2,487 examples ordered to give every man a *capote*. Rather than *culottes*, the regiment was wearing tricot *pantalons*, 1,936 pairs being in use. We also note 1,082 *chapeaux* in service and 1,060 *schakos*. Armament wise, the *sous-officiers* of *voltigeurs* were armed with 131 An XI light cavalry *mousquetons* as well as 27 *carabines rayé*, with 9 *voltigeur* officers armed with these weapons. The *voltigeurs* themselves had no sabres, but were issued 366 *fusils de dragon*.[84]

A letter dated 8 January 1808 tells us the regiment for its greater part was dressed in linen *pantalons de route*, all of which needed replacing; the *capotes* were also 'falling to pieces'. The writer goes on to say that the men wore their *capotes* and *pantalons de route* as habitual clothing in barracks and their rooms, that new entrants to the regiment were to be issued 'used' clothing from old soldiers, and they were to be issued new, as the conscripts often arrived with just a linen *veste* and *pantalons*. The letter also tells us the regiment's *habits* did not conform to regulations as they enclosed the hips, and that all new *habits* were to conform to the model sent by the war minister. New *habits* were to be made for the drum major, drummers, musicians and *sapeurs*, but we are ignorant as to their appearance.[85]

20ᵉ *de Ligne*

The 3ᵉ and 4ᵉ battalions were reviewed on 13 March 1808. We note 358 *schakos* were in use and 184 *chapeaux*, while the two war battalions had a further 785 *schakos* and

2,147 *chapeaux*. The *voltigeurs* in both battalions had chamois distinctions as 27m 30 of chamois broadcloth had been used for this purpose. We also note 2,445 *capotes* had been issued, made from 1,146m 01 grey tricot.[86] The war battalions were reviewed on 29 May 1808, when 2,686 *chapeaux* or *schakos* were in service, and the two *voltigeur* companies had four cornets. Only *sous-officiers* and grenadiers carried sabres.[87]

21ᵉ *de Ligne*

The decree of 15 January 1807 equipped the war battalions with 922 white *habits*, 1,153 *vestes*, 1,152 pairs of *culottes*, 3,726 *capotes*, 197 *capotes* in 'kit form', 5,162 pairs of shoes and 767 shirts.[88] Inspected on 1 December 1807, the report reveals that of the regiment's 4,595 *habits*, 2,292 needed total replacement, and since 1805 4,011 *habits* had been made. The huge numbers needing replacement may imply the presence of white *habits* in use with the regiment: sufficient blue broadcloth to make 2,453 *habits* had been used, indicating well over 1,500 white *habits* had been made. We also note every pair of tricot *culottes* needed total replacement. No *schakos* were in use, but 288 bearskins for grenadiers were. When we look however at the store's returns, we find 288 bearskins, were in the *dépôt* and were not issued. We also find 2,509 brand-new *capotes* had been made, and all bar two issued. They were made from a mix of beige broadcloth – some 2,194m being used to make *capotes*, as well as beige tricot – some 4,645m 76 being used; *sous-officiers* had broadcloth and other ranks tricot. No chamois or yellow broadcloth existed for *voltigeurs'* distinctions. The regiment was issued 102 cavalry *mousquetons*. Of these, 12 were issued to the band, drum major, and drum master, 20 to sergeant majors and sergeants, 4 to corporals of the *voltigeur*

Sapeur of the 21ᵉ *de Ligne* as observed in summer 1808. (*Collection KM*)

Grenadier officier and private of the 21ᵉ *de Ligne* in summer 1808. (*Collection KM*)

Voltigeur officer and private of the 21ᵉ *de Ligne* in summer 1808. We can date this image to 1808 when we compare what is depicted in the regiment's archive. (*Collection KM*)

Officer and fusilier of the 21ᵉ *de Ligne*, in summer 1808. Plumes were strictly non-regulation for any other than grenadiers, but were tolerated as long as they were not paid for from government or regimental funds. (*Collection KM*)

companies and 66 were issued to the drummers and cornets. Therefore, the drummers wore both cross belts as they must have been issued *gibernes* to carry the cartridges for their firearm. The regiment had 396 *voltigeurs*, who were armed with standard infantry muskets, had no sabres, and seemingly had no distinctions to mark them out from the fusiliers.[89] A document dated 1 December that authorised prices the regiment was to pay for cloth and items of equipment makes no mention of chamois broadcloth for *voltigeurs*, lists *schakos* to cost 9fr 25 and remarkably reports black pleated neck stocks made from horse hair – *col noir en crin* – to cost 1fr 15 and white stocks to cost 40 centimes.[90]

Reviewed on 1 May 1811, the inspector noted the regiment had 62 officers, 2,438 men and 94 horses. He added 8 officers were needed to bring the regiment up to capacity. Clothing wise, a lot needed replacing: 10 *vestes*, 1964 pairs of *culottes*, 481 *schakos*, 55 *gibernes* and belts, 119 bayonet scabbards, 16 *baudriers*, 31 muskets and 7 sabres. Needing repairs were 125 *gibernes* and belts, 19 musket slings, 18 muskets and 3 drums. Missing were 202 *baudriers*, 202 sabres and 48 drums.[91]

Reviewed on 1 July 1811, the 4ᵉ and 6ᵉ battalions we wearing 1,255 *habits*, 1,255 sleeveless *vestes*, 1,255 pairs of tricot *culottes*, 1,255 *schakos*, 1,255 *bonnets de police*, and 1,255 *capotes*. Equipment wise, 1,229 *gibernes* and belts were issued, 1,869 *baudriers*, 1,229 musket slings and 20 drums. Armament was 1,229 muskets, 1,229 bayonets, and 186 sabres.[92]

The regiment's battalion artillery was equipped with four 3-pdr field guns, six caissons, five infantry munition caissons, one field forge, five stores waggons, one ambulance, and one wagon for rations. The regiment had 36 gunners, 50 drivers and 108 horses.[93]

22ᵉ de Ligne

The decree of 15 January 1807 equipped the war battalions with 1,404 white *habits*, 2,028 *vestes*, 2,033 pairs of *culottes*, 1,579 *capotes*, 1,641 pairs of shoes and 1,953 shirts.[94] Reviewed on 21 December 1807 at Wesel, the regiment had fully adopted the *schako*, complete with chinscales, some 3,183 being in use, and having been issued 1,677 *chapeaux* since 1805. Since 1805, 3,349 *habits* had been made, which needed 5,190m of broadcloth: we note 3,722 of blue broadcloth had been used to make *habits*, and 3,005m of white broadcloth, indicating the production of more white *habits*. In addition, 1,315 *redingotes* were in use, 567 being made since 1805, and 772 needing replacement. Furthermore, the inspecting officer noted that the clothing was well made, except the *culottes*, which were too large on the men's legs. Not an inch of chamois cloth broadcloth existed and no equipment for *sapeurs* existed either. The *redingotes* were made from grey tricot, some 2,702m being used for this purpose. Remarkably 41 grenadiers – surely *voltigeurs*? – were armed with An XI light cavalry *mousquetons*, as were all 54 drummers, who must have been issued *gibernes* and belts as well as the eight men in the band and the drum corporal. The unit had no drum major and had 16 children on regimental strength.[95]

Sapeur of the 22ᵉ *de Ligne*, who had retained his white *habit* into late spring 1808. (*Collection KM*)

Regulations in Practice 117

Grenadiers of the 22ᵉ *de Ligne* in summer 1808. Otto correctly shows the use of *schakos* for grenadiers. Bearskins had been abolished for campaign use in August 1805, and removed from use in March 1806. (*Collection KM*)

Voltigeur officer and private of the 22ᵉ *de Ligne* in summer 1808 at the point of transition from white to blue uniform. (*Collection KM*)

23ᵉ de Ligne

Inspected on 1 September 1804, the regiment had nine *sapeurs*, but no bearskins for them, at least officially. The clothing was all considered excellent, well sewn and made from good-quality cloth for the rank and file, the inspector remarked. He raised concerns that the band was being lavished with money over and beyond the day's pay per month from each officer.[96] Inspected again on 9 August 1805, the inspector noted:

> the turnbacks of the tails of the *habits* are decorated with small pieces of broadcloth cut in the shape of a heart: they are to be changed to numbers to match the other regiments.

This order neatly tells us what the regulation ornaments to the tails were to be. He carried on:

> There exists four companies that wear epaulettes and sword knots, as well as hunting horns on the tails of their *habits*; they have braided their hair into long tresses. They are equipped as *chasseurs* [...] The band, drummers, *sapeurs* and *fifre* are clothed according to the regulation. The equipment is bad [...] many bayonet scabbards are missing and not one *baudrier* in buff leather exists to carry the eagles [...] the manner of fastening the collar of the *habit* is incorrect, the shirt collars are thrown up and a cravat is worn, which is to be immediately abolished and a black regulation stock worn by the *sous-officiers* and men.

The inspector noted 1,988 1777-model muskets were in use and 397 of the 1763 model. The four *chasseur* companies had been sent back to the regiment from the *Grenadiers Réunis*.[97]

Reviewed on 19 January 1808, we remark the regiment had 1,702 *capotes* in use, more than a 1,000 being lost during the previous campaign. Remarkably, every one of the 2,834 men under arms had a *schako*, all brand new. Just 2 *sapeurs*' aprons existed and 3,240 *chapeaux* had been taken from service days before the inspection. The *capotes* had been produced from 2,461m beige tricot, and not an inch of chamois or yellow broadcloth existed for *voltigeurs* but they were issued 515 An XI light cavalry carbines and, as per regulation, no sabres.[98]

24ᵉ de Ligne

Inspected at Brest in October 1804, the inspecting officer noted the *chapeaux* were in deplorable condition; most were non-regulation, being over tall and too wide corner to corner. The inspector authorised that new *chapeaux* were to be made, to match the regulation exactly. The regimental accounts report in the year to 1 September 1804, 45,600fr had been spent on *capotes*, smocks and *pantalons de route*, with a further 55,497fr

Sapeur of the 24ᵉ *de Ligne* in summer 1808. Nothing shown in this image is recorded in the regiment's paper archive. We see both the full dress with a *habits-veste* and a sombre undress *surtout*. (*Collection KM*)

20 spent on making 1,600 *capotes* and the same number of *pantalons de route* and smocks, as well as 1,600 pairs of shoes. The inspector noted that the epaulettes of *sous-officiers* and soldiers were a point of avarice, i.e. far too costly and showy, and added that *sous-officiers* in the line did not have their own pattern epaulettes, these were reserved for the Garde Impériale! The inspector also noted that the regiment had blackened cow hide *porte-gibernes* in use, which were to be exchanged for whitened buff to accord with the recent regulations.[99]

The decree of 15 January 1807 equipped the war battalions with 1,019 white *habits*, 2,184 *vestes*, 2,117 pairs of *culottes*, 1,496 *capotes*, 1,075 *capotes* as 'kits', 3,909 pairs of shoes

Grenadiers of the 24ᵉ *de Ligne* in summer 1808. The regiment officially had no bearskins between 1803 and February 1808, but inherited some from Oudinot's Grenadiers when part of this formation was disbanded into the 24ᵉ *de Ligne* in later summer 1808, which may well date the illustration. The double-breasted *surtout* is extremely atypical. (*Collection KM*)

and 2,178 shirts. The regiment also received new campaign equipment: 292 *marmites* with lids and bags, 2,937 *petit bidons*, 152 hatchets and cases and 292 *gamelles*.[100]

The regiment was inspected on 29 January 1808. The regiment had 2,758 *capotes* in service, 2,658 being made since July 1805, of which 1,519 needed total replacement. The

Voltigeurs of the 24ᵉ *de Ligne*. The colpack and double-breasted *surtout* are not recorded in any other document from the epoch. The 24ᵉ *de Ligne* in February 1808 possessed not an inch of chamois broadcloth, epaulettes, sword knots, plumes or *schako* cords for *voltigeurs*: this image clearly post-dates 21 February 1808. (*Collection KM*)

regiment furthermore was in the process of swapping *chapeaux* for *schakos*, 1,598 *chapeaux* were to be written off, and 2,701 *schakos* were in use, of which 1,140 needed replacing. Given these were recently issued, how had the become so damaged as none were with the war battalions? When we look at the *dépôt* contents, we find that the *capotes* were made from beige broadcloth – some 1,800m being used for this purpose – for *sous-officiers*, as well grey tricot, some 2,408m 38 being employed for other ranks. Not an inch of chamois broadcloth existed. Interestingly, no *mousquetons* were issued, and grenadiers alone had sabres, while the drummers and *cornets* had 72 sabres between them. As one would expect at the end of the Eylau and Friedland campaign, the regiment's clothing was noted as in bad condition and over 1,000 muskets had been lost in the campaign of 1807.[101]

To make up for manpower losses in the 1807 campaign, General Oudinot sent a detachment of grenadiers and *voltigeurs* from the 6ᵉ *regiment des Grenadiers Réunis*, to be taken into the regiment on 1 October 1808; some 108 men, notably 61 grenadiers in bearskins, and 68 *voltigeurs*. The men came from the 54ᵉ, 63ᵉ, 94ᵉ and 105ᵉ *de Ligne*:[102]

Regiment	Habit					
	Replace in 6 months	Replace in 12 Months	Replace 12–18 months	Replace 18–24 Months	Replace after 24 months	Replace after 36 months
54ᵉ de Ligne		1			1	
63ᵉ de Ligne	7		36	25	3	
94ᵉ de Ligne			1			
105ᵉ de Ligne	9	12		10	7	
TOTAL	16	13	37	35	7	

These bearskins were, it seems, the only examples the regiment ever had, at least according to extant documents:[103]

Regiment	Bearskin or *Schako*					
	Replace in 6 months	Replace in 12 Months	Replace 12–18 months	Replace 18–24 Months	Replace after 24 months	Replace after 36 months
54ᵉ de Ligne			2			
63ᵉ de Ligne			67	4		
94ᵉ de Ligne			1			
105ᵉ de Ligne			34			
TOTAL			104	4		

No mention is made of epaulettes, sword knots, plumes etc, but we assume they existed.

The paper archive of the 24ᵉ *de Ligne* states that on 28 December 1809, 1,069fr was paid by Colonel Chabert personally to reinstate the costs of the artillery to allow it to complete its clothing. Some 280fr was spent the following year, 1810, on equipment and clothing.[104]

25ᵉ de Ligne

Reviewed on 28 October 1804, the inspector noted that the men wore their queues 'fantastically long' and that despite the clothing being new, half needed replacing as the materials used were 'cheap and very low quality'. Moreover, the cut of the garments did not match the model sent by the War Ministry.[105]

Although no prints exist showing the regiment wearing the white uniform, archive paperwork categorically makes it clear that the white *habits* were indeed made. The decree of 15 January 1807 equipped the war battalions with 1,003 white *habits*, 2,002 *vestes*, 2,004 pairs of *culottes*, 2,421 *capotes*, 186 *capotes* in 'kit form', 4,013 pairs of shoes and 1,660 shirts.[106] Furthermore, regimental accounts tell us some 302m 95 of capucine broadcloth was used, to produce 1,122 *habits*. In total the regiment in December 1807 had 1,288 good *habits* in use, 895 needing repairs and 797 to be written off, a total of 2,920, thus roughly half the regiment had white *habits*. The inspection returns note some 2,974 *habits* had been issued, along with 4,328 *vestes* and 5,615 pairs of *culottes*. We also note that 251m 66 of scarlet broadcloth had been used, 4,254m 80 white broadcloth – arguably for white *habits* and *vestes* – and 2,809m 53 blue broadcloth as well as 13,423m white tricot for *culottes*. Some 213m 69 of capucine broadcloth remained in the *dépôt*. Was this used for facings of the drummers, band and *sapeurs* from 1808? Yes, according to the Otto MS. The regiment was equipped with 2,000 *schakos*, of which 1,751 needed immediate replacement, 1,725 *chapeaux* were destined for the rubbish heap and 568 needed repairs – some 2,293 being in use. *Schakos* were clearly not in universal usage. Just 909 *capotes* were in service and 2,842 were authorised for production. For *sous-officiers*' *redingotes*, 122m 50 of beige broadcloth had been used. The *voltigeurs* were armed with standard infantry muskets and 74 light cavalry *mousquetons* were in use, 58 being issued to drummers and 17 to the band as well as battalion adjutants, the drum major and drum master – clearly these men had *gibernes* and belts. For the year 1808 the inspector authorised the production of 1,628 *habits*, 2,842 *capotes*, 1,500 *vestes*, 2,718 *bonnets de police*, 1,751 *schakos*, 606 *gibernes*, and 435 musket slings.[107]

Reviewed on 1 May 1811, the inspector noted the 1ᵉ and 2ᵉ battalions had 52 officers, 2,433 men and 101 horses. He added 18 officers were needed to bring the regiment up to capacity. Clothing wise, a lot needed immediate replacement: 182 *habits*, 209 *vestes*, 181 pairs of *culottes*, 8 *schakos* and 1,878 *capotes* among other items. The battalions were missing 196 muskets and bayonets and 300 sabres. The men had not been paid since 1806.[108]

Reviewed in May 1811, the 4ᵉ battalion was re-formed from men transferred from the *Compagnie de Marche* of the 15ᵉ *de Ligne*, which had been sent to the 8ᵉ Corps of the Army of Portugal, some 446 men. The clothing was in shreds: of 446 *habits*, 110 were in good condition, 160 needed repairs and 176 were to be written off. The clothing was less than six months old but the long march to the rear area of the army of Portugal had basically destroyed two thirds of the battalion's *habits*! Not a single *schako* was in good condition, 299 needed repairs and 147 were to be written off. Likewise, the *culottes*

Sapeur of the 25ᵉ *de Ligne* in summer 1808. Using the remaining facing cloth from the regiment's white *habits* to dress the head of column troops was a logical and economical way of making the dress highly distinctive. (*Collection KM*)

were either serviceable or life expired, the *capotes* were again in need of repair, some 114 examples, with a total replacement of some 173 garments, leaving just 159 in usable condition. The leather work was in better condition, with just 20 *gibernes* needing repairs. Just 55 sabres and *baudriers* were issued to the *sous-officiers*, while the *voltigeurs* and grenadiers were not issued sabres.[109]

The 5^e battalion was formed around a cadre of 423 men drawn from the 1^e *Provisoire Bataillon de Marche* in June the same year. The men had numerous items of clothing missing, for 423 men we note 421 *vestes*, 325 *bonnets de police*, and 225 *capotes*. Not a single sabre or *baudrier* was issued, which is remarkable as the detachment had 6 drummers, 3 sergeant majors, 11 sergeants, 3 fourriers and 23 corporals, all of whom were allowed to carry a sabre! We also note the presence of seven gunners.[110]

These two reports show that it is potentially wrong to assume that *sous-officiers* wore sabres. Clearly in these two cases, *sous-officiers* and drummers had none. How widespread this practice was in the army is we cannot say, but it is clear that we have to change our assumptions about the armament of *sous-officiers*, drummers and elite companies.

26^e *de Ligne*

Reviewed on 1 September 1803, we find 38,000fr had been spent buying 1,600 *capotes*, linen smocks, and the same number of *pantalons de route*. The regiment had 9 *sapeurs*.[111] Inspected on 27 February 1808, we note 1,626 *chapeaux* were in use with the war battalions, which also had 650 *redingotes* in service and 1,143 to be disposed of, and 72 bearskins were with the 1^e battalion, all of which we are told had been purchased after January 1807. Of the *redingotes*, they were made from beige broadcloth for *sous-officiers* and grey tricot for other ranks. *Voltigeurs'* clothing had required just 3m 80 of chamois broadcloth. The inspecting officer authorised 449 *schakos* and 598 *redingotes* produced. *Voltigeurs*, as could be expected from regulations, had no sabre. No mention is made of the s*apeurs'* aprons and axe cases recorded in 1805.[112]

27e *de Ligne*

When inspected on 30 November 1807, the regiment had sufficient cloth to make 212 white *habits*, and materials for 303 *vestes* in *dépôt*. We know some of the regiment were in white, as 395m 58 of capucine broadcloth had been used to produce 1,644 *habits* and *vestes*. The inspection return also shows that the *voltigeur* companies had chamois collars to the *habit* as 19m 86 of chamois broadcloth had been used for this purpose. The *dépôt* companies had *schakos*, 1,009 examples, everyone else had *chapeaux*, 1,909 examples. Some 1,556 *capotes* had been produced by the regiment, and out of 2,329 in use the balance came from captured stores. We notice also, that the eight-strong regimental band and drum corporal were issued An XI light cavalry *mousquetons* and also *gibernes*, as were presumably 18 *voltigeur sous-officiers* who also carried these firearms, as did a further 76 *voltigeur* corporals, drummers and *cornets*: in total, 105 such firearms were in use and 18 *carabines rayé* were with *voltigeur* officers. *Voltigeurs* had no sabres.[113] Rousselot, like Boucquoy, indicates that the regiment's drummers had dark orange facings. i.e., capucine.[114] Arguably, applying the capucine broadcloth that remained in the *dépôt* to face drummers' *habits* makes perfect economic sense, and is implied by the Otto MS, however no archive documents support this notion.

28ᵉ de Ligne

The regiment had been authorised to wear white *habits* in 1806. Although no prints exist showing the regiment wearing the white uniform, archive paperwork categorically makes it clear that the white *habits* were indeed made. The decree of 15 January 1807 equipped the war battalions with 1,001 white *habits*, 2,005 *vestes*, 2,006 pairs of *culottes*, 2,072 *capotes*, 326 *capotes* in 'kit form', 2,417 pairs of shoes and 1,467 shirts.[115] Further confirmation that the regiment wore white comes from the inspection report of 26 December 1807, which reports 511m 60 of scarlet *and* capucine broadcloth had been used since 1805 to make a minimum of 1,500 additional white *habits*. Therefore, we can be certain that most men had received new *habits* by the end of 1807. We also see that 2,794 *chapeaux* and *schakos* were in use, and 2,329 *capotes* were in use made from grey broadcloth. Indeed, out of 2,652 *habits*, 1,372 needed immediate replacement and 240 repairs. The inspector authorised 1,313 *habits* made and 1,484 *schakos*. Two suppliers had been chosen to fulfil this contract: a supplier in Lille for 2,955fr and Maison Frebure of Paris were to supply *schakos* with cords for 3299fr. *Voltigeurs* were issued 189 sabres, carried infantry muskets, and had no distinctions. Yet we note the regimental band, 8 men, the drum major and drum corporal as well as 34 fusiliers and 36 drummers had *gibernes* and An XI light cavalry *mousquetons*. In total, 104 weapons were in use. The inspector noted that the *schakos* were issued to the *dépôt* battalions and that the *habits* 'were cut a little short in the tails' compared to the regulations.[116]

29ᵉ de Ligne

At the time of the 1804 inspection, quite remarkably the regiment was wearing 1,531 *schakos*, and naturally enough the inspector ordered that they were to be replaced with *chapeaux*.[117] The next review describes the headdress as 'a type of helmet with a large copper plate to the front', which makes us think of an Austrian-type helmet and is plausible as the regiment was garrisoned in Verona, or more likely it is simply a bad description of a *schako*. Either way, the *schakos* were to have been abolished more than nine months earlier.[118] The *dépôt* battalion was reviewed in March 1808, and had issued 532 *schakos*. We also note that 22m 20 of chamois broadcloth had been used for *voltigeur* distinctions, and 2,587m of grey broadcloth had been used to make *redingotes*, of which 1,035 were in service. *Voltigeurs* in all three battalions had no sabres and carried infantry muskets.[119] The war battalions, garrisoned in Lille, were given a shake-down review in April 1808. We note 1,512 *chapeaux* and *schakos* were in service, the 6 *voltigeur* cornets were fit only for the scrap metal merchant, and half of the *gibernes* – 808 examples –

needed total replacement. For *voltigeur* clothing in the war battalions, just 1m 10 of chamois broadcloth had been used since 1805: insufficient for any distinction other than a line of piping on a few garments. Stores held 109 brand-new *schakos* and 100 *chapeaux*. Nothing is recorded for grenadiers or *sapeurs*.[120]

30ᵉ *de Ligne*

The inspection of September 1804 reveals that 45,600fr had been spent buying 1,600 *capotes*, the same number of linen smocks, pairs of shoes and *pantalons de route*.[121] Reviewed in summer 1805, regimental accounts tell us that the War Ministry had sent *effects de modèle* for the regimental tailor to copy. The report also mentioned 90 An XI light cavalry *mousquetons* were in use: 36 with *sous-officiers* and 54 with drummers. We also note for the band, drummers and *sapeurs*, white broadcloth had been dyed *bleu de ciel*, no doubt for facings costing 177fr 30.[122] Rousselot suggests the base colour of these uniforms was scarlet: this is perfectly possible as in the period 1805 to 1807, 626m 94 was used to make 3,321 *habits*. This number of *habits* would officially have needed 498m 15, leaving 128m 79 of cloth unaccounted for, presumably for the *habits* of the drummers, *sapeurs* and musicians.

Under the January 1807 decree, the regiment was equipped with 997 *habits*, 2,003 *vestes manches*, 2,162 pairs of *culottes*, 2,902 *capotes*, 3,527 pairs of shoes and 109 shirts. The *habits* may have been white as the regiment was ordered to adopt them in March 1806.[123] These were the only such garments the unit had, as stores at the end of 1807 reported 5,139m of blue broadcloth being used to produce 3,321 *habits*.

Inspected on 26 November 1807, every man was wearing a *chapeau*, with

Grenadier officer of the 30ᵉ *de Ligne* depicted by Suhr sometime in 1808.

Regulations in Practice 129

Voltigeur officer of the 30ᵉ *de Ligne* in summer 1808 from a naïve artwork by Suhr.

Fusilier officer of the 30ᵉ *de Ligne* drawn in a naïve style by Suhr sometime in 1808.

3,522 in service and 1,761 scheduled for replacement. Not an inch of chamois or yellow broadcloth had been purchased, yet contrary to regulations, *voltigeurs* carried sabres, and were armed with infantry muskets. The band and drummers were armed with 62 An XI light cavalry carbines.[124]

Inspected on 1 July 1811, the 5ᵉ and 6ᵉ battalions had the following clothing and equipment:[125] 1,206 *habits*, 1,206 *vestes*, 1,206 pairs of *culottes*, 1,206 *capotes*, 1,206 *bonnets de police*, and 1,206 *schakos*.

The two battalions had no grenadiers or *voltigeurs*. We note 189 sabres were issued to drummers and *sous-officiers*. In 4ᵉ battalion 95 sabres were issued to 2 *adjutant-sous-officiers*, 6 sergeant majors, 24 sergeants, 6 *fourriers*, 45 corporals and 12 drummers. In 6ᵉ battalion 94 sabres were issued to 2 adjutant-sous-officiers, 5 sergeant majors, 24 sergeants, 6 fourriers, 47 corporals and 10 drummers – one man clearly had no sabre. Every man had a stock buckle, a pair of knee buckles and waistbelt buckle for the *culottes*. Likewise, every man had linen stockings, a pair of black and a pair of black long gaiters, a *havresac* and black stock. No man had a *schako* cover, linen *pantalons* or *giberne* cover.[126]

Reviewed on 1 May 1811, the inspector noted the regiment had 55 officers, 2,141 men and 100 horses. He added 16 officers were needed to bring the regiment up to capacity. Clothing wise, 1,627 *habits*, 1,327 *vestes*, 206 pairs of *culottes*, 207 *schakos*, 959 *capotes*, 874 *gibernes*, 750 *giberne* belts and 57 *baudriers* needed repairs. Needing to be replaced were 944 *schakos* and 478 *capotes*. Missing items included 204 *baudriers*, 30 drums and carriages, and 204 sabres.[127]

31ᵉ *de Ligne*

No regiment of this designation.

32ᵉ *de Ligne*

At the time of the September 1805 inspection, the regiment had 16 *sapeurs*, each armed with an An XI light cavalry *mousqueton*, yet officially no axes and cases existed and just a single apron. The unit's 63 drummers were also armed with *mousquetons* and issued *gibernes*. The regiment's three adjutants and drum major were issued their own pattern sabre.[128]

The regiment is particularly well documented for the use of the white *habit*. Two prints by Martinet show a grenadier – a bearskin is shown but none existed in reality – and a fusilier in white *habits*. Martinet is quite correct. The decree of 15 January 1807 equipped the war battalions with 1,000 white *habits*, 2,000 *vestes*, 2,000 pairs of *culottes*, 1,722 *capotes*, 38 *capotes* in 'kit form' to be made by the men, 2,985 pairs of shoes and 1,703 shirts.[129] Further confirmation of white *habits* comes from the inspection on 31 December 1807. The report tells us the regiment had used 44mm 55 of capucine broadcloth, sufficient for 247 new *habits* and *vestes*. A further 297 white *habits* appear in an inspection return of 15 December 1807. Presumably we are dealing with just two

Grenadier of the 32ᵉ wearing the regulation white *habit* by Martinet. Officially, no bearskins were adopted when the regiment was wearing white.

Fusilier of the 32ᵉ *de Ligne* wearing regulation white uniform. The white gaiters are the exception, as they were abolished in 1805, but I am sure some colonels kept these items in store for use on special occasions.

companies? The returns further show that the regiment was wearing a mix of *chapeaux* and *schakos*, and that *voltigeurs* had chamois collars, some 8m 12 of chamois broadcloth being used to make *habits*. A total of 300 *schakos* were in service with 3ᵉ battalion, the war battalions had *chapeaux*.[130] Purchased in 1808 were 1,000 *schakos* and 100 set of *schako* cords for fusiliers and 185 *schakos* for grenadiers to replace the existing *chapeaux*.[131]

The regimental accounts signed off on 1 January 1809 reveal the following expenses for equipping the 4ᵉ and 5ᵉ battalion:[132]

500 pairs of shoes, total 2,625fr
2,000 shirts, total 9,000fr
1,000 pairs of black gaiters, 1,000 pairs of grey gaiters, total 6,450fr
270m of white tricot, total 1,053fr
10,272m linen for linings, total 13,732fr 46
185 *schakos*, total 1,850fr
266 grammes of gold lace for *sous-officiers*, 7 ounces of gold lace; total 158fr 19
1,000 pairs of woollen stockings, total 2,000fr
1,000 musket worms and 1,000 *epinglettes*, total 600fr
1,000 *schakos*, total 9,500fr
1,000 *schako* cords, 140 pairs of grenadiers' epaulettes, 140 pairs of *voltigeurs*' epaulettes, 140 grenadiers' sword knots, 140 grenadiers' pompoms, 140 *voltigeurs*' pompoms, 560 fusiliers' pompoms; total 2,737fr 40
276 *capotes*, total 5520fr
1,000 *havresacs* and straps, total 10,050fr

Of interest is the presence of *schako* cords, the first documented use in regimental accounts, along with sword knots for grenadiers. *Voltigeur* epaulettes are a surprise but not unexpected.

33ᵉ *de Ligne*

The decree of 15 January 1807 equipped the war battalions with 1,075 white *habits*, 2,000 *vestes*, 2,215 pairs of *culottes*, 1,357 *capotes*, 330 *capotes* in 'kit form' to be made by the men, 2,821 pairs of shoes and 159 shirts.[133] Regimental records reveal the colonel requested the price for violet broadcloth. We assume the regiment also produced white *habits* in the *dépôt*, but at the time of the inspection on 22 November 1807, not one inch of such cloth is reported as being used. The men were wearing *chapeaux* in the war battalions, some 1,752 examples, all needing to be replaced. We also note the regimental band – 8 men – the drum major, drum corporal and adjutants were armed with An XI light cavalry *mousquetons* and issued *gibernes*; six *sapeurs* were likewise armed, along with 36 fusiliers and 34 drummers; 90 such weapons being issued.[134]

Reviewed on 1 May 1811, the inspector noted the regiment had 57 officers, 2,171 men and 76 horses. He added that 25 officers were needed to bring the regiment up to capacity. Clothing wise, 1,666 *habits* needed repairs, as did 958 *habits*, 826 *vestes*, 1,583 pairs of *culottes*, 723 *capotes*, 669 *schakos*, 614 *bonnets de police*, while 121 *bonnets* needed to be replaced. He added that the unit needed the following immediately as men had lost these items: 106 *vestes*, 14 *bonnets de police*, 46 *gibernes*, 116 *baudriers* – we must imagine some form of improvised sling to carry the *giberne* – 78 musket slings and 268 sabres. Needing repairs, the inspector noted, were 13 *marmites*, 32 *grand bidons*, 20 gamelles, 17 hatchets, and 229 muskets – a further 32 needed replacing. The driving harness either needed repair – 12 sets – or was missing, some 23 sets. He added that the men had last been issued new clothing in 1807, and many men were too old for service.[135]

The 4ᵉ and 6ᵉ battalions of the regiment were given a shake-down inspection in July 1811 at Mayence (Mainz). Of interest, the 4ᵉ battalion had a grenadier company, some 113 *sous-officiers* and men, each armed with a sabre as well as a musket. In the 2ᵉ, 3ᵉ, 4ᵉ, 5ᵉ companies, just the sergeant majors, sergeants and *fourriers*, as well as drummers, had sabres. The same is true of the *voltigeur* company. Only corporals of the grenadier company had sabres, we note. Every man in the battalion had two pairs of shoes and two shirts. The grenadiers had no epaulettes, and no plumes or *schako* cords existed as we would expect following the 1810 decree. In the 6ᵉ battalion, no man carried a sabre, and not a single musket sling existed either.[136] Clearly, issues that faced the regiment earlier in the year were not yet fully resolved. We assume they were before the Niemen was crossed.

34ᵉ *de Ligne*

At the time of the October 1804 inspection, the regiment had blackened cow hide leather work, which was to be bleached or replaced with buff leather.[137] These items had not been changed by August 1805. The 72 drummers were issued *gibernes*, sabres and An XI light cavalry *mousquetons*.[138]

Faced with violet, the 34ᵉ *de Ligne* would have looked highly distinctive when it adopted white *habits*. We know this was indeed the case as the regiment purchased 484m 67 of violet broadcloth and used 341m 66 in the production of 1,263 *habits* and *vestes*, 600 of these 'being sent to the war battalions'. The men were wearing *chapeaux* at the time of the review in the war battalions. We note that *sous-officiers* had beige broadcloth *redingotes*, and other ranks grey tricot *capotes*. *Voltigeurs* had chamois facings, 14m 40 chamois broadcloth being used. *Voltigeurs* and grenadiers had 741 pairs of epaulettes in use, and 4 more sets in stores waiting to be issued, along with 340 sword knots in use with 6 in stores. Some 3,610 pompoms were in use, we also note. The war battalions had 3,611 *chapeaux* in use, and the 3ᵉ battalion 1,073. The regiment's 72 drummers and *cornets* were issued *gibernes* and An XI light cavalry *mousquetons*; the seven-strong band, drum major, drum master and three adjutants were issued *gibernes* and *carabines rayé*.[139] In 1814 three white *habits* were in the regiment's *dépôt*.[140] Confirming the use of white *habits*, we note the decree of 15 January 1807 equipped the war battalions with 674 white *habits*.[141] Clearly the *dépôt* and one war battalion were in white.

35ᵉ de Ligne

Inspected during 1803, we notice white linen for gaiters, horn buttons for white gaiters and *culottes*, bearskins and grenades for grenadiers' *gibernes*. Again, drummers' lace is reported but none was in stores. The same is true of grenadiers' epaulettes, pompoms and sword knots, as well as drummers' sword knots and epaulettes.[142] No bearskins are reported in 1804 or 1805.

At the time of the review of 8 January 1808, 1,348 *capotes* were in service, and every man was wearing a *schako*. Remarkably, 55m of chamois broadcloth had been used to make *voltigeurs*' distinctions: did the cornets have chamois facings? Presumably. Stores reported that 1,886 *chapeaux* had been issued prior to January 1808, implying the *schakos* were all recently issued.[143] Between 10 April and 1 June 1809 the war battalions lost a huge amount of kit: 350 bearskins, 1,890 *schakos*, and 1,350 *capotes* among other items in action at Essling.[144] The absence of bearskins in 1803, 1805 and 1808 implies these items had been purchased during the 1808 reorganisation of the line at a time of relative peace and plenty.

36ᵉ de Ligne

The regiment was inspected on 27 December 1807. Since the previous inspection, 3,646 *habits* had been made. We note 2,977 *chapeaux* were with the war battalions and 300 *schakos* were with the *dépôt* battalion. Just 320 bearskins were in use, of which 80 had been made and issued since September 1805, with 13 remaining in store. Also in use were 2,377 grey tricot *redingotes*. The *voltigeurs* lacked sabres and were armed with infantry muskets. Drummers and *cornets* were issued An XI light cavalry carbines, as were 8 fusiliers, 12 grenadiers and 2 corporals. Of interest to us is the fact that the regiment purchased 271m 25 of violet broadcloth. Some 146m 75 had been used in the production of 232 *habits* and *vestes*.[145] In 1814 the *dépôt* held 79m 08 of violet broadcloth, which indicates either the production of more white *habits*, or more reasonably the cloth had been utilised for the facings for the drummers and band between 1808 and 1812.[146] Confirming the use of white *habits*, we note the decree of 15 January 1807 equipped the war battalions with 1,001 white *habits*.[147]

37ᵉ de Ligne

Unit accounts in summer 1805 report the production of 1,600 *capotes*, smocks, pairs of shoes and *pantalons de route* costing 55,631fr, and a further 6,000fr was spent buying 200 bearskins for grenadiers.[148]

The 1807 review is missing, but partial regimental accounts show that the *schakos* in the regiment had cords, pompom and chinscales from 1807, and in the same year, the regiment bought 270 *chapeaux* costing 5fr 75 each as well as 400 *schakos* costing 11fr 50 each, including cords, plate and chinscales. Also purchased in 1807 was 3,333m of linen, for 344fr 27, 607 *porte-giberne*s costing 3fr 85, and 553 musket slings costing 1fr 60 each. A further 216 *schakos* were obtained in 1808, along with 2,050m of linen for linings costing 104fr 52. In 1809 1,425m of linen was purchased for 171fr, and 1,040 *schakos* costing 11fr 50 each for the 4ᵉ battalion. In 1811 a further 1,146m 65 of linen was purchased, 300 *schakos* costing 11fr 50, 25 pairs of black twill gaiters costing 5fr 50 a pair, 65 pairs of grey gaiters costing 2fr 55 a pair, and 8 pairs of stockings for 1fr 80 a pair. In 1812 the regiment's master shoe maker produced 7,842 pairs of shoes for 3,921fr in two orders, 4 January 1812 and 18 August 1812. The master gaiter maker was ordered on 19 August 1812 to make 803 pairs of black half gaiters according to the new regulation. Each pair cost 3fr 40. Also ordered on 19 August were 1,724 pairs of socks costing 2fr 50 a pair, and 2,175 pairs of *pantalons* costing 4fr 25 each. In 1813 the regiment's master shoemaker made 2,972 pairs of shoes at 5fr 50 a pair.[149] The accounts alas don't give us any indication of the clothing made and cloth usage.

Reviewed on 1 May 1811, the inspector noted the regiment had 58 officers, 1,875 men and 69 horses. He added 10 officers were needed to bring the regiment up to capacity. Clothing wise, a lot needed replacement: 26 *habits*, 143 *vestes*, 1,633 pairs of *culottes* and 1,259 *bonnets de police* among other items.[150]

38ᵉ de Ligne

No regiment of this designation.

39ᵉ de Ligne

Reviewed on 15 December 1807, we note 3,424 *chapeaux* were in use, not an inch of chamois broadcloth had been used for *voltigeurs*' distinctions, and as in 1804 and 1805 not a single bearskin existed. The 53 drummers were armed with An XI light cavalry carbines, and issued *gibernes*, as was the drum major, 18 *sous-officiers* and 6 fusiliers who were also issued sabres.[151]

40ᵉ de Ligne

Under the terms of the decree of 15 January 1807, the unit was issued 1,013 white *habits*, 2,013 *vestes manches*, 2,165 pairs of *culottes*, 3,501 *capotes*, 5,096 pairs of shoes and 1,902 shirts.[152] The regiment was inspected on 9 December 1807. The inspection returns note the men were all uniformly dressed, and the garments were well cut and well sewn. The list of materials used indicates that 1m 80 of 'celeste' coloured broadcloth was bought and 3m used in producing *habits*. 'Celeste' is surely *bleu celeste*, which is rather odd as the regiment in theory used violet facings! Was this cloth, in fact, destined for drummers rather than facings for the white *habits*? Arguably so and the regiment does not seem to have adopted white *habits*. We also note just 256 *schakos* were in use with the *dépôt* battalion. The *sous-officiers* had grey broadcloth *redingotes* and the other ranks grey tricot *capotes*. A further 16m 75 of chamois broadcloth had been used to make *voltigeurs*' clothing, who did not carry sabres but were armed with infantry muskets. We note the three war battalions had 3,279 *chapeaux* and the *dépôt* battalion 256 *schakos*, while 1,822 *capotes* were in use made from grey broadcloth for *sous-officiers* and grey tricot for soldiers.[153]

41ᵉ de Ligne

No regiment of this designation.

42ᵉ de Ligne

Inspected on 8 February 1808, the regiment was totally decked out in white *habits*, some 2,645 examples, yet no *capotes* seem to have been issued. The *voltigeur* companies had six *cornets*, yet not an inch of chamois for *voltigeurs*' distinctions. We note 312 sabres were issued to the grenadiers, while the *voltigeurs* had no sabres and infantry muskets.[154] We note, following the decree of 2 February 1808, the 3ᵉ battalion created four *sapeurs*, presumably reflecting practice in the war battalions.[155]

43ᵉ de Ligne

The decree of 15 January 1807 equipped the war battalions with 1,000 white *habits*, 2,005 *vestes*, 2,007 pairs of *culottes*, 1,775 *capotes*, 72 *capotes* in 'kit form', 2,228 pairs of shoes and 1,553 shirts.[156] Reviewed on 24 December 1807, the inspection reports the *dépôt* had made 864 *capotes* from grey tricot, of which 531 were in use, while 1,493 *chapeaux* were in service alongside 1,012 *schakos*. Also in use were 531 new *capotes* with the *dépôt* battalion; none were with the war battalions. Not an inch of chamois broadcloth existed, while we note *voltigeurs* lacked sabres but were armed with 412 An XI light cavalry carbines. These were issued to the *sous-officiers* of the company, and also to the 64 drummers and *cornets*, and had been since summer 1805 along with *gibernes* and belts.[157]

44ᵉ de Ligne

Regimental accounts report that in the year to 12 September 1804, 9,513fr 62 had been spent on buying *capotes* and shoes, with a further 3,722fr spent the following year.[158] We are ignorant of their colour.

The decree of 15 January 1807 allocated the unit 211 *marmites* with covers and bags, 1,673 *petit bidons*, 161 hatchets with cases, and 211 *gamelles*. The regiment also received 1,041 *habits*, 2,017 *vestes manches*, 2,021 pairs of *culottes*, 274 ready-made *capotes* with 572 as 'kits', 2,450 pairs of shoes, and 2,846 shirts.[159] Inspected almost a year later on 28 January, the unit reported 3,236 grey tricot *capotes* in service, 6 *voltigeur* cornets, 825 *chapeaux* and 2,840 *schakos*. Some 14m 40 chamois broadcloth had been used to make *voltigeur* clothing. Stores held 1,204 *schakos* yet to be issued. The regiment band of 8 men, 22 *sapeurs* and 36 drummers were all issued An XI light cavalry *mousquetons* as well as sabres and *gibernes*.[160]

Reviewed on 27 January 1809 during the siege of Saragossa, the regiment was in appalling condition: the unit needed 550 *habits* and the same number of *vestes manches*, 705 pairs of *culottes*, 24 *schakos*, 159 bearskins, 459 *capotes* as well as 450 smocks. More than 1,000 pairs of shoes were needed, 1,000 pairs of gaiters, 460 black stocks, 240 musket slings, 130 *baudriers*, 260 bayonet scabbards, 150 *gamelles*, 150 *grand bidons*, 1,500 *petit bidons*, 2,600 shirts and 4,000 pairs of socks. What had been a smartly dressed unit nine months earlier was a total shambles.[161]

45ᵉ *de Ligne*

A perusal of the regiment's accounts ending 5 September 1805 informs us that in the year up to 23 September 1804 some 2,880fr had been spent buying grenadiers' bearskins and up to 20 June 1805 a further 1,440fr was spent buying bearskins for the 3ᵉ battalion – clearly all battalions had grenadiers swaggering in bearskins and no doubt fringed scarlet epaulettes.[162]

The decree of 15 January 1807 totally reclothed the war battalions with 1,519 white *habits*, 2,480 *vestes*, 2,498 pairs of *culottes*, 2,188 *capotes*, 103 *capotes* in 'kit form', 3,799 pairs of shoes and 1,788 shirts.[163] Reviewed on 29 November 1807, every man was wearing a *chapeau*. No *capotes* existed, no bearskins, not an inch of chamois broadcloth had been purchased, but we do remark that stores reported 60m of black broadcloth had: presumably for the production of gaiters. Drummers were armed with 42 An XI light cavalry carbines.[164]

Confirming the adoption of white *habits* is a portrait of the regiment's major decked out in the white uniform faced in *bleu celeste*.[165]

The regiment's accounts in 1808 admit to the purchase of 104m of scarlet worsted lace costing 52fr, 375m of white worsted lace costing 131fr 25, and 1,200m of white worsted

Sapeur of the 45ᵉ *de Ligne* sometime in late spring or summer 1808. (*Collection KM*)

Grenadier and drum major of the 45ᵉ *de Ligne* in the first half of 1808. The use of sky blue broadcloth left over from making white *habits* was a cost-effective way of using this material to give the regiment a highly distinctive look as it transitioned from white to blue. (*Collection KM*)

cording costing 72fr. The white lace and cord was destined to decorate the regiment's *bonnets de police*, which the inspector noted were to have no decoration. The regiment also bought 6m 96 white broadcloth costing 8fr 60 and 65m 60 linen costing 83fr 16 to make 388 *bonnets de police:* arguably the white cloth was used to pipe the turban.[166] Presumably these items were blue, but the use of two colours of lace is inexplainable. In 1809 125 pairs of grenadier epaulettes were purchased costing 5fr 50 a pair, rather than the regulation 4fr 75, so we must imagine these were rather extravagant items![167]

46ᵉ *de Ligne*

Reviewed on 22 September 1804, the regiment's accounts note 9,600fr had been spent buying 1,600 *capotes*, smocks, linen *pantalons de route* and the same number of pairs of shoes. To the general chagrin of the inspector, the regiment had abolished the queue, the blue broadcloth used to make the *habits* was very low quality, and the *habits* themselves were badly made, notably too tight on the collar and chest. The tails of the *habits* were too long – indeed when a man was on bended knee the tails should not touch the floor, but the back of the man's knee. The *culottes* were also badly cut and made. In addition, the regiment's equipment was badly fitted and needed cleaning, while the men wore their *chapeaux* at 'odd angles'. The gaiters in use were cut too long, because the legs of the *culottes* were too short, and rather than buttoning to the *culottes*, the gaiters were held up with gaiter straps. The regiment's clothing was mostly new but in bad condition. Of the 1,950 *habits* in use, 1,186 had been issued less than a year, yet despite

Sapeur of the 46e *de Ligne* in the first half of 1808. The use of sky blue broadcloth left over from making white *habits* was a cost-effective way of using this material to give the regiment a highly distinctive look as it transitioned from white to blue. (*Collection KM*)

Voltigeur officer and private of the 46ᵉ *de Ligne* sometime in the first half of 1808, certainly after the February 1808 inspection when the regiment was still dressed in white. An extant white *habit* for the regiment exists in the museum at Montpellier. (*Collection KM*)

this fact 586 needed urgent repairs and 492 total replacing. Likewise, 410 *vestes* needed repairs and 492 replacing, 732 pairs of *culottes* need replacing and 1,287 *chapeaux*. The regiment's leather work was in very poor condition. Of 1,879 *gibernes* in service, 871 needed urgent repairs and 622 were fit only for scrap. The *giberne* belts were in a better state. Of the 1,879 in service, 169 needed repairs and 266 replacing. To make up the shortfall, *dépôt* held stocks of brand-new clothing and equipment, namely 42 *habits*, 62 *vestes*, 248 pairs of *culottes*, 30 *chapeaux*, 85 *bonnets de police*, 24 *gibernes*, 26 porte-*gibernes*, 93 musket slings and 21 *baudriers*.[168]

Reviewed again on 15 August 1805 at Lille, regimental accounts note 1,314fr 40 had been spent on buying clogs for the 1^e and 2^e battalion. The regiment's clothing was still in poor condition. Of the 492 *habits* that needed replacing 11 months earlier, just 58 *habits* had been issued. Of the 1,992 *habits* in use, 1,467 were life expired: 73 per cent of the regiment's *habits* were falling to pieces and desperately needed replacing. Again, of the 1,992 pairs of *culottes* in use, 1,808 pairs had to be replaced – 90 per cent of the regiment's *culottes* were fit only for the rag merchant to take away! Every single *bonnet de police* had to be replaced and 1,370 *chapeaux* – or 68 per cent of all in use – had to be replaced. Equipment was still in terrible condition: 4,360 *gibernes* and belts had to be replaced urgently. The 3e battalion had be clothed like new, but the war battalions were in rags! *Dépôt* held virtually nothing for immediate issue: 65 new *habits* and 132 needing repairs, 82 pairs of *culottes* and 24 *chapeaux*. Armament wise, the band, drum major and drum corporal were issued 10 *sabres briquet* and belts, 10 *gibernes* and belts and 10 light cavalry *mousquetons*. The drummers were likewise issued 54 *sabres briquet* and *baudriers*, 54 *gibernes* and belts and 54 *mousquetons*.[169]

The decree of 15 January 1807 totally reclothed the war battalions with 1,000 white *habits*, 2,000 *vestes*, 2,000 pairs of *culottes*, 1,563 *capotes*, 352 *capotes* in 'kit form', 3,112 pairs of shoes and 1,796 shirts. A second report tells us the 46^e received a further 850 *capotes* and 508 pairs of shoes.[170]

Reviewed on 20 December 1807, the regiment was wearing a mix of blue and white *habits*: some 500 white regulation *habits* had been issued along with 1,000 pairs of *culottes* and 1,000 *vestes*. Some 600 *schakos* were in service. Not an inch of chamois cloth existed for *voltigeurs*. Since 1805, 1,322 *habits* and 1,180 *vestes* had been repaired and 387 *habits*, 368 *vestes*, 430 pairs of *culottes*, 27 *chapeaux* and 3 *bonnets de police* had been produced in *dépôt* – all remained brand new and unissued. The regiment had no *capotes*. The regiment's 58 drummers were issued with 58 light cavalry carbines, 58 sabres, as well as 58 *gibernes* and belts. We note the drum major, 6 *sous-officiers*, 7 grenadiers – *sapeurs*? – and 7 fusiliers were also issued *mousquetons*, making 72 in use. The regiment's Administrative Council agreed on 1 October 1807 to the purchases of *schakos* for 19,350fr, some 1,530fr worth of tricot, 7,691fr 15 of leather to make *gibernes*, and 6,720fr was spent buying bearskins for grenadiers.[171] The bearskins, we assume, were replacements for those lost in the 1805–07 campaign and were ordered for the newly raised battalion. The regiment had 13 *sapeurs*, the report dated 22 September 1804 states 13 axes, aprons and bearskins for *sapeurs* had been purchased for the sum of 1,413fr 28.[172] We also note that the drummers had been equipped with *gibernes* and firearms since the camp of Boulogne.[173]

In the first quarter of 1810, the 4ᵉ battalion, while based at Valladolid, spent 31fr on buying two fanions, and purchased 728 *capotes* at 1fr 20 each, and a further 873 at 60 centimes each – these must have been very simple and presumably very crude garments given they cost little more to make than a pair of overalls! In the second quarter of the year a further 772 *capotes* were made for 1fr 20 and 926 *capotes* for 40 centimes, while in the third quarter 586 *capotes* were purchased for 1fr 20 each as well as 67 *capotes* for 1fr 20 and 8 *capotes* for 40fr. Ordered in the second quarter of 1810 for delivery by the fourth quarter were:[174]

201 black stocks, total 52fr 90
423 shirts, total 105fr 75
123 pairs of stockings, total 43fr 05
432 pairs of shoes, total 280fr 80
159 pairs grey gaiters, total 47fr 70
147 pairs black gaiters, total 257fr 25
194 *havresacs*, total 320ftr 10
169 musket worms, total 16fr 90
168 *epinglettes*, total 3fr 28

On 15 May 1811, the regiment passed 331 other ranks to the 15ᵉ de Ligne. They were clothed and equipped as follows:[175]

Item	Total	Good condition	Need repairs	To be written off
Habits	331	2	63	260
Vestes	109	48	1	60
Culottes	128	103	1	24
Schakos	331	8	161	162
Bonnets de police	157	17	25	115
Capotes	308	5	129	174
Gibernes	331	331		
Porte-gibernes	331	331		
Baudriers	44	44		
Muskets and bayonets	330	330		
Sabres	44	44		
Bayonet scabbards	300	300		

Of interest, men were clearly not on parade with no legwear; we assume they were wearing linen *pantalons*. Men clearly were on parade in *habits* with no *vestes*! Only the *sous-officiers* had sabres and *baudriers* as insufficient existed to equip the grenadiers and *voltigeurs* with these. Based on the return, to quote a well-known forces phrase the men must have looked 'a complete shower'. One can only imagine the bad impression that a *habit* worn over a no doubt dirty shirt, tucked we hope, into a pair of dirty and patched overalls would have created. Not every man had a *capote* nor a *bonnet de police*. This inspection gives us a vivid snapshot of how regiments in Spain, hundreds of miles from their *dépôt*, actually looked in the field.

The regiment in July 1811 was ordered to send the 2ᵉ, 3ᵉ, and 4ᵉ companies of the 5ᵉ battalion to reinforce the 60ᵉ *de Ligne*. The inspection makes interesting reading and shows how clothing made several years earlier was still in service:[176]

Item	1808	1809	1810	1811	Comment
Habits	11	367	64		442
Vestes	5	361	74		442
Culottes	1	136	302		439. Three pairs needed
Schakos	12	368	62		442
Bonnets de police	12	373	50		435. Seven items needed
Capotes	3	269	103	17	392. Fifty needed
Gibernes	13	380	49		442
Porte-gibernes	13	380	49		442
Musket slings	10	331	40		381
Muskets					442
Bayonets					442
Bayonet scabbards	12	370	43		425. Twenty-three needed

Some 1,100 pairs of black gaiters were purchased for 1,430fr in the fourth quarter of 1811. In the third quarter of 1812, 837 pairs of pantalons were made for the sum of 1fr 20 a pair. In 1813 *schako* covers were purchased for 1fr 75 but alas we do not know the quantity obtained, and 137 grenadiers sword knots were purchased for 1fr 25 rather than the allowed for 1fr.[177]

With the men stripped from the 5ᵉ battalion, the 4ᵉ and 5ᵉ companies of the 5ᵉ battalion were re-raised and were inspected on 2 May 1812. The clothing of the conscripts was entirely new, the clothing was all complete and had been perfectly fitted to the height of the men. Each man had three shirts and three pairs of shoes in his *havresac*. The companies were perfectly dressed according to the regulation – we assume not Bardin as it did not come into force until September 1812.[178]

47ᵉ *de Ligne*

Reviewed in late summer 1804, the unit had 12 *sapeurs*, yet officially at least, they had no axes, axe cases or bearskins.[179] The summer 1805 inspection reported 8,640fr had been spent buying buff leather equipment to replaced blackened cow hide equipment then in use, which was to be placed into government stores. Even after this expense, 412 blackened cow hide *giberne* belts, 80 *baudriers* and 628 musket slings still needed to be changed.[180] Reviewed on 2 February 1808, we note 3,036 *schakos* were in use and 306 *chapeaux* were in service. No *capotes* existed, nor bearskins for grenadiers, and not an inch of chamois broadcloth either.[181]

48ᵉ *de Ligne*

In October 1804, we note the regiment had 12 *sapeurs* led by a sergeant who, officially at least, had no axes and cases or bearskins.[182] In July 1805, 22 fusiliers and 54 drummers were issued An XI light cavalry *mousquetons*.[183] A letter dated 1 May 1806 tells us that two fusilier companies were disbanded to form *voltigeurs*, more than nine months since the formation decree had been issued.[184] Inspected on 1 December 1807, the war battalions were wearing 2,100 *chapeaux*, and the men at the *dépôt* 1,278 *schakos*. Every single *chapeau* was noted to be replaced with a *schako* with immediate effect. Not an inch of chamois broadcloth had been purchased and no grenadier bearskins, just like 1804 and 1805. In 1804 13 *sapeurs*' aprons existed, but no mention of these is made in 1808: presumably lost on campaign. No *capotes* were in use, we note. The drummers were armed with 52 An XI light cavalry carbines, while officers of the *voltigeurs* carried nine *carabines rayé*.[185]

50ᵉ *de Ligne*

The decree of 15 January 1807 issued 1,001 *habits* 2,004 *vestes manches*, 2,003 pairs of *culottes*, 480 *capotes*, 2,446 pairs of shoes and 1,621 shirts.[186]

Inspected on 20 December 1807, 3,200 *chapeaux* were in use with the three war battalions and 283 *schakos* with the *dépôt* battalion. We note, 14m 40 of chamois broadcloth had been used since January 1807 to make *voltigeur* clothing, 1,926m 78 grey tricot had been used to make *capotes*, 10,604m 55 black twill for gaiters, and 1,618m 38 linen for grey gaiters. We note also 652 *vestes sans manches* made from broadcloth existed for *sous-officiers* and 3,223 *vestes manches* made from white tricot. Furthermore, 186 bearskins in were in service, 71 *gibernes* for drummers and musicians, 304 grenadier pompoms, as well as 315 *houpettes*, 316 pairs of epaulettes and 316 sword knots. For *voltigeurs* were 360 pompoms, *houpettes*, pairs of epaulettes and sword knots. The band, drum major, drum master and 53 drummers were armed with 62 An XI light cavalry *mousquetons*.[187]

In October 1811 the regiment purchased 76m 12 red broadcloth, 65m 20 white broadcloth, 1,103m 22 white serge, 130m 60 red serge and 1,824m of linen. The red broadcloth was for cuffs and collars. The only application of the red serge was to line the tails of *habits*, likely those of the regimental artillery.[188]

51ᵉ *de Ligne*

Reviewed on 23 November 1807, we note 2,900 *schakos* were in use and 3,084 *capotes* as well as 6 *voltigeurs*' horns. The *sous-officiers* had beige broadcloth *redingotes*, and other ranks grey tricot. Between August 1805 and October 1807, 3,448 *chapeaux* had been issued. Not an inch of chamois broadcloth had been purchased, and no grenadiers' bearskins existed. We note the 8-man regimental band, 19 *voltigeur sous-officiers* and 51 drummers and *cornets* were issued An XI light cavalry *mousquetons* and *gibernes*. In addition, 207 dragoon muskets were issued to *voltigeurs*, who also had sabres as did 25 *voltigeur* corporals.[189]

52ᵉ *de Ligne*

The war battalions were reviewed in April 1808. We note 1,632 *schakos* were in use with the war battalions and 435 with the *dépôt*. No bearskins were reported and not an inch of chamois broadcloth had been obtained. The *sous-officiers*, drummers and 96 grenadiers were armed with sabres.[190] The *dépôt* battalion was reviewed in March: 441 *schakos* were in use by 474 men, clearly some men had another form of headdress not recorded. The *dépôt* had made 193 *capotes* from 562m of grey tricot and for *voltigeurs*, while 2m 40 of chamois broadcloth had been purchased but not used. Stores held 417 brand-new *schakos* to be issued to the war battalions.[191]

53ᵉ *de Ligne*

Inspected on 14 January 1808, the inspector noted that the regiment needed 1,385 *habits* and *vestes*, 923 *capotes* and an additional 692 *schakos*. Stores had used 16m 08 chamois broadcloth to make *voltigeur* clothing, leaving 12m 32 in stores. We also note 1,820 *capotes* were in use and stores held 1,806m 59 of grey tricot to make further examples. Also in use were 1,800 *chapeaux* and 1,409 *schakos*, the later with the *dépôt* battalion. We also note 24 corporals were issued An XI light cavalry *mousquetons*.[192] Reviewed at the end of July 1808, the inspector noted that the majority of the regiment's clothing and equipment had to be replaced during 1808, and needed 2,788 muskets, 24 An XI light cavalry *mousquetons* and 1,056 sabres. Stores held just 134 muskets and 283 sabres.[193] These *habits* due for replacement may well have been white: we think this because 1,115 white *habits* had been issued under the decree of 15 January 1807 to the war battalions.[194]

The portrait of Colonel Songeon wearing a white *habit* is an indicator that the regiment wore white *habits*. His *habit* has rose collar piped white, rose *revers* piped white, rose cuffs piped white and white cuff flaps. He wears an épée from a black sabre belt. As a field officer, he wears a *gorget*, with a silver eagle in laurel wreath – an item often attributed to the Imperial Guard. His *schako* has a white heron *aigrette*. The top band is decorated with a band of gold embroidered stars within a gold border – again features often attributed solely to the Fusilier Grenadiers of the Imperial Guard. The side chevrons of the *schako* are likewise decorated with gold stars with a gold border. It has gold cords and chinscales hooked up to the back of the *schako*.

We also glimpse Songeon's horse furniture, a light cavalry *schabraque* in blue with '53' in the back corner. The horse's harness is standard heavy cavalry, but he uses light cavalry stirrups and breastplate as well as a light cavalry *schabraque*. Songeon was named Colonel of the 53ᵉ *de Ligne* on 1 February 1805, having previously served as Major of the 28ᵉ *de Ligne* since 25 March 1804. In 1809 he was promoted to adjutant-commandant.¹⁹⁵

54ᵉ *de Ligne*

Under the decree of 15 January 1807, the regiment was issued 1,018 *habits*, 1,051 *vestes manches*, 1,037 pairs of *culottes*, 3,000 *capotes*, 4,496 pairs of shoes and 1,696 shirts.¹⁹⁶ Inspected at the end of 1807, the *dépôt* battalion was dressed in *schakos*, some 1,547 examples, and the regiment needed 2,387 additional *schakos* to replace *chapeaux*, some 1,997 being issued. We know by this date that *voltigeurs* had chamois distinctions as the *dépôt* had used 36m of chamois broadcloth prior to the inspection for this purposed. *Capotes* for *sous-officiers* had been made from 1,200m of beige broadcloth and for the other ranks some 1,710m 36 of grey tricot had been used, leaving 332m 99 of grey tricot in the *dépôt*. In total, 883 *capotes* had been made but only 454 had been issued to the *dépôt* battalion, leaving 429 brand-new examples in *dépôt*. Since 1805 the *dépôt* had made 3,524 2814 *habits* and repaired 847. Some 657 brand-new *habits* remained in *dépôt* accompanied by 669 *vestes* and 131 pairs of tricot *pantalons*. Alas, we can say nothing about drummers or grenadiers. Nothing is mentioned about the 13 *sapeurs*' aprons and axes with cases in September 1804.¹⁹⁷

55ᵉ *de Ligne*

Under the decree of 15 January 1807, the regiment was issued 1,000 *habits*, 2,000 *vestes manches*, 2,000 pairs of *culottes*, just over 3,000 *capotes*, 3,676 pairs of shoes and 1,580 shirts.¹⁹⁸ When inspected on 15 December 1807, the regiment had 3,504 *chapeaux*

Sapeur of the 76ᵉ *de Ligne* in the first half of 1808. In theory the 54ᵉ had pink facings under the white colour scheme, so we cannot be certain why this vivid red was used. (*Collection KM*)

in service, no *schakos* or bearskins existed, not one of the *capotes* remained in use that had been issued earlier in the year. We do note 23m 21 chamois broadcloth had been used, the amount implying that more than collars were made from this material. The regiment was armed with 2,393 infantry muskets, and 96 light cavalry *mousquetons*: some 16 examples being issued to *voltigeur sous-officiers*; 54 were with the drummers and the remainder with the band, drum major and drum master. The *voltigeurs*, we note, had no sabres. Regiment accounts prepared since 23 September 1805 record:[199]

203fr. Bearskin plates for grenadiers
16fr 60. Assorted lace
1,058fr 48. Assorted cloth
936fr. *Havresacs*
1,835fr 75 broadcloth for gaiters
405fr. Stockings
192fr. Assorted passementeries
49fr 88. Assorted passementeries
840fr. Buttons
575fr. *Chapeau*.
TOTAL 6,467fr 93

The accounts were agreed on 2 January 1808; does this mean that bearskins were either an innovation of 1808 or had they existed previously and had all been lost? Sadly, without further archive evidence, we cannot say which hypothesis is correct.

Reviewed again on 3 February 1808, some 10,535fr had been spent replacing the items to be written off, and some 7,328fr 55 had been taken from the ordinary fund to pay for repairs. At the time of the review the regiment had 2,370 muskets, 208 light cavalry carbines issued to the *voltigeurs*, 2,541 bayonets and 751 sabres used by grenadiers, *voltigeurs*, drummers and *sous-officiers*.[200]

56e *de Ligne*

Inspected at the close of 1807, the regiment had 1,309 *schakos* in use, and 1,849 *chapeaux*, of which 1,517 were to be written off as life expired. Also, in use were 8 *voltigeur* cornets and 3,123 *capotes*. The regiment's 462 *voltigeurs* had chamois collars, as some 19m 20 of chamois broadcloth had been purchased and employed to make collars for *habits*. They were armed with light cavalry *mousquetons*, and were not issued sabres as per regulation. The band, drum major, drum master and three adjutants were armed with 12 *carabines rayé*, 20 sergeants and sergeant majors also had *carabines rayé*, as did 4 *fourriers* and corporals. The grenadiers were issued 302 sabres and it seems they did not wear bearskins as none are mentioned. Perhaps the epaulettes were counted with the *habits*?[201] One source gives the band and drummers orange *revers*. This seems odd as under the 1806 colour scheme, the 56ᵉ had rose facings. Certainly, no mention is made of such uniforms in the regiment's paperwork.²⁰²

In summer 1809, the 3ᵉ *marche bataillon* of the 58ᵉ *régiment de la Ligne* was taken into the regiment, some 230 men. Given this was a temporary formation of new conscripts that had marched to Germany as replacements following the great battle of Aspern-Essling and Wagram, it comes as a surprise to find that men had items of clothing missing. Of the 230 men in the detachment, only 194 arrived; 20 had been hospitalised and 11 were AWOL. Those men that did arrive were wearing 192 *habits* – 2 missing, 193 *vestes* – 1 missing, 192 pairs of *culottes*, 190 *bonnets de police*, 194 *schakos*, 194 *capotes*, 193 *gibernes* and belts, 188 musket slings, and 192 bayonet scabbards. They had 166 shirts, 263 pairs of shoes, 191 pairs of black gaiters, 186 pairs of grey gaiters, 190 black stocks, 192 *havresacs*, 194 muskets and 191 bayonets. The officer railed that the men were incompetent at their drill and in maintaining their uniforms.²⁰³

57ᵉ de Ligne

Inspected on 24 August 1805, the inspector recorded that 2,055fr 95 had been spent on lace for *sous-officiers* and other distinctions. In addition, 5,184fr had been spent on the purchase of 216 bearskins for the grenadiers, costing 24fr each. The grenadiers alone were issued sabres, 190 men excluding their *sous-officiers* and drummers. Fourteen grenadiers were armed with light cavalry *mousquetons* – the *sapeurs* we wonder? – and every drummer was issued a *giberne* and belt, sabre and light cavalry *mousqueton*. Likewise, the band had 10 *gibernes* with belts, 10 *sabres briquet* and *baudriers*, and were likewise armed with *mousquetons*.²⁰⁴ Issued under the terms of the decree of January 1807, the unit was issued just over 1,000 *habits* – presumably white, 2,003 *vestes*, the same number of pairs of *culottes*, 1,353 *capotes*, a further 248 as 'kits', 2,911 pairs of shoes and 247 shirts.²⁰⁵

Reviewed in Strasbourg on 10 November 1807, the regiment had 2,441 *chapeaux* in use, of which 1,858 were to be replaced by *schakos*, with the same number of *habits*, *vestes manches*, and *bonnets de police* and every single pair of *culottes* also to be replaced. No *capotes* existed but 6 *voltigeur* cornets did. Again. not an inch of chamois cloth existed for *voltigeurs'* collars. We note further that the *voltigeurs* did carry sabres in three battalions, and they were armed with infantry muskets. Seventy-four light cavalry carbines had been issued, 10 to the regimental band, drum major and drum master, 13 to grenadiers – we assume *sapeurs* – and 51 were with the drummers, ergo the drummers had *gibernes* and belts issued as well as sabres. The inspector further noted the clothing was well made but shabby, the men's discipline was mediocre, and their drill was terrible. The men also carried their muskets at the shoulder in a slovenly manner, i.e. weapons were carried badly at whatever angle suited the man. Nothing was said about drummers, but the band was too expensively and flamboyantly dressed.²⁰⁶

Rousselot, based on the work of Boersch, a secondary source from after the epoch, states that the band wore dark blue *habits* with bright yellow facings with white lace to collar, cuffs and *revers*, and by 1809 had swapped the costly yellow facings for *bleu celeste*.²⁰⁷

Regulations in Practice 149

Grenadier officer of the 57ᵉ *de Ligne* sometime in 1808 after a naïve drawing by Suhr.

Voltigeur officer of the 57ᵉ *de Ligne* sometime in summer 1808.

150   Napoleon's Line Infantry – From the Battle of Jena to the Invasion of Iberia

Fusilier officer of the 57ᵉ *de Ligne* drawn in a naïve style by Suhr sometime in summer 1808.

Drummer of the 57ᵉ *de Ligne* drawn in a naïve style by Suhr sometime in summer 1808. The use of sky blue facings is strictly non-regulation.

The petit Suhr manuscript, which contains only 30 images rather than more than 60 in the full one, does indeed show a drummer of the 57ᵉ with dark blue *habit* faced in *bleu celeste*. The image is painted by the brother of the artist who created the Bourgeois of Hamburg, and is a little-known source, although it exists as copies only. Thus, it seems reasonable that a dark blue uniform with light blue facings existed at some point. However, without archive sources to confirm or deny these comments, we can add nothing to the hypothesis presented by previous authors beyond the 1808 report that indicates that the band was dressed flamboyantly. Indeed, a letter of 8 June 1805 indicates the regiment had 25 musicians and had spent 3,850fr on clothing the band.²⁰⁸ Presumably this lavish uniform was still in use in 1807? We wonder if the official establishment of eight musicians on the regiment's books overlooked the hired-in musicians? Without further archive sources we cannot tell. Arguably, the 1807 report indicates that the band was over strength.

Inspected again in 1808, a report of 12 January 1808 states that the clothing was 'passable', i.e. in serviceable condition, and was excellently made. The regiment had received as replacement weapons for those lost in the campaign of 1805 to 1807, 625 muskets, 61 *mousquetons*, 686 bayonets and 402 sabres.²⁰⁹

Voltigeur cornet of the 57ᵉ *de Ligne* drawn in a naïve style by Suhr sometime in summer 1808. The use of sky blue facings is strictly non-regulation. He has a cavalry trumpet rather than the expected hunting horn.

58ᵉ de Ligne

When inspected on 5 January 1808, the regiment had 2,897 *schakos* in use and 1,497 *chapeaux*, all scheduled for replacement. No cloth existed for *voltigeurs* or to make *capotes*, and none were in use. The seven-strong regimental band, the drum major and drum master were issued nine An XI light cavalry *mousquetons*, as well as *gibernes*. For the *voltigeur* companies, the *sous-officiers* were issued 40 *mousquetons* and sabres, and the *voltigeurs* themselves 403 *mousquetons* and sabres.[210]

Fusilier of the 58ᵉ *de Ligne* drawn by Martinet sometime in 1808.

Voltigeur of the 58ᵉ *de Ligne* drawn by Martinet sometime in 1808.

59ᵉ de Ligne

In summer 1804, the regiment purchased 1,600 linen smocks, 1,600 *capotes* and the same number of *pantalons de route* and pairs of shoes. We also note 236 grenadier bearskins were in use.[211] In early summer 1805 the regiment had 93 An XI light cavalry *mousquetons* in use, with 36 issued to drummers, and 14 to the band, drum major, drum master and adjutants.[212]

Inspected on 4 April 1808, we note 1,571 *chapeaux* had recently been taken from use and every man had a *schako*, 2,927 being in use. Since 1805, 4,214 *capotes* had been made, with 2,032 in use. In terms of cloth use, 31m 44 chamois broadcloth had been used making *voltigeur* clothing, *sous-officiers* had beige broadcloth *redingotes* and other ranks grey tricot *capotes*. The drum major was issued an An XI light cavalry *mousqueton*, while the band were issued sabres. The regiment's 18 *sapeurs* were likewise armed with *mousquetons*, as were the 18 *voltigeur cornets*. Following the inspection, the *voltigeurs* were ordered to hand in their sabres and *baudriers*.[213]

In 1809, for men newly admitted to the grenadier or *voltigeur* company of the 3ᵉ battalion, 271fr 70 was spent on making them new *habits*, 239fr 88 was spent repairing 60 bearskins and 16 brand-new bearskins were purchased for 23fr 50 each, a total of 376fr. The 4ᵉ battalion in the second quarter of 1809 was reclothed after it had suffered heavily in the action at Ebelsberg. A sum of 1,273fr 80 was spent buying blue, red, green and yellow broadcloth, as well as white serge and line. The yellow was clearly used to mark out *voltigeurs*, yet of what purpose was the green? The grenadiers and *voltigeurs* of the battalion were dressed as new. Was the green used for facings for drummers and *cornets*? We simply cannot say. The tailoring bill for repairs to the clothing of 1ᵉ and 2ᵉ battalion in 1809 to 1811 were as follows:[214]

862 *habits* at 1fr 50 each
894 *schakos* at 1fr 50 each
20m blue broadcloth at 12fr 78 a metre
3m red broadcloth at 15fr 50 a metre
9m white broadcloth at 10fr 66 a metre
93m linen at 2fr 67 a metre

Costs incurred in the following year were as follows:[215]

496 *schakos* repaired at 1fr 50 each
787 *habits* at 1fr 75 each
718 *vestes* at 75 centimes each
392 *schakos* at 1fr 40 each

The regiment's leather work was described as mediocre, and was in a terrible condition, with most of it impossible to repair following the invasion of Portugal. Following

Masséna's retreat in 1811, the following costs were incurred in patching up the regiment's overtly worn-out clothing as no new clothing had arrived since the regiment had entered Spain:[216]

30m beige broadcloth costing 16fr 50 a metre
40m white broadcloth costing 11fr a metre
250m blue serge costing 1fr 35 a metre
450m of linen costing 1fr 35 a metre
1,357 *habits*, 1,213 *vestes*, 583 pairs of *culottes* repaired for 2,836fr 25
1,605 *schakos* repaired for 802fr 50
60 cow hides, total 99fr
5 dozen basane hides, total 67fr 50
1,478 *gibernes* repaired
456 *porte-gibernes* repaired

The inspecting officer urged the War Ministry to release funds so the regiment could purchase new clothing and equipment in France. We cannot say if this was done as the regimental accounts lack any detail for 1812 and later. The blue serge had one purpose only, to line *habits* or *vestes*. Given that *vestes manches* were white, it is unlikely they were lined blue. This therefore suggests that the blue serge was used to line *habits*, which conceivably were destined either for:

Drummers: red *habits* lined in blue
Regimental artillery: blue *habits* lined in blue

Personally, I really like the idea of drummers in reversed colours, adorned with yellow lace perhaps. Certainly, at this date, regiments on service in Spain in theory, did not have regimental artillery. Therefore, are we seeing drummers clothing? Yet what of the green broadcloth? We are left with two questions we seemingly cannot answer with any degree of certainty.

60ᵉ *de Ligne*

Reviewed on 27 January 1808, the four battalions were universally equipped with 3,273 *schakos*, but only 4 cornets were issued to the *voltigeur* companies in the 1ᵉ and 2ᵉ battalion, the other two battalions had drummers in these company. No *capotes* existed, and no distinctions for grenadiers or *voltigeurs*, at least officially. The *voltigeur* companies were armed with 537 An XI light cavalry *mousquetons*.[217] Dispatched to the regiment on 24 November 1811 from the stores at Bayonne while serving the Armée du Nord under General Reille were 492 *capotes*, 248 *schakos*, 280 *bonnets de police*, 600 pairs of *culottes de drap*, 11 *vestes manches*, and 40 pairs of *culottes de peau* presumably destined for the regimental baggage wagon drivers.[218]

61ᵉ de Ligne

The decree of 15 January 1807 totally reclothed the war battalions with 1,051 *habits*, 2,003 *vestes manches*, 2,008 pairs of *culottes*, 3,283 *capotes*, 199 *capotes* in 'kit form', 2,217 pairs of shoes and 365 shirts.[219] Inspected on 10 November 1807, every man had a *chapeau*, some 3,715 examples. The regimental band, drum major and drum master were issued *gibernes* and An XI light cavalry *mousquetons*, so too 13 *sapeurs* and 54 drummers. Not an inch of chamois broadcloth existed, nor any of the *capotes* issued earlier in the year. Only grenadiers and *sous-officiers* carried sabres, while 15 *voltigeur* officers were armed with *carabines rayé*.[220]

Reviewed on 1 May 1811, the inspector noted the regiment had 59 officers, 2,174 men and 64 horses. He added that 12 officers were needed to bring the regiment up to capacity. Clothing wise, 214 *habits*, 14 *vestes*, 1,954 pairs of *culottes*, 6 *schakos*, 195 *bonnets de police* and 13 *capotes* needed to be replaced. Missing items included 152 *baudriers*, 30 drums and carriages, 4 *voltigeur* cornets, and 238 sabres.[221]

62ᵉ de Ligne

Records for the regiment's clothing are sporadic. The regiment's accounts, which start in 1806, are very piecemeal. In 1806 30m 27 of scarlet broadcloth costing 451fr 02 for 1,613 *habits* was purchased, in 1807 24m 50 beige tricot to make 70 *capotes* cost 113fr 92 and in 1808 122m of beige tricot costing 569fr 62 was purchased to make 210 *capotes*. The captain clothing officer noted each *capote* in theory required 4m 31 of cloth and were tailored to a 'very large dimension'.[222]

At the time of the 20 March 1808 review, every man was issued a *chapeau*, 1,892 being in service. Not an inch of chamois broadcloth existed to make *voltigeurs*' clothing, yet four cornets were in use. Only grenadiers and *sous-officiers* carried sabres.[223] Reviewed again on 8 June, we still note no chamois broadcloth and no *schakos* existed nor *capotes*.[224]

On 5 May 1811, 65 driving horses were purchased for the regimental artillery for 32,500fr! In May 1813 26m of gold lace and 80m of worsted lace was obtained for 107fr, and on 8 September 1813 19m 50 of gold lace was purchased for 165fr 75 and 8 pairs of grenadiers' epaulettes for 27fr 11.[225]

63ᵉ de Ligne

Under the scheme for white *habits*, the 63ᵉ *de Ligne* was to adopt aurore facings. Remarkably we have a whole palimpsest of sources that agree on this point. Firstly, we have an eyewitness report by an officer of the regiment:

> The 63ᵉ *de Ligne* was a regiment of good discipline and its good appearance, and no doubt for coquettish reasons, the colonel adopted for the officers the distinctive colour (collar and piping in aurore) which the regiment had adopted with the white *habits*.[226]

Sapeur of the 63ᵉ *de Ligne*. The use of aurore broadcloth left over from making white *habits* was a cost-effective way of using this material to give the regiment a highly distinctive look as it transitioned from white to blue. (*Collection KM*)

Regulations in Practice 157

Officer and grenadier of the 63ᵉ *de Ligne*. The aurore facings and collar to the officer's *surtout* is recorded in the regiment's paper archive, so we can be sure what is shown is an accurate depiction of the regiment in the first half of 1808. (Collection KM)

Confirming this observation, the decree of 15 January 1807 clothed the war battalions with 1,115 white *habits*.[227] Conversely, when we look at the regiment's inspection report of 31 January 1808 we find no aurore broadcloth, and only a small amount of white broadcloth had been used, suggestive that the white *habits* issued in 1807 were the only such garments. About the dress of the regiment:

> The inspector general reports with much malcontent that there is great irregularity in the clothing, which I order the officers to have rectified within 15 days of this order being issued. The captain in charge of the clothing will rectify the great abuse in the amount of lace applied to the uniforms [of the band? ed] and other irregularities in the dress [tenured] of the regiment.
>
> It is strictly forbidden from the date of this order for the *sous-officiers* to wear boots when off duty; it is forbidden for them to wear a *surtout* and épée. I order the commanding officer of the *dépôt* to replace the aurore collars worn by the officers; they are to wear simple *frac*, likewise it also expressly forbidden [illegible]. It is forbidden for *sous-officiers* to wear gold lace *ganse* on their hats; I order that the yellow collars of the drummers' *habits* are to be changed.

Clearly, officers had adopted aurore distinctions and the *sous-officiers* had adopted affectations akin to those used by the *Garde Impériale*. We note the Otto MS confirms officers using aurore cloth on their *surtouts*. Not an inch of yellow broadcloth existed but 14m 40 of chamois broadcloth had been ordered, the report notes, and 2,909m of grey tricot had been used to make 2,383 *capotes*. The regiment was sporting 1,775 *chapeaux* and 2,254 *schakos*. When we look at the regiment's armament, we see 27 *carabines rayé* were issued – presumably to *voltigeur* officers and *sous-officiers* – 15 being lost in the campaign of 1807 along with 1,100 muskets and 281 *sabres briquet*![228]

64ᵉ *de Ligne*

Inspected at Rocroi in November 1804, the regiment had 21 *sapeurs*, rather more than the regulation, 12 led by a sergeant.[229] The decree of 15 January 1807 issued the regiment 1,605 *habits* – potentially white – 2,205 *vestes manches*, 2,325 pairs of *culottes*, 2,121 *capotes*, 3,047 pairs of shoes and 1,623 shirts.[230] Reviewed on 9 November 1807, some 2,914 *chapeaux* were in use with the war battalions, while 760 *schakos* were issued to the *dépôt* battalion. We also note 9m 90 of chamois broadcloth had been used to make *voltigeurs'* clothing. Stores held 381 smocks, 236 pairs of *pantalons de route* and 864 *capotes* to dress new entrants to the regiment. We also remark that 96 An XI light cavalry *mousquetons* were in use.[231]

65ᵉ *de Ligne*

The decree of 15 January 1807 issued the regiment 1,097 *habits* – potentially white given the 63ᵉ adopted white – 2,002 *vestes manches*, 2,004 pairs of *culottes*, 3,180 *capotes*,

4,752 pairs of shoes and 321 shirts.²³² Inspected on 25 November 1807, the two war battalions were equipped with 2,420 *chapeaux*, with the *dépôt* battalion equipped with 1,034 *schakos*. Despite six cornets being issued to *voltigeur* companies, not an inch of chamois broadcloth existed, but stores did hold a further 1,326 *schakos* to replace the *chapeaux* of war battalions. We remark that grenadiers, *voltigeurs*, *cornets* and drummers were armed with sabres, the *voltigeurs* also being issued 349 An XI light cavalry carbines – the hussar model rather than the longer *mousqueton* it seems – as were drummers and *cornets*. The inspector remarked that the blue piping to the collar and cuffs of the *habit*, contrary to regulation, had been replaced with white. He wrote to the War Ministry for an answer if this 'slight amelioration to the regulation could be tolerated'. The officers were reprimanded for wearing large, baggy *pantalons* in the Russian manner and failing to appear like French officers.²³³ Regimental accounts commencing in new year 1808 report:²³⁴

Clothing Fund
1808
630m Linen for lining. Total 252fr
2,121m 76 linen for linings. Total 424fr 34
9 drums. Total 126fr 68
140 pairs epaulettes for *voltigeurs*. Total 420fr
59m gold lace at 11fr 63 a metre. Total 184fr 65
50m yellow worsted lace. Total 10fr 87
1,244m 70 white tricot. Total 5,204fr 97
4 pairs of epaulettes for *adjutant-sous-officier*. Total 68fr
4 sword knots for *adjutant-sous-officier*. Total 68fr
3m 30 gold lace for *sous-officiers*' distinctions. Total 1fr 95
1,200m of linen for lining. Total 240fr
979m 80 white tricot. Total 342fr 93
392 *schakos* at 11fr each. Total 1,069fr 09
1,229 *schakos* at 10fr 50 each. Total 2,122fr 71
2,500 pairs of shako chinscales. Total 3,517fr 85
206 grenadiers' bearskins. Total 3,597fr 29
100 grenadiers' bearskins. Total 1,700fr
100 grenades in copper for *gibernes* of grenadiers, 100 plume holders, 100 bearskin covers. Total 308fr 34
26 grenades in copper for the gibernes of the grenadiers, and 46 plume holders. Total 97fr 50
300 plumes for grenadiers costing 4fr 25
100 pairs of grenadiers epaulettes and sword knots. Total 240fr
242 *habits*, 12 *vestes*, 137 pairs of *culottes*, 102 *bonnets de police*. Total 932fr 03
3 *sapeurs*' aprons, 3 axe cases. Total 117fr 63
1 trumpet and cord. Total 44fr 88

1809
4 *sapeurs'* aprons, 4 pairs of gauntlets for *sapeurs*, two axe cases.
318m linen for *sacs à distribution*. Total 95fr 40
3m lace at 8fr 71 a metre.
27 *schakos* at 10fr 50 each
842 *schakos* at 10fr 50 each
129 *schakos* at 64fr 50 each
317 pairs of epaulettes and sword knots for grenadiers, delivered 20 March 1809. Total 1,902fr
Additional pairs, delivered 5 April 1809. Total 430fr 50
370 pairs of epaulettes and sword knots for *voltigeurs*, delivered 20 March 1809, total 2,220fr
700 pompoms for fusiliers, delivered 24 July 1809. Total 350fr
1 trumpet with cord delivered 5 August 1809. Total 46fr 50
80 red *schako* cords for grenadiers, supplied 24 July 1809. Total 240fr
400 yellow shako cords for *voltigeurs*, supplied 24 July 1809. Total 840fr
120 sets of cords for grenadiers' bearskins, 132 sets of grenadiers' *schako* cords. Total 599fr 40
120 plates for grenadiers' bearskins. Total 176fr 70
13 pairs of epaulettes and sword knots for *sapeurs*. Total 23fr 80
22 bearskins at 29fr 90 each
80 bearskins for grenadiers. Total 640fr
17m of linen for lining
40 pairs of epaulettes for grenadiers at 6fr a pair, 40 sword knots for grenadiers at 1fr 50, 190 sets of yellow *schako* cords for *voltigeurs* at 2fr each.

1810
285 *schakos* at 10fr 50 each

1811
Two fine gold lace borders for adjutants' *schako*. Total 12fr
11 *sapeurs'* aprons, 20 drum carriages, 20 drums, 36 drumstick holders, 36 sets of drumsticks.

1812
247 yellow *houpettes* at 75 centimes each
150 pairs of shoes. Total 825fr
150 of gaiters. Total 555fr

1813
49 plumes for grenadiers at 4fr 90
137 pompoms for grenadiers, 685 pompoms in diverse colours, 12 white pompoms for *état-major*. Total 437fr 89.

Thus, we see that the grenadiers of the 1ᵉ, 2ᵉ, and 3ᵉ battalions had bearskins, while the 3ᵉ, 4ᵉ and 5ᵉ battalion swapped into *schakos* during 1808 and 1809. We also know the grenadiers, at least 120 men, had plates to their bearskins. *Voltigeurs* remarkably had their own-pattern epaulettes and yellow *schako* cords, but it seems they did not have plumes. Rather than horns, the *cornets* had, it seems, trumpets! We note some of the *schakos* were noted as costing far more than a standard type: were these for *sous-officiers*? We also see *sapeurs* had axes, axe cases, aprons and bearskins: we assume they also had epaulettes, plumes etc. We know nothing about the drummers and band alas. Ernest Forte, based on Wurtz, gives the *sapeurs* white epaulettes with red crescents and the drummers aurore facings laced in yellow. Aurore was the regiment's facing colour under the 1806 regulation, so this is not impossible. He further shows a very non-regulation heart-shaped bearskin plate. We know the grenadiers' bearskins had plates but we are ignorant of the design.

66ᵉ *de Ligne*

Inspected on 28 February 1808, the two war battalions were decked out with 1,441 *chapeaux* or *schakos*. We also note 4 *voltigeur* cornets were in use, yet not an inch of chamois broadcloth existed. Grenadiers and *voltigeurs*, we note ,were armed with sabres, as were the drummers and *cornets*. Of interest, the band and 12 *sous-officiers* of *voltigeurs* were armed with *carabines rayé*.[235]

67ᵉ *de Ligne*

Inspected on 7 December 1807, 1,650 *schakos* were in use alongside 2,050 *chapeaux*. Stores had used 21m 30 of chamois broadcloth to make *voltigeurs*' clothing and 2,091m 14 grey broadcloth was in stores to make *capotes*. The *voltigeurs* lacked sabres but were armed with 372 An XI light cavalry *mousquetons*. We note 27 *carabines rayé* were in use, 7 with the band, 1 with the drum major, 1 with the drum master and 18 with *voltigeur sous-officiers*.[236]

68ᵉ *de Ligne*

No regiment of this designation.

69ᵉ *de Ligne*

Reviewed on 13 August 1805, the inspector noted the regiment's band of 8 men was costing more than the regulation allowance, reporting that 52,777fr 95 had additionally been spent on 'Clothing for service at sea' *capotes* and wooden clogs. Stores held nothing to issue to new entrants to the unit. Armament wise, the band as well as drum major and drum corporal were issued An XI light cavalry *mousquetons* and *gibernes*, so too 12 sergeants, 22 fusiliers and 35 drummers. Of interest, 2 *enfants de troupe* were also armed as fusiliers.[237]

Inspected on 30 March 1808, the inspector ordered the regiment to adopt *schakos*; 2,161 were in use and 565 were needed. Not an inch of chamois broadcloth existed. Grenadiers and *sous-officiers*, as well as drummers, were armed with 719 sabres. We also note 111 An XI light cavalry carbines were in use, 19 issued to *voltigeur* officers, 30 to *voltigeur sous-officiers*, 22 to *voltigeurs* and 40 to drummers, who were also issued *gibernes*.[238]

70ᵉ de Ligne

Reviewed on 10 February 1808, 365 *chapeaux* were in service alongside 3,000 *schakos*. Stores furthermore reports the use of 14m 40 of chamois broadcloth to make clothing for *voltigeurs*, who were armed with 291 An XI light cavalry *mousquetons*, and 1,700m of beige broadcloth was held to make *capotes*. The 54 drummers were also armed with An XI light cavalry *mousquetons*. Regimental accounts tell us 28,500fr was spent with DeGront of Paris buying *schakos*, a further 600 costing 6,540fr came from Meunier of Paris, who also supplied the regiment's buttons and *schako* plates for 4,950fr.[239]

The 3ᵉ battalion of the regiment was present at the siege of Saragossa when it was inspected on 1 January 1809. The report tells us the battalion needed 150 *habits* and *vestes manches*, 300 pairs of *culottes*, 100 *schakos*, 100 bearskins, 300 *capotes* and smocks, 400 pairs of shoes, 200 pairs each pf grey and black gaiters, 100 *havresacs*, 50 *gibernes*, 10 *baudriers*, 100 musket slings, 100 bayonet scabbards, 20 *gamelles*, 20 *grand bidons* and 300 *petit bidons*.[240] Presumably the grenadiers in the first two battalions also had bearskins, as well as epaulettes.

71ᵉ de Ligne

No regiment of this designation.

72ᵉ de Ligne

On 15 January 1807 the regiment was issued 641 *habits*, but we are ignorant of their colour: presumably blue. At Friedland, the regiment lost 799 *gibernes* and belts, 246 sabre belts, 2 *gibernes de tambour*, 16 drum carriages and 7 drums. Reviewed on 20 November 1807, the inspection report tells us 2,969 *chapeaux* were in use with the war battalions and 769 *schakos* with the *dépôt* battalion. No *capotes* existed and we note 10m 96 of chamois broadcloth had been used to make *voltigeur* distinctions, who were armed with 352 dragoon muskets, while 92 An XI light cavalry *mousquetons* were in use and 27 *carabines rayé*: 7 with the band, 2 for the drum major and drum master, and 18 with the senior *sous-officiers* of *voltigeur* companies. As expected from the regulations, the *voltigeurs* had no sabres.[241]

73ᵉ de Ligne

No regiment of this designation.

74ᵉ de Ligne

No regiment of this designation.

75ᵉ de Ligne

The paper archive of the regiment is particularly complete. Chef du Bataillon Tixier wrote to the regiment's colonel on 20 April 1804 informing him that he had received from Maison Cailloin of the Palais Royale, Paris, a tri-colour feather panache for the *chapeau* of the drum major.[242]

Inspected on 28 July 1805, the inspector had an apoplectic fit about the poor condition of the regiment's leather work and the unit's shabby appearance, ranting that 'it appears to me that not a single buckle or any buff work has ever been cleaned […] nor have the soldiers and *sous-officiers* paid attention to the buttons on their uniforms […]'[243]

Inspected on 13 September 1805, the 3ᵉ battalion's inspection has some surprises. We find 20 bearskins for grenadiers, 63 sets of cords and plumes for bearskins, 13 *sapeurs'* aprons as well as clothing for the drum major that comprised 1 new *frac*, 1 new *habit*, 1 new *veste*, 1 new pair of *culottes*, 1 new *chapeau*, 1 new sabre and 1 new mace! Also present was the cash box for the band.[244]

At the start of March 1806, Captain Gomeret wrote to the regiment's major about difficulties he faced in clothing the regiment. He had no option but to buy 400 shirts from local suppliers at inflated prices in Montreuil, that not a metre of blue broadcloth was in the *dépôt*, and not an inch of scarlet or white broadcloth existed. Concerning the band, he noted they were 'very prettily dressed' as their *habits* were lined in rose, i.e. hot pink, but he noted that the cloth was expensive, and was not really worth the money as the colour faded very rapidly. We wonder if the pink facings were retained, and also what the rest of the uniform was like? Imperial blue facing pink would have been very distinctive.[245] Furthermore, he commented that 40 grenadier bearskins were received at the regiment's *dépôt* complete with 'their fittings'.[246]

At the close of March 1806, Captain Gomeret wrote to the regiment's major informing him that *schakos* had been introduced to replace the *chapeaux*. He reported that *chapeaux* had been ordered to replace those that needed replacing, and that the *schako* would be introduced from 1807 as *chapeaux* became due for replacement.[247] A report of 25 September 1806 records the delivery of 160 further bearskins, which had cost 4,320fr.[248]

The decree of 15 January 1807 issued the regiment 1,001 *habits*, 2,001 *vestes manches*, 2,001 pairs of *culottes*, 1915 *capotes*, 3,532 pairs of shoes and 225 shirts.[249] For *voltigeurs* a document dated 1 July 1807 reports 14m 40 chamois broadcloth had been used, 317m

Drum major of the 75ᵉ *de Ligne* sometime in summer 1808. The regiment's archive tells us that prior to the adoption of scarlet-faced blue *habits*, the drum major wore a uniform cut from pink broadcloth and his *chapeau* had a tricolour panache.

Drum major of the 75ᵉ *de Ligne* sometime in 1810, by which time the uniform is now a blue *habit* faced in crimson with gold lace. The drummers in the background also have crimson *revers* to their *habits*.

50 of beige broadcloth for *sous-officiers' redingotes*, and 1,379m of grey tricot for 1,000 *soldats' capotes*.²⁵⁰ A document of 15 August 1807 reports that 168m of blue serge had been obtained to line the *habits* of the musicians and cost 517fr, while 85m of chamois serge was purchased to line the *habits* of 8 *sapeurs* and cost 85fr. We assume therefore that the *sapeurs* had chamois facings. The reverse of the same report lists 26 *habits* for *sapeurs* in the *dépôt* that had cost 5fr 20 each to produce, also stating that 40fr 60 had been spent

Author's reconstruction of the uniform of the *sapeur* of the 75ᵉ *de Ligne* according to the regiment's paper archive. A document of 15 August 1807 reports 85m of chamois serge was purchased to line the *habits* of 8 *sapeurs* and cost 85fr. We also find that 17m of chamois broadcloth was allocated to the *sapeurs'* uniforms. The *sapeurs* had bearskins, scarlet epaulettes and carried light cavalry *mousquetons*. A document of 1806 mentions painting the handles of the *sapeurs'* axes blue.

Author's reconstruction of a grenadier drummer of the 75ᵉ *de Ligne* in the 1805–08 period based on the regiment's preserved paper archive. The regiment's archive is one of the most complete for any *ligne* regiment in 1805 to 1808.

Author's reconstruction of a *voltigeur* drummer of the 75ᵉ *de Ligne* in the 1805–08 period based on the regiment's preserved paper archive.

on new band *habits*, and a further 245fr buying 91m white broadcloth to make *vestes* and *culottes* for the band. A further 1,500fr was spent on instruments and *habits*.[251] The archive is clear that the band was faced pink, while the *sapeurs* had chamois distinctions. By 1810 the *sapeurs* and band had scarlet facings and grenadiers had *schakos*, leaving some *sapeurs* with bearskins. On 25 September, Captain Gomeret reported that the master tailor had made 282 smocks, 22 *habits*, 167 *vestes manches*, 10 pairs of *culottes*, 262 *bonnets de police* and repaired 8 habits for the 3ᵉ battalion. More than 1,000 would be made. For the war battalions, 452 *capotes* costing 23fr, 339 costing 22frfr and 345 costing 16fr had been obtained: the price difference surely represents lower-grade materials and single rather than double-breasted garments.[252]

Reviewed on 6 January 1808, the report notes that the regiment had 2,187 *schakos* in use and 1,083 *chapeaux*, all of which needed total replacement with *schakos*. Some 1,344 *capotes* were in use, 893 of which needed repairs and 451 total replacement. The *capotes* were made from grey tricot, some 1,379m 120 being used for this purpose, stores holding 317m 50 beige broadcloth to make *sous-officiers' redingotes*. In addition, 19m 80 of chamois broadcloth had been used to make *voltigeurs'* distinctions. Dépôt held 89 brand-new *habits*, 104 *schakos*, 61 *bonnets de police* and 322 *capotes*. In terms of weapons, the *voltigeurs* had had their sabres taken from them and were armed with 223 dragoon muskets, while 24 drummers were armed with light cavalry *mousquetons* and 25 were armed with infantry muskets. Every one of the 49 drummers was issued a sabre, *giberne* and belt. Oddly, or remarkably, 26 non-French muskets were in the regiment's possession.[253]

76ᵉ de Ligne

Inspected in September 1804, the reviewing officer noted the men wore their hair too long, and their faces were hidden by enormous side beards. He ordered the men to cut their hair in accordance to regulations. He added that many of the men's *vestes* were too short, and did not cover the waistband of the *culottes*, the latter not being made as exact copies of the *effets de modèle* sent by the War Ministry.[254] The decree of 15 January 1807 issued the regiment 1,004 *habits*, 2,003 *vestes manches*, 2,001 pairs of *culottes*, 525 *capotes*, 3,032 pairs of shoes and 2,004 shirts.[255] Inspected on 15 December 1807, the report tells us no *capotes* or bearskins existed, nor *schakos* and the men were wearing 2,495 *chapeaux*. Not an inch of chamois broadcloth had been purchased. We note the *voltigeurs* did not have sabres and that 60 An XI light cavalry *mousquetons* were in use, 54 being issued to drummers and *cornets*.[256]

77ᵉ de Ligne

No regiment of this designation.

78ᵉ de Ligne

No regiment of this designation.

79ᵉ de Ligne

The review of September 1804 tells us 1,600 *capotes*, smocks and pairs of *pantalons de route* had been made. The *capotes* were made from tricot and *etoffe* (twill) of an unspecified colour. We also note in stores 481m 50 of black twill to make gaiters, 109 stock buckles, 3,605 fusilier pompoms, 273 pairs of grenadier epaulettes, 166 grenadier sword knots, 166 grenadier pompoms and 200 scarlet plumes. Remarkably, we find 613 pairs of mittens.[257] Inspected on 20 January 1808, we note 612 *chapeaux* were in service alongside 3,262 *schakos* and 1,916 *capotes*, which had been made from 2,517m 90 of grey broadcloth for *sous-officiers* and grenadiers as well as 2,075m grey tricot for other ranks. Stores also reported 30m 31 linen was used to line black gaiters, for which 198m 58 black twill had been used. A mere 7cm of silver lace had been used to adorn a musician's uniform. The *voltigeurs* had four *cornets*, who were armed with 519 dragoon muskets – 310 of which were Austrian – and had no sabres as the regulations dictated. Stores report that 19m 20 of chamois broadcloth had been used to make *voltigeurs'* clothing. We note 64 linen smocks were in use and 467 pairs of linen *pantalons de route*. We also notice 1,852 pompoms for fusiliers, 554 pairs of grenadier epaulettes, 403 grenadiers' sword knots, 153 sets of bearskins cords – yet no bearskins existed, at least officially – 35 stock buckles, 30 plumes and 4 pairs of adjutant's epaulettes. We also note the unit had 17 *sapeurs*.[258]

80ᵉ *de Ligne*

No regiment of this designation.

81ᵉ *de Ligne*

The 1808 inspection report cannot be located, but a report of 20 September 1819 reveals that in the period 1807 to 1809, the regiment purchased 3,413 *schakos* for the sum of 41,348fr 63. The regulation states *schakos* were to cost 10fr, yet the 81ᵉ were buying those costing 12fr 50 with cords plumes and chinscales, and the *sous-officiers schakos* cost 22fr 50 each! Presumably these had gold lace and rather extravagant red and gold *schako* cords like those of the Garde Impériale. The War Ministry refused to pay for the embellishments, ordered the lace and cords stripped off and agreed to pay 11fr 65 per *schako*, leaving the regiment out of pocket to the sum of 2,086fr 88. This is one of very few cases where *sous-officiers* in the ligne were dressed in imitation of the Garde Impériale: the atypical should not be treated as the typical. In the same period, 1,983 *havresacs* were purchased, but the inspector rejected a claim for 1,156fr 42 for luxury items. Some 550 tassels for *bonnets de police* along with 1,630 toises [1 toise = 6ft 6] of cording for *bonnets de police* costing 210fr was purchased in April 1806, along with 162 bearskins costing 30fr including plate, cords and plume, and 2 pairs of epaulettes for the *adjutant-sous-officier*. A second report reveals that on 1807 1,125fr was spent buying *schakos*, 154fr 60 was spent buying a pair of epaulettes, a *chapeau*, a pair of boots and a sword knot for the *adjutant-sous-officier*.[259]

82ᵉ *de Ligne*

Reviewed on 8 March 1808, 1,825 *chapeaux* and *schakos* were in use, and 4 *voltigeur* cornets. Stores report the use of 1,383m 73 beige broadcloth and grey tricot to make *capotes*, all of which were lost on campaign. Likewise, chamois broadcloth of an unknown amount had been used to make *voltigeurs*' clothing. We note 72 grenadiers' bearskins and the same number of grenadiers' epaulettes had existed in 1803, but not are mentioned five years later. We also note that 205 An XI light cavalry *mousquetons* were issued: 28 to *voltigeur sous-officiers* and 171 to *voltigeurs* themselves. We also note 12 *carabines rayé* were issued to *voltigeur sous-officiers*. A further 77 *mousquetons* were issued to the staff, band, *sapeurs*, drummers and *cornets*.[260]

83ᵉ *de Ligne*

No regiment of this designation.

84ᵉ de Ligne

In July 1805 we note the regiment had 12 *sapeurs*, the band, 3 *sous-officiers*, 62 fusiliers and 54 drummers were armed with An XI light cavalry *mousquetons*.[261] Reviewed on 4 January 1808, 1,073 *chapeaux* were in use alongside 2,030 *schakos*. We also note 6 *voltigeurs'* horns were in service and stores reports 21m 27 of chamois broadcloth had been used to make *voltigeurs'* clothing. Also in service were 1,037 *capotes* made from grey tricot, and the drummers and *cornets* were armed with 54 An XI light cavalry carbines.[262]

To replace the *chapeaux* in 1ᵉ battalion, on 10 February 1808 the regiment purchased 982 *schakos* costing 12fr each with 982 covers made from black oil cloth for the sum of 13,226fr 10, along with 920 copper buckles for *schakos*, costing 126fr 38. The *schakos* without buckles cost 10fr each. This is one of the few instances we have that show the use of *schako* covers before 1813. A year later 880 *schakos*, 880 *schako* covers, and 880 pompoms were purchased for the sum of 12,568fr 40. A further 200 *schakos* with 200 cockades were purchases for 2,370fr. The *schakos* purchased in 1808 and 1809 were of a 'superior quality', being made entirely from cow hide, which must have made them rather heavy. The leather was covered in black broadcloth.[263]

85ᵉ de Ligne

Inspected in Strasbourg on 16 November 1807, the regiment had 2,664 *chapeaux* in the war battalions and 647 *schakos* with the *dépôt* battalion. The regiment used 14m 40 of chamois broadcloth in the same period for *voltigeur* distinctions, and remarkably had not a single *capote*! The *dépôt* held 5 *habits*, 61 *vestes*, 129 pairs of *culottes*, 64 *chapeaux*, 95 *bonnets de police*, and 53 *schakos*. Clearly the regiment wore a mix of headdress, and its clothing and equipment was utterly worn out.[264] Reviewed again on 1 December 1807, the inspector noted that the war battalions had lost a considerable amount of leather work and equipment in the campaign of 1807 on the field of battle or captured by the enemy. The 3ᵉ battalion had supplied some of the missing items, and in consequence needed

Sapeur of the 85ᵉ *de Ligne* sometime in the first half of 1808. (*Collection KM*)

Grenadier private and officer of the 85e *de Ligne* sometime in the first half of 1808. (*Collection KM*)

new equipment. The report further notes that a mix of *chapeaux* and *schakos* were worn, of the 3,518 *habits*, half needed repairs, and of the 4,293 items of headdress, 1,876 needed repairs and 642 were to be disposed of as life expired. In addition, 286 men needed new tricot *pantalons*, 642 men an item of headdress, 1,629 a *bonnet de police*, 464 a *giberne*, 42 a *giberne* belt and 53 a sabre belt. The regiment had 64 drummers and 8 *cornets* in the *voltigeur* companies. No *capotes* were in service and no chamois cloth existed for *voltigeur* distinctions. Brand-new clothing in the *dépôt* included 170 *habits*, and 16 needing repairs, 184 *vestes*, 79 pairs of *culottes*, 62 *chapeaux* and 6 *bonnets de police*. The regiment had an eclectic mix of firearms: 4,103 muskets, 40 An XI light cavalry *mousquetons* were issued to drummers, and 34 *carabines rayé* with *voltigeur sous-officiers*.[265]

172 Napoleon's Line Infantry – From the Battle of Jena to the Invasion of Iberia

Voltigeur officer and private of the 85ᵉ *de Ligne* sometime in the first half of 1808. (*Collection KM*)

86ᵉ de Ligne

Reviewed on 25 January 1808, every man was wearing a *schako*, 3,525 examples, with a further 89 brand-new examples in stores. We also notice 19m 20 of chamois broadcloth had been used to make *voltigeurs'* clothing and 1,700m of beige tricot had been used to produce 1,629 *capotes*. *Voltigeurs* were armed with 339 dragoon muskets and 27 *voltigeur sous-officiers* were issued *carabines rayé*.²⁶⁶

87ᵉ de Ligne

No regiment of this designation.

88ᵉ de Ligne

Inspected in Strasbourg on 16 November 1807, the regiment had 2,664 *chapeaux* with the war battalions and 647 *schakos* with the *dépôt* battalion. The regiment used 14m 40 of chamois broadcloth in the same period for *voltigeur* distinctions, and remarkably had not a single *capote*! The *dépôt* held 5 *habits*, 61 *vestes*, 129 pairs of *culottes*, 64 *chapeaux*, 95 *bonnets de police*, and 53 *schakos*. Clearly the regiment wore a mix of headdress, and the regiment's clothing and equipment was utterly worn out. *Voltigeurs* did not carry sabres, and were armed with infantry muskets.²⁶⁷

89ᵉ de Ligne

No regiment of this designation.

90ᵉ de Ligne

No regiment of this designation.

91ᵉ de Ligne

No regiment of this designation.

92ᵉ de Ligne

Inspected on 14 November 1803, the report is hugely informative: it reports 304m of black twill was in stores along with 3,780 small copper buttons for gaiters, 43m 50 drummers' lace, tricolour *aigrettes* for *chapeaux* were listed but none existed, likewise musicians' lace. Stores held also 149 pairs of grey gaiters, 445 pairs of black, 346 pairs of shoe buckles, 477 pairs of knee buckles and 776 stock buckles. Listed but none existed were pins for the queue as well as spare *rabats* (the white piping that slotted into the black stock), of which 145 black examples were in stores and 615 white. Cloth in stores included 150m 40 green broadcloth, and 1,024m 5 fine linen for shirts. Listed, but again none existed, were epaulettes for grenadiers, epaulettes for drummers, as well as sword knots and pompoms for grenadiers and drummers' sword knots, copper grenades for grenadier *gibernes* as well as *sapeurs*' aprons, axe and axe case.[268] Inspected on 27 July 1805, every man was wearing a *chapeau*, and we note 35 drummers out of 72 were armed with An XI light cavalry *mousquetons*.[269] No other inspection reports can be found at the time of writing.

93ᵉ *de Ligne*

Officer of the 93ᵉ *de Ligne* in naïve drawing by Suhr sometime in summer 1808.

Colonel of the 93ᵉ *de Ligne* depicted by Suhr. The image dates to summer 1808.

Inspected on 8 August 1805, we remark that stores had issued 375 *capotes* to new entrants, along with 289 smocks and just 9 pairs of linen *pantalons de route*; some 720 pairs remained in stores, with 2,611 black stocks, 137 pairs of grey gaiters and 111 pairs of black. We note for the war battalions 1,600 *capotes*, smocks and *pantalons de route* had been made. Only grenadiers, drummers and *sous-officiers* were issued sabres.[270]

The 1807 inspection is missing from the regiment's archive, but partial accounts do exist:[271]

Year	Month and Day	Item	Amount	Contracted price	Delivery price	Difference	Total cost increase
1809	15 November	*Havresacs*	337	6fr	8fr 50	2fr 50	842fr 50
		Socks	42 dozen pairs	16fr 50	22 50	4fr	239fr 40
		Giberne and *Porte-gibernes*	150	4fr 50	4fr 60	10c	37fr 50
	4 December	Large buttons	626 dozen	38c a dozen	75c a dozen		231fr 62
		Small buttons	2,039 dozen	24c a dozen	37c a dozen		275fr 26
1810	15 February	*Gibernes*	150	4fr 45	4fr 60	15c	22fr 50
		Sabre belts	150	4fr 40	4fr 50	10c	15fr
		Giberne belts	150	4fr 50	4fr 60	10c	15fr
		Linen for lining	650	1fr 40 a metre	1fr 88	48c	312fr
		Shoes	476 pairs	5fr a pair	5fr 50 a pair	50c a pair	238fr
		Grey gaiters	410 pairs	1fr 80 a pair	2fr 50 a pair	70c a pair	287fr
		Black gaiters	276 pairs	3fr 25 a pair	5fr 50 a pair	2fr 25	621fr
		Havresacs	150	6fr	8fr 50	2fr 50	375fr
	10 March	Red broadcloth	28m	11fr a metre	20fr 50		266fr
		White broadcloth	49m	9fr 50 a metre	12fr 20		132fr 30
		Yellow broadcloth	6m	44fr 45 a metre	19fr 40		47fr 70
		Linen for lining	319m	1fr 40 a metre	2fr 90		478fr 50
		White serge for lining	219m	1fr 40 a metre	1fr 90	50c	109fr 50
		Red worsted lace	74m	60c a metre	75c		11fr 10
		Red *houpettes* for grenadiers	411		1fr 40		267fr 15

Year	Month and Day	Item	Amount	Contracted price	Delivery price	Difference	Total cost increase
		Yellow houpettes	411		1fr 20		246fr 60
	24 April	Linen for lining	85m 52	1fr 40 a metre	1fr 84 a metre	44c a metre	37fr 62
		Shoes	90 pairs	5fr a pair	5fr 50 a pair	50c	395fr
		Black gaiters	302 pairs	3fr 35 a pair	5fr 50 a pair	2fr 15 a pair	679fr 50
1811	21 February	*Schako* cords	152		3fr 10		471fr 20

The regiment fell foul of changing regulations. *Schako* cords were abolished with the circular of 9 October 1810. The War Ministry refused to sanction this purchase, rather unsurprisingly. The *voltigeurs* had yellow distinctions.

94ᵉ *de Ligne*

Sapeur of the 94ᵉ *de Ligne* with sky blue facings sometime in the first half of 1808. (*Collection KM*)

Grenadier and *voltigeur* of the 94ᵉ *de Ligne* sometime in the first half of 1808. (*Collection KM*)

In summer 1805, in the list of the regiment's weapons we note that the 13 *sapeurs* with the regiment were armed with An XI light cavalry *mousquetons*.²⁷² The *voltigeur* companies were formed on 18 October 1805.²⁷³

Inspected at Wesel on 3 December 1807, every man was wearing a *chapeau*, 3,196 examples being in use, 1,971 being issued since August 1805 and 1,626 in need of replacing. Also in service were 6 *voltigeur* cornets. Stores report no *sapeurs*' equipment or any chamois broadcloth. We note 13 *sapeurs* were issued An XI light cavalry carbines, and the *voltigeurs* carried sabres as well as infantry muskets. Furthermore, a huge number of *habits* – 2,460 examples – had been issued to the regiment from government stocks along with 3,044 *vestes manches* and 3,067 pairs of *culottes*. Some 172m 24 of blue broadcloth had been used to repair 964 *habits*.²⁷⁴ The inspector authorised the regiment to replace *chapeau* with *schakos* to cost 10fr 70. The regiment also had 379 sabres and 173 muskets that needed to be replaced and required 463 muskets with bayonets and 85 sabres for the newly levied battalion.²⁷⁵ A price list of effects the regiment was to obtain included the *grand modèle havresac*, favoured rather than retaining the use of the *petit modèle* reserved for light infantry.²⁷⁶

95ᵉ *de Ligne*

Inspected on 27 November 1807, the regiment had 3,549 *chapeaux* in use. No *schako* had been purchased and not a single *capote* existed. *Dépôt* held brand-new ready to be issued 397 *habits*, 869 *vestes*, 766 pairs of *culottes*, 269 *chapeaux* and 307 *bonnets de police*. Not an inch of chamois or beige broadcloth had been purchased or used. *Voltigeurs* did not carry sabres, and were armed with infantry muskets.²⁷⁷

96ᵉ *de Ligne*

At Landau on 15 December 1807 the regiment possessed 2,379 *chapeaux*, 1,067 *schakos* and 6 *voltigeurs*' horns, among other items. Of the 3,634 *habits*, 1,237 needed repairs, and 456 total replacement, so too half the *chapeaux*. The men had no *capotes*, and not an inch of chamois broadcloth existed. The inspector authorised 1,673 *schakos* be purchased with celerity and the remaining *chapeaux* repaired. The band, drum major and 15 *voltigeur sous-officiers* were armed with An XI light cavalry *mousqueton*s, as were 13 *sapeurs*.²⁷⁸

97ᵉ *de Ligne*

No regiment of this designation.

98ᵉ *de Ligne*

No regiment of this designation.

180 Napoleon's Line Infantry – From the Battle of Jena to the Invasion of Iberia

Grenadier and fusilier drummer of the 95ᵉ *de Ligne* sometime in summer 1806. The men's *habits* seem to have gold (yellow?) lace around the *revers*. The uniform is incredibly sombre.

A group of officers of the 95ᵉ *de Ligne* in summer 1806. The *voltigeur* officer is notable for his chamois collar.

99ᵉ *de Ligne*

No regiment of this designation.

100ᵉ *de Ligne*

The regimental accounts signed off on 9 December 1803 state 5,112fr 17 was spent buying 'bearskin caps for grenadiers'. Clearly bearskins had existed, no doubt along with

Grenadiers of the 95ᵉ *de Ligne*. Clearly, grenadiers, as we expected from the 1791 regulation, had both a bearskin and *chapeau*. Yet officially bearskins were not to be taken on campaign. The light beige gaiters are presumably the grenadier's campaign items.

Regulations in Practice 183

This group of officers, men and bandsmen of the 95ᵉ *de Ligne* in summer 1806 gives us some exceptional details not recorded in the regiment's archive. We see on the left a bandsman with sky blue facings and of African origins. We also see *voltigeurs* with chamois collar, and the drum major wearing what must be a sombre campaign uniform. In front of the drum major we see the bandmaster wearing, again, sky blue facings. Both bandsman and musician have sky blue trefoils with gold lace at the shoulder.

epaulettes as 677fr was spent on 'distinctions for grenadiers'. The regiment had 8 *sapeurs* led by a corporal.[279] Inspected on 31 October 1807, the regiment had 3,712 *chapeaux* with the war battalions and just 175 *schakos* with the *dépôt* battalion. The regiment's clothing was worn out at the end of the 1807 campaign despite 1,600 *habits* and *vestes manches* being issued in January 1807. Nearly everything had to be replaced, and we note not an inch of chamois cloth had been purchased for *voltigeur* distinctions and not a single *capote* existed.[280]

Sapeur of the 95ᵉ *de Ligne* in summer 1806.

Sapeur of the 95ᵉ *de Ligne* in summer 1808. We see, as with the bandsmen, the *sapeurs* had sky blue facings. The similarity between the two contemporary depictions of the *sapeurs* of the 95ᵉ are notable. (*Collection KM*)

Officer and grenadier of the 95ᵉ *de Ligne*. Compared to the 1806 image, the grenadier's bearskin has gained a peak and chinscales. The officer's dress identical to that shown in 1806. (*Collection KM*)

Sapeur of the 96ᵉ *de Ligne* sometime in summer 1808. This is the second *habit-veste* shown by Otto long before the Bardin regulation. Presumably these garments were inspired by Prussian fashion rather than French. (*Collection KM*)

Grenadier of the 96e *de Ligne* by Martinet.

Fusilier of the 96e *de Ligne* by Martinet. It is labelled as such on the obverse of the original image.

Drum major of the 96ᵉ *de Ligne* as he appeared in the first half of 1808. (*Collection KM*)

Grenadier and fusilier of the 96ᵉ *de Ligne* as they appeared in the first half of 1808. (*Collection KM*)

Officer of *voltigeurs* and *voltigeur* of the 96ᵉ *de Ligne* in the first half of 1808. (*Collection KM*)

Regulations in Practice

Regimental accounts for the regiment reveal small details about how the regiment was actually dressed compared to the regulations. But we must stress that just because the 100e *de Ligne* had certain items that were strictly non-regulation, it does not mean that all the regiments in the French army had the same 'forbidden' items obtained in 1809:[281]

808 *schakos* for other ranks, total 9,2892fr
3 *schakos* for *sous-officiers*, total 78fr
620 pompoms
170 sets of *schako* cords, total 204fr
2 *voltigeur* horns and cords, total 68fr 45
4m gold lace, total 41fr
10m gold lace, total 85fr
560 pompoms, total 420fr
70m of drummers' livery, total 52fr 5
4 *sapeurs'* axes '*modèle de la garde impériale*', 4 axe cases, 4 *sapeurs'* aprons in cow hide, 4 pairs of gauntlets, total 416fr
100 *voltigeur* pompoms, 57 pairs grenadiers' epaulettes, 153 grenadier pompoms, total 1,456fr
100 *voltigeur* pompoms, total 400fr
40 grenadiers' *schako* cords, 40 *voltigeurs'* *schako* cords, total 452fr
50 pairs grenadiers' epaulettes, 60 grenadier pompoms, 40 *voltigeur* pompoms, total 830fr
1 pair *adjutant-sous-officier* epaulettes, total 126fr
20 *baudriers*, total 150fr
148 *schakos*, total 1702fr
150 pompoms, total 115fr
150 bearskins, 150 sets of bearskin cords, 150 plumes for bearskins, total 4,875fr

Of interest, no *sapeurs'* sabres were purchased, arguably therefore they used standard line-pattern sabres. The drummers had their own pattern lace, but alas we have no idea at all as to its appearance; we assume it was the 1808 issue of 1786 pattern. The War Ministry ordered lace and ornaments be stripped from the *sous-officier schakos*, stating these were forbidden items.

101e *de Ligne*

Inspected on 15 July 1807, we note 1,641 *schakos* were in stores waiting to be issued. We also note, 244m 92 of scarlet and crimson broadcloth had been used; the 101e was allocated crimson facings under the March 1806 decree. More than 1,742m of white broadcloth had been used since 1805, and just 205m of blue broadcloth to make 579 *habits* and repair 1,329 examples. Presumably the balance of the *habits* were white. As the remaining 71m 85 scarlet and crimson cloth did not exist by June 1808, presumably the crimson was used for drummers' facings. Not an inch of chamois broadcloth existed, so clearly *voltigeurs* did not have distinctive uniforms at thus date.[282] Confirming this observation, the decree of 15 January 1807 totally reclothed the war battalions with 1,036 white *habits*, 1,961 *vestes*, the same number of *culottes*, 595 ready-made *capotes*, 1,934 *capotes* supplied as 'kits', 3,799 pairs of shoes and 2,559 shirts.[283]

Reviewed on 6 March 1808, the 3ᵉ battalion was wearing 454 brand-new *schakos*, and had 200 *capotes* made from 790m 37 of grey tricot. Stores reports the two war battalions had 1,173 *chapeaux*. The *voltigeurs* had chamois distinctions as 14m 35 of chamois broadcloth had been used.[284] The war battalions were reviewed in June, by which time 2,145 new *schakos* had been issued, and a further 20m of chamois broadcloth had been used to make *voltigeurs'* clothing. Only grenadiers, drummers and *sous-officiers* were issued sabres, while *voltigeurs* carried regular infantry muskets.[285] This neatly shows it took more than two years from the decree introducing *schakos* for war battalions to be issued these: only possible once the army was back on French soil. It also shows that despite the decree being issued in late summer 1805, it was not until spring 1808 that *voltigeurs* gained chamois distinctions, a pattern repeated across the army as a whole.

102ᵉ *de Ligne*

Reviewed on 30 September 1804, we note the regiment had 12 *sapeurs*, and that 1,475 *chapeaux* out of 2,280 in use were life expired, as was every single one of the 1,466 *bonnets de police*: not enough existed for each man to have one. The inspector ordered 1,140 *habits* to be made, accompanied by 1,140 *vestes*, 2,280 pairs of *culottes*, 1,140 *chapeaux*, 100 *gibernes* and belts as well as 6 *sapeurs'* aprons.[286] Reviewed again on 9 December 1805, the inspector noted 1,536 new *chapeaux* had been delivered, 607 *habits*, 982 *vestes* and 969 pairs of *culottes*, as well as 6 *sapeurs'* aprons. This still left thousands of new *habits*, *vestes*, *culottes*, *chapeaux* and *bonnets de police* needed. Stores held 1,423 black stocks, 1,766 white stocks and 1,656 pairs of stockings. The *voltigeur* companies had not been created by this date.[287]

Inspected again on 7 March 1808, the *dépôt* battalion was equipped with 580 *schakos*, 502 *capotes* and the *voltigeur* company had one *cornet* and one drummer. Stores had issued 932 *chapeaux* to the war battalions prior to the review and a further 1,200 at the point of review. Since 28 July 1806, 1,435m 53 of blue broadcloth, 100m 56 white broadcloth, 1,251m 42 scarlet broadcloth and 14m 40 chamois broadcloth had been used. The huge amount of scarlet broadcloth used comes as a surprise and suggests usage other than piping, collars and cuffs of *habits*.[288]

103ᵉ *de Ligne*

The 103ᵉ was created during the last days of the monarchy, along with the 102ᵉ, 104ᵉ and 105ᵉ regiments, in accordance with the Law of 28 August 1791, but its organisation was actually completed only on 24 January 1792. The 1ᵉ Battalion consisted mainly of elements of the National Guard of Paris, while the 2ᵉ battalion was fed by levees of the Upper Rhine.

Inspected on 7 November 1807, the war battalion's status was not known by the inspecting officer as they had been on campaign constantly since 1806. The *dépôt* between 1805 and 1807 had used 1,599m 17 white broadcloth, 14m 80 yellow broadcloth for *voltigeur* distinctions, 6,252m 21 blue broadcloth, 2,138m 11 beige broadcloth for making *capotes*, 649m scarlet broadcloth, 14,320m white tricot for *vestes* and *culottes*, 3,251m 84 beige tricot for *capotes*, and 23,160m 90 white serge to line *habits*. Some 4,443 *capotes* had been made and issued made from tricot and broadcloth. No *schakos* existed, so we presume they were purchased in 1808 – this neatly demonstrates the huge delay in enacting the 1806 regulation![289]

104ᵉ *de Ligne*

No regiment of this designation.

105ᵉ *de Ligne*

Reviewed on 9 October 1804, the inspector lamented that the cloth, clothing and equipment did not adhere to the *effects de modèle* sent from the War Ministry, but did accept the model of garments adopted by the regiment were all very uniform. Alas, we do not know how the items differed from regulation. Regimental accounts report 44,729fr 53 was spent buying *redingotes*, *pantalons de route* and smocks.[290] The decree of 15 January 1807 reclothed the war battalions with 1,004 – presumably white – *habits*, 2,003 *vestes manches*, 2,003 pairs of *culottes*, 193 ready-made *capotes* and a further 717 supplied as 'kits', 2,637 pairs of shoes and 1,967 shirts. We also note the unit received 227 *marmites* with lids and bags, 1,767 white metal *petit bidons*, 115 hatchets and cases and 227 *gamelles*.[291]

Reviewed again on 28 January 1808, 2,569 *capotes* were in service, of which 858 needed repairs and 1,121 replacing. We note also 1,111 *chapeaux* were in use, all scheduled for replacement, and 2,108 *schakos*, of which 1,311 needed replacing and 605 repairing. Cloth used by the regiment included 14m 40 of chamois broadcloth for *voltigeurs*, 800m beige broadcloth for *sous-officiers*, and 5,470m 25 grey tricot for other ranks' *capotes*. Only *sous-officiers* and grenadiers carried sabres, as did the 54 drummers. *Voltigeurs* were armed with infantry muskets.[292]

106ᵉ *de Ligne*

The report of 1 September 1805 tells us the regiment had 13 *sapeurs* with aprons, equipped with the same number of axes with cases and belts. We assume they also had bearskins, but no archive document supports this hypothesis. The report identified 342 *habits* were needed under the usual terms of renewal, but the inspector added that in fact 1,000 *habits* were needed and 1,200 *chapeaux* rather than the 470 that fell for renewal.[293]

In an undated report from 1807, not an inch of chamois broadcloth existed, but 2,400 *schakos* did, all brand new, and also 6 *voltigeur* cornets. None of the *sapeurs'* equipment existed.[294] Inspected on 4 January 1808, we note 13 An XI light cavalry carbines had been issued to *sapeurs* on 23 May 1807, all being lost on campaign. Some 14m 40 of chamois broadcloth had been used to make *voltigeurs'* clothing, who were armed with infantry muskets and were not issued sabres. We also note 2,557 *schakos* were in use, 400 needed to be replaced, so too did all 6 *voltigeur* cornets and 4 drums.[295] A second report, dated 5 January 1808, adds that during the year 1807 the regiment received 400 pairs of *culottes*, 400 *schakos*, 800 *bonnets de police*, 845 *gibernes* and belts, 600 *baudriers*, 450 musket slings and 2 drums. An almost identical list of needs was prepared for 1808.[296]

A report made on 1 June 1809 for losses of equipment since 1 April reports 47 men killed, 591 wounded and 104 prisoners of war after Essling. In terms of equipment, 1,365 *schakos* were lost, 264 bearskins, 1,415 *habits*, 1,365 *vestes*, 1,765 pairs of *culottes*, 1,067 *capotes* and 1,689 *bonnets de police*. The grenadier bearskins had all been purchased after January 1808. Also lost at Essling were 13 *mousquetons* and 3 *sapeurs'* axes, plus 4 *voltigeur* cornets, 19 drums and carriages, 225 sabres, 1,592 bayonets and 1,592 muskets. Huge losses, when the unit mustered 2,997 men, with an almost 50 per cent loss of effective weaponry and clothing after one battle.[297]

107ᵉ de Ligne

No regiment of this designation.

108ᵉ de Ligne

Regimental accounts of 24 September 1803 report 45,569fr spent on *redingotes*, smocks and linen *pantalons de route*.[298] Reviewed on 27 July 1805, we note 61 An XI light cavalry *mousquetons* were in service: 53 with the regiment's drummers, who were also issued *gibernes*, 7 with fusiliers and a solitary example with a sergeant major.[299] Inspected on 30 November 1807, every man on parade was wearing a *chapeau*, some 2,899 examples being in use, alongside 1,369 *redingotes*. *Dépôt* had made 1,089 examples, with 492 issued, 591 in stores to be issued and 20 to be disposed. The *voltigeur* companies had 9 cornets but not an inch of chamois broadcloth had been obtained for their uniforms, and we note they did not carry sabres. The regiment's 49 drummers, band of 8 men, the drum major and drum corporal and 26 senior *sous-officiers* carried An XI light cavalry carbines, 84 being in use.[300]

109ᵉ de Ligne

No regiment of this designation.

110ᵉ de Ligne

No regiment of this designation.

111ᵉ de Ligne

Reviewed on 23 November 1807, 2,283 *schakos* were in service and 1,486 *chapeaux*. No *capotes* existed, and not an inch of chamois broadcloth, yet the *voltigeurs* were armed with 336 sabres and the same number of An XI light cavalry *mousquetons*.[301] The drummers had been issued 36 such weapons in 1805, with the band, drum major and drum corporal being allocated 10 weapons and *gibernes* with belts. Following the review, the inspector issued a list of items and prices for items the regiment needed to obtain. It reports *garance* (madder red) broadcloth costing 14fr 75 for cuffs and piping, *schakos* to cost 10fr 50, as well as white and black stocks, wool stockings, black and grey gaiters, and notes that the tailoring cost of a *habit* was 2fr 20, a *veste* 1fr, 90 centimes for *culottes* and 1fr for a *capote*.[302]

Reviewed on 1 May 1811, the inspector noted the regiment had 71 officers, 2,507 men and 96 horses. He added 9 officers were needed to bring the regiment up to capacity. Clothing wise, a lot needed immediate replacement, which included 30 *habits*, 1,616 pairs of *culottes*, 396 *capotes*, 350 *bonnets de police*, 65 *schakos*, 12 muskets, and 15 *gibernes* with belts. The men, he noted, had not been paid properly since 1808 and had received almost no new clothing.[303]

112ᵉ de Ligne

Created on 9 September 1803, the 1808 inspection cannot be found at the time of writing.[304]

113ᵉ de Ligne

Created on 23 May 1808 as the *régiment d'infanterie Toscan*. Officially the 113ᵉ de Ligne from 1 January 1810. No archives for the dress of the regiment can be located at the time of writing.

114ᵉ de Ligne

Created on 7 July 1808 by merging the 1ᵉ and 2ᵉ *régiments provisoires des armées d'Espagne*, the regiment was mobilised at Miranda de Ebro in Spain on 30 August 1808. It was disbanded in summer 1814. Reviewed on 27 January 1809 during the siege of Saragossa, the regiment was in appalling condition: the unit needed 3,200 *habits* and the same number of *vestes manches* and *culottes*, 3,000 *schakos*, 400 bearskins, 1,000 *capotes* as well as 2,000 smocks. Furthermore, 3,000 pairs of shoes were needed, 1,500 pairs of black gaiters were needed and the same number of grey, 1,000 black stocks, 150 *gamelles*, 150 *grand bidons*, 1,500 *petit bidons*, 2,600 shirts and 4,000 pairs of socks. What had been a smartly dressed unit nine months earlier was a total shambles.[305]

115ᵉ *de Ligne*

Formed in 1808 from an amalgam of the 3ᵉ et 4ᵉ *régiments provisoires des armées d'Espagne*, with the decree of 7 July 1808. It was a collection of conscripts with very few veteran *sous-officiers* and officers. Reviewed on 27 January 1809 during the siege of Saragossa, the regiment was in appalling condition: the unit needed 400 *habits*, 3,400 *vestes manches* and the same number of pairs of *culottes*, 600 *schakos*, 400 bearskins, 500 *capotes* as well as 2,000 smocks. In addition, 340 pairs of shoes with the same number of grey and black gaiters, 150 *gamelles*, 150 *grand bidons*, 1,500 *petit bidons*, 2,600 shirts and 4,000 pairs of socks.[306]

116ᵉ *de Ligne*

The regiment was formed 7 July 1808 from the 5ᵉ and 6ᵉ *régiments provisoires des armées d'Espagne*. Reviewed on 27 January 1809 during the siege of Saragossa, the regiment was in appalling condition: the unit needed 800 *habits*, 830 *vestes manches* and the same number of pairs of *culottes*, 200 *schakos*, 200 bearskins, 500 capotes as well as 500 smocks. In addition, the unit needed 600 *havresacs*, 200 *gibernes* and belts, 400 musket slings, 800 *baudriers*, 100 bayonet scabbards, 500 bayonets, 300 *gamelles*, 300 *grand bidons*, 2,000 *petit bidons*, 1,500 shirts and 1,000 pairs of socks.[307]

117ᵉ *de Ligne*

Created with the decree of 7 July 1808 from the 9ᵉ and 10ᵉ *Regiment provisoires d'Infanterie* for service in Spain. Reviewed on 27 January 1809 during the siege of Saragossa, the regiment was in appalling condition: the unit needed 3,000 *habits*, and the same number of *vestes manches* as well as of pairs of *culottes*, 2,000 *schakos*, 400 bearskins, 3,000 *capotes* as well as 2,000 smocks. In addition, the unit needed 700 *havresacs*, 300 *gamelles*, 300 *grand bidons*, 2,000 *petit bidons*, 1,500 shirts and 1,000 pairs of socks. By March, some new clothing had arrived, leaving a shortfall of 190 *habits*, 150 *vestes manches*, 200 pairs of *culottes*, 525 *schakos* and 1,000 *capotes*.[308]

118ᵉ *de Ligne*

Formed in 1808 for service in Spain with the decree of 7 July from the 11ᵉ *régiment provisoire des armées d'Espagne* and three battalions of conscripts from the *dépôt général*. No archives for the dress of the regiment can be located at the time of writing.

119ᵉ de Ligne

Formed in 1808 from the 13ᵉ and 14ᵉ *Regiments Provisoires de Infanterie* to serve in Spain. No archives for the dress of the regiment can be located at the time of writing.

120ᵉ de Ligne

Formed on 7 July 1808 to serve in Spain from the 17ᵉ and 18ᵉ *Regiments Provisoires de Infanterie*. No archives for the dress of the regiment can be located at the time of writing.

121e *de Ligne*

The regiment was formed on 1 January 1809 from the 1ᵉʳ and 2ᵉ *Legion de reserve*. No archives for the dress of the regiment can be located at the time of writing. Dressed in white, they would have stood out from the bulk of the blue-clad line. Inspected on 24 March 1809 at the siege of Saragossa, the unit was missing 100 *habits*, 1,000 *capotes*, 200 pairs of shoes, 150 pairs of black gaiters and 700 pairs of long grey gaiters.[309]

122e *de Ligne*

The 122ᵉ *Regiment d'infanterie de Ligne* was formed in 1809 from the 3ᵉ and 4ᵉ battalions of the 3ᵉ *Legion de reserve* and the 4ᵉ battalion from the 4ᵉ and 5ᵉ *Legion de reserve*. The regiment's paperwork says nothing on clothing.[310]

Régiment de la Méditerranée

By decree of 8 June 1808, a battalion was organised in Corsica to serve as a *dépôt* for refractory conscripts from the Italian departments of the Empire. Made up of six companies of *chasseurs*, it took the name of the 'Mediterranean Battalion' in August 1809, filled out with a cadre from the 6ᵉ *régiment de Ligne*. The decree of 27 January 1810 transformed this unit into a light infantry regiment of five battalions, without an elite company: the Mediterranean Regiment. At the beginning of 1811, the unit was garrisoned in Corsica, Elba and Corfu and took part in several naval expeditions. Due to the overcrowding of the regiment, Napoleon ordered – by decree of 11 March – the formation of the 2nd Mediterranean Regiment in Bastia and Elba. This time it was a line infantry unit formed by stripping the 1ᵉ and 2ᵉ battalion of the 6ᵉ *régiment de Ligne*, some 50 officers and 1,839 other ranks. It was reviewed on 25 October 1811. The grenadier companies were adorned with *schakos*, and carried sabres, as did the *sous-officiers*.[311]

By decree of 20 September 1812, the 1st Mediterranean Regiment became the 35ᵉ *Légère* and the 2nd Regiment, the 133ᵉ *Ligne*. In anticipation of the Saxon campaign (1813), both were assigned to General Durutte's 32nd Infantry Division, attached to Marshal Augereau's XI Corps. Both units were disbanded on 12 May 1814.

Chapter 10
Conclusions

This study has brought to light several important conclusions about how the Grande Armée was dressed, which is of major concern to artists, figure painters, re-enactors and wargamers. It allows us to present the following details. So, what did a French fusilier wear in 1806? The archive documents tell us:

Chapeaux with pompom, *bonnets de police* for other duties. *Voltigeurs* had no distinctions but were primarily armed with An XI light cavalry *mousquetons*.
Shirt, stock and underwear, long linen socks.
Habit worn over sleeved veste.
Culottes worn with long grey linen gaiters, black gaiters for exceptional circumstances.
Linen *pantalons*. Worn with short linen gaiters these were worn on campaign, in battle and around barracks.

A soldier in 1808 would have exchanged his *chapeau* for a *schako*, often with chinscales, and would be wearing a *capote*. More often than not, the *chapeau* would have been Prussian, and the cloth for his *capote* from Germany or Poland. The 1806 *schako* is largely a myth; none were worn at Jena, Eylau or Friedland. As the next sections show, it is wrong to assume that every regiment had its grenadiers in bearskins, and that every regiment had its *voltigeurs* with distinctive clothing.

Officer of fusiliers by Martinet.

Sergeant of fusiliers by Martinet. White gaiters were abolished in 1805, but some units adopted these items after August 1814.

Corporal of fusiliers by Martinet. The collar patches are unexpected, so too the white gaiters.

Fourrier of fusiliers, by Martinet. The collar patches are unexpected, as is the gold lace to the *schako*.

Battalion colour (?) carried by a grenadier sometime in 1805–07.

Two fusiliers showing the typical dress of the French line infantry from the 1790s through to spring 1808.

Two *voltigeurs*, with extensive use of yellow facings to their uniforms. It may be an accurate depiction of a specific regiment, and should not be used to give credence that this is how *all voltigeurs* were dressed.

Regimental bands uniforms and instruments were paid from stoppages in officers' pay: this meant in most cases their uniforms were cheap and therefore sombre, as shown here.

Conclusions 207

Sapeurs had been part of the French army since 1786. The apron was not to be worn on campaign, which is accurately depicted here.

Regimental drummers marched at the head of column on parade, and colonels often paid for embellishments to their uniforms: those of the 16ᵉ *de Ligne* were dressed as shown here with scarlet *revers* to the *habit*.

Conclusions 209

 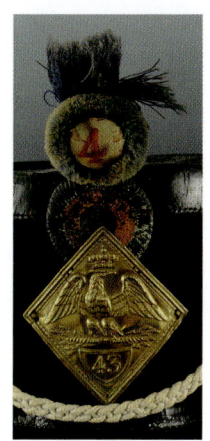 

An incredibly well-preserved example of the 1806 *schako* complete with what are presumably its original cords, and adorned with an 1808 pompom designating 4ᵉ battalion. The 1806 model was perhaps the most commonly used type of the era. Examples were collected off the field of Waterloo. (*Photograph and Collection of Bertrand Malvaux*)

On campaign, from 1804, French soldiers wore a shapeless greatcoat. In this image by Geisler we see a drummer in his greatcoat, and to his left a fusilier of the 57ᵉ *de Ligne*. The drummer may also be from the 57ᵉ. Of interest, his epaulettes are green with red crescents and this may make him a *voltigeur* drummer: we remember that not all *voltigeur* companies had hunting horns, and many had drums.

Conclusions 211

Grenadier c.1810 by Martinet, who correctly shows the grey campaign gaiters that were carried up to the knee. It was only from 1813 that the campaign gaiters, like the parade examples, became much shorter.

French line infantry in greatcoats c.1808.

French infantry in bivouac c.1811.

Conclusions 213

French fusilier wearing his greatcoat, campaign pantalons and *bonnet de police*. As the greatcoat is double breasted, we assume he is a sous-*officier*, which may account for the elaborate *bonnet de police*.

Grenadiers

The following regiments have archive paperwork to attest to the presence of bearskins, which we assume to be accompanied by scarlet epaulettes and plumes:

Regiment	1804	1805	1808	Comments
1ᵉ de Ligne	Nil	Nil	Nil	1809 63 bearskins for grenadiers in use.[1]
3ᵉ de Ligne	164 in good condition, 40 needing repairs, 38 written off, total 242 examples.[2]	288 in use.[3]	126 with 1ᵉ battalion, remainder in schakos.[4]	Extracted from the standing orders of the 3ᵉ de Ligne, the following snippets of very useful information. 13 October 1806. 'Make arrangements to purchase 240 pairs of epaulettes, sword knots and pompoms, 200 plumes and 60 bearskins for grenadiers. 330 pairs of epaulettes, pompoms, and sword knots for the *voltigeurs*, 700 *houpettes* for the fusiliers of the 3ᵉ battalion. 1,400 *houpettes* for the first two battalions.'[5]
6ᵉ de Ligne	Nil	Nil	Nil	4 *sapeurs*' bearskins 1811.[6]
7ᵉ de Ligne		Bearskins written off 24 July 1805.[7]	The regiment in the course of the period 23 September 1804 to 10 November 1807 had issued 343 pairs of grenadier epaulettes accompanied by 354 grenadier pompoms and 344 sword knots.[8]	513 grenadier pompoms, 500 pairs scarlet epaulettes, 500 grenadier sabre knots in November 1807.[9]
8ᵉ de Ligne	8,053fr 40 was spent on bearskins.[10]	Nil	Nil	Otto MS shows bearskins 1808
9ᵉ de Ligne	Nil	Nil	Nil	91 bearskins reported lost at Essling.[11]
11ᵉ de Ligne				
12ᵉ de Ligne	Nil	Nil	275 made since 1805.[12]	
13ᵉ de Ligne				

Conclusions

Regiment	1804	1805	1808	Comments
16ᵉ de Ligne	252 in use, 42 needed.¹³		210 good condition, 42 to be written off. 90 made and issued since 1805.¹⁴	
17ᵉ de Ligne	Nil	Nil	Nil	180 bearskins needed repair, 1 May 1811.¹⁵
18ᵉ de Ligne	Nil	Summer 1805 stores reports 70 grenadier pompoms, 87 pairs of grenadier epaulettes, and 52 sword knots.¹⁶	31 bearskins in service. 240 made since 1805, with 209 in stores.¹⁷	341 grenadier pompoms, 356 pairs grenadier epaulettes, 336 grenadier sword knots.
19ᵉ de Ligne	Regimental accounts list in the second quarter of 1809 the purchase of 390 pairs of grenadier epaulettes costing 6fr 50 each in lieu of the government tariff of 3fr 50. In the fourth quarter of the year 90 pairs of grenadier epaulettes were purchased costing 3fr 75 a pair.¹⁸			
21ᵉ de Ligne	Nil	Nil	288 made since 1805.¹⁹	
24ᵉ de Ligne	Nil	Nil	Nil	104 bearskins inherited from 54ᵉ, 63ᵉ, 94ᵉ and 105ᵉ de Ligne in October 1808.²⁰
26ᵉ de Ligne	Nil	Nil	72 in use 27 February 1808.²¹	
32ᵉ de Ligne	Nil	Nil	Nil	Purchased 1809 140 pairs of grenadier epaulettes, 140, 140 grenadier sword knots, 140 grenadier pompoms.²²
35ᵉ de Ligne	Nil	Nil	Nil	350 bearskins lost at Essling.²³
36ᵉ de Ligne	Nil	3,400 in use	320 in use, 93 made since 1805, 80 issued, 13 in stores. 60 ordered for production.²⁴	Inspected on 1 September 1814, the regiment possessed 52 grenadier bearskins.²⁵
37ᵉ de Ligne	6,000fr spent on bearskins.²⁶			
45ᵉ de Ligne	The report of 5 September 1805 informs us that in the year up to 23 September 1804 some 2,880fr had been spent buying grenadier bearskins and up to 20 June 1805 a further 1,440fr was spent buying bearskins for the 3ᵉ battalion.²⁷ In 1809 125 pairs of grenadier epaulettes were purchased costing 5fr 50 a pair, rather than the regulation 4fr 75, so we must imagine these were rather extravagant items!²⁸			

Regiment	1804	1805	1808	Comments
46ᵉ de Ligne	The report dated 20 December 1807 states 6,720fr was authorised to be spent on bearskins on 1 October 1807.[29] Drawn up for inspection on 1 August 1814, the stand-out feature from the men on parade is that the grenadier company was wearing 183 bearskins! A further 11 worn-out bearskins were in *dépôt*.[30]			
50ᵉ de Ligne	Nil	186 in stores	186[31]	438 grenadier pompoms, 440 grenadier *houpettes*, 438 pairs of grenadier epaulettes, 439 sword knots.
55ᵉ de Ligne	Nil	Nil	203fr was spent buying bearskin plates in January 1808.[32]	
57ᵉ de Ligne	24 August 1805, the inspector recorded the purchase of 216 bearskins for the grenadiers, costing 24fr each.[33]		Nil	
59ᵉ de Ligne	During 1809, 239fr 88 was spent repairing 60 bearskins and 16 brand-new bearskins were purchased for 23fr 50 each, a total of 376fr.[34]			
63ᵉ de Ligne	64 bearskins passed to 24ᵉ de Ligne at the end of 1808.[35]			
65ᵉ de Ligne	Nil		306 bearskins bought during 1808. 100 pairs of grenadiers epaulettes.	120 set of bearskin cords, 120 bearskin plates, 102 bearskins obtained 1809.[36]
75ᵉ de Ligne	20 bearskins for grenadiers, 63 sets of cords and plumes for bearskins.[37]	In March 1806 40 grenadier bearskins were received at the regiment's *dépôt* complete with 'their fittings'.[38] A report of 25 September 1806 records the delivery of 160 further bearskins, which had cost 4,320fr.[39]		
79ᵉ de Ligne	No bearskins. Stores held in late summer 1803, 273 pairs of grenadier epaulettes, 166 grenadier sword knots, 166 grenadier pompoms, and 200 scarlet plumes.[40]	Nil	New year 1808 stores reported 554 pairs of grenadier epaulettes, 403 grenadier sword knots, 153 bearskins with cords and plume in service.[41]	

Regiment	1804	1805	1808	Comments
81ᵉ *de Ligne*	162 bearskin costing 1,042fr were purchased in 1806.⁴²			
82ᵉ *de Ligne*	72 grenadier bearskins and the same number of grenadier epaulettes had existed in 1803.⁴³			
100ᵉ *de Ligne*	Accounts signed off 9 December 1803 state 5,112fr 17 was spent buying 'bearskin caps for grenadiers'.⁴⁴			In new year 1810, the 100ᵉ *de Ligne* replaced the bearskins of its grenadiers. The clothing officer reported that the bearskins needed replacing as they had been in service for 25 years and were 'absolutely no longer fit for service or repair'. 256 purchased for 5,332fr 30.⁴⁵
103ᵉ *de Ligne*	Stores in late summer 1804 reports 37 pairs of grenadier epaulettes and 76m of red worsted fringe, no doubt for making epaulettes.⁴⁶			
105ᵉ *de Ligne*	38 bearskins passed to 24ᵉ *de Ligne* in October 1808.⁴⁷			
106ᵉ *de Ligne*	A report made 1 June for losses of equipment since 1 April 1809 reports 264 bearskins lost.⁴⁸			
114ᵉ *de Ligne*	Raised in 1807 for service in Spain. The grenadiers of the 114ᵉ *de Ligne* possessed 60 bearskins in summer 1814.⁴⁹			
121ᵉ *de Ligne*	Raised for service in Spain in 1809, at the time of disbandment in 1814 the regiment had 16 old bearskins in *dépôt*.⁵⁰			

From this data resume, it is abundantly clear that grenadiers wearing bearskins were, prior to 1808, a rare phenomenon. It is clear that only a few grenadier companies were so adorned. Regardless of what the regulations said, regimental finances dictated in most cases that grenadiers wore the same headdress as the fusiliers.

Archive evidence is abundantly clear that grenadiers had two headdress: either a *chapeau* and bearskin or *schako* and bearskin. Bearskins were not worn during campaign; they were parade items ostensibly, even with the Garde Imperiale.⁵¹ The cords and plumes were always *both* removed: it is a huge error to see bearskins with cords and no plumes. It is wrong to suppose grenadiers had bearskins at Austerlitz, Jena, Eylau and Friedland. Bearskins were expensive, hence the use of cheaper headdress for campaign use.

Voltigeurs

What follows is a summary of archive records for the adoption for *voltigeurs'* distinctive items. Unless otherwise stated, *voltigeurs* were not issued sabres and carried infantry muskets.

Regiment	Clothing	Armament
1ᵉ de Ligne	The 1ᵉ and 2ᵉ battalions when inspected on 17 June 1808 had not an inch of chamois cloth.[52] In comparison, the 3³ battalion had used 9m 60 of chamois broadcloth.[53]	
2ᵉ de Ligne	26 November 1807, we note 19m 20 chamois broadcloth had been used to make *voltigeurs'* clothing.[54]	Issued to the *voltigeurs* on 18 February 1806 were 448 light cavalry *mousquetons* and 34 *carabines rayé*, a further 60 *mousquetons* being issued 2 April 1807. Remarkably, every man carried a sabre.[55]
3ᵉ de Ligne	At the time of the November 1807 inspection the regiment had no chamois cloth at all. The first purchase was made on 29 April 1808. Yet in 1806 they had sported green *schako* cords, as well as epaulettes and sword knots:[56] '13 October 1806. Make arrangements to purchased 240 pairs of epaulettes, sword knots and pompoms, 200 plumes and 60 bearskins for grenadiers. 330 pairs of epaulettes, pompoms, and sword knots for the *voltigeurs*, 700 *houpettes* for the fusiliers of the 3ᵉ battalions. 1,400 *houpettes* for the first two battalions.' No further *voltigeur* epaulettes were purchased until 24 June 1809, when 44 pairs were purchased costing 324fr. The *voltigeurs* never had plumes and always had *houpettes*, 52 *houpettes* were purchased on 30 July 1808 and a further 130 on 1 March 1809, 85 on 24 June 1809 and a further 60 on 7 September 1809.[57]	
4ᵉ de Ligne		1 November 1807 no clothing, but sabres issued to *voltigeur* company.[58]
6ᵉ de Ligne	3m 50 chamois use for 3ᵉ battalion, January 1807 to March 1808. 1811, 21m 86 of yellow broadcloth for *voltigeurs'* distinctions along with 2 horns.[59]	
7ᵉ de Ligne	Cloth used by the regiment in the course of the period 23 September 1804 to 10 November 1807 included the purchase of 74m 52 of chamois broadcloth, of which 21m 90 was used. 6 Cornets in use.[60]	Officers and *sous-officiers* armed with 34 *carabines rayé*. Other ranks issued sabres.

Conclusions

Regiment	Clothing	Armament
10ᵉ de Ligne	June 1808, 14m 80 of yellow broadcloth had been used in the production of *voltigeurs*' clothing.	140 An XI light cavalry carbines in use with 3ᵉ battalion.[61]
12ᵉ de Ligne	21 March 1808, *dépôt* reports 14m 40 chamois broadcloth used and 6 cornets in service.[62]	Sergeant major and sergeants armed with 15 An XI light cavalry *mousquetons*, corporals and *voltigeurs* armed with 339 dragoon muskets. Sabres only with *cornets* and *sous-officiers*.
13ᵉ de Ligne	Reviewed on 7 January 1808, since December 1807, 43m 13 of chamois broadcloth had been employed.[63]	No sabres, infantry muskets.
15ᵉ de Ligne	Inspected on 13 February 1808, 22m 13 chamois broadcloth used.[64] A letter dated 27 January 1806 from the Minister of War to the regiment's colonel stated that epaulettes for *voltigeurs* were to be discontinued, no pairs were authorised for production and in future *voltigeurs* were to have the same epaulettes as fusiliers.[65]	485 An XI light cavalry carbines were in use and 36 *carabines rayé* by officers and *sous-officiers* of *voltigeur* companies. No sabres carried by *sous-officiers*.[66]
16ᵉ de Ligne	Inspected on 22 November 1807, dressed in white, the *voltigeurs* had chamois collars as 42m 68 of chamois broadcloth had been used. This is a huge amount, so where else was the cloth used? 2 cornets in use with 6 more authorised for purchase.	Officers, sergeant major, sergeants, *fourriers* armed with 52 *carabines rayé*. Voltigeurs issued sabres and infantry muskets.[67]
17ᵉ de Ligne	Inspected on 1 January 1808, the *voltigeur* companies clearly existed by winter 1807 as some 18m 37 chamois broadcloth had been used to make collars for *voltigeur habits*. 8 cornets were in use as well.[68]	Since 1804 114 light cavalry carbines were in use with the *voltigeur* company, along with 302 dragoon muskets, and 18 *carabines rayé* were in use, 3 were issued to officers and 5 to *sous-officiers*.
18ᵉ de Ligne	Between 1805 and 1808, the regiment had used 14m 40 of yellow broadcloth for the collars of *voltigeurs*' habits, also for *voltigeurs* were 543 pompoms, 420 pairs of epaulettes and 360 sword knots.[69]	Armed with 170 *sabres briquet*, *sous-officiers* and men issued 198 An XI light cavalry *mousquetons*.
19ᵉ de Ligne	When inspected on 27 December 1807 the regimental *dépôt* held 19m 61 of chamois cloth for *voltigeurs*' collars.[70] In the third quarter of 1808, two new *voltigeur* horns were purchased with yellow cords and tassels.[71]	131 An XI light cavalry *mousquetons* as well as 27 *carabines rayé*, with 9 *voltigeur* officers armed with these weapons. The *voltigeurs* themselves had no sabres, but were issued 366 *fusils de dragon*.
20ᵉ de Ligne	13 March 1808, 27m 30 of chamois broadcloth had been used for *voltigeur* clothing.[72]	
26ᵉ de Ligne	3m 80 chamois broadcloth used January 1807 to January 1808.[73]	

Regiment	Clothing	Armament
27ᵉ de Ligne	When inspected on 30 November 1807, dressed in white, the *voltigeur* companies had chamois collars to the *habit* as 19m 86 of chamois broadcloth had been used for this purpose.[74]	103 An XI light cavalry *mousquetons* and also *gibernes*, issued to 76 *voltigeur* corporals, drummers and *cornets*. 103 examples in use. *Voltigeurs* had no sabres. 18 *carabines rayé*.
29ᵉ de Ligne	March 1808, 22m 20 of chamois broadcloth had been used for *voltigeur* distinctions.[75]	
32ᵉ de Ligne	The inspection returns of 15 December 1807 show that *voltigeurs* had chamois collars, some 8m 12 of chamois broadcloth being used to make *habits*.[76] The regimental accounts signed off on 1 January 1809 reveal the following expenses:[77] 140 pairs *voltigeur* epaulettes, 140 *voltigeur houpettes*, 140 *voltigeur* sword knots. These were allocated to 1ᵉ battalion only. Therefore, the 2ᵉ and 3ᵉ battalions lacked these distinctions, unless paperwork is missing.	
34ᵉ de Ligne	14m 40 chamois broadcloth being used. *Voltigeurs* and grenadiers had 741 of epaulettes in use, and 4 more sets in stores waiting to be issued, along with 340 sword knots in use with 6 in stores.[78]	12 *carabines rayé*.
35ᵉ de Ligne	8 January 1808, 55m of chamois broadcloth had been used to make *voltigeurs'* distinctions: did the cornets have chamois facings?[79]	
40ᵉ de Ligne	9 December 1807, 16m 75 of chamois broadcloth had been used to make *voltigeurs'* clothing.	*Voltigeur soldat* did not carry sabres but were armed with infantry muskets.[80]
43ᵉ de Ligne		24 December 1807, *voltigeurs* lacked sabres but were armed with 412 An XI light cavalry carbines, which were issued to the *sous-officiers* of the company, and also to the 64 drummers and *cornets*.[81]
48ᵉ de Ligne		9 *carabines rayé*.
50ᵉ de Ligne	Inspected on 20 December 1807, 14m 40 of chamois broadcloth had been used since January 1807 to make *voltigeur* clothing. For *voltigeurs* were 360 pompoms, *houpettes*, pairs of epaulettes and sword knots.[82]	
51ᵉ de Ligne		23 November 1807, 19 *voltigeur sous-officiers* and 51 drummers and cornets were issued An XI light cavalry *mousquetons* and *gibernes*. In addition, 207 dragoon muskets were issued to *voltigeurs*, who also had sabres, as did 25 *voltigeur* corporals.[83]

Conclusions

Regiment	Clothing	Armament
52ᵉ de Ligne	14 January 1808 stores had used 16m 08 chamois broadcloth to make *voltigeur* clothing, leaving 12m 32 in stores.[84]	
54ᵉ de Ligne	30 November 1807, 36m of chamois broadcloth used.[85]	
55ᵉ de Ligne	15 December 1807, the regiment had used 23m 11 of chamois broadcloth in making *voltigeur habits*.[86]	
56ᵉ de Ligne	27 November 1807, 19m 20 chamois broadcloth used.[87]	26 *carabines rayé*.
58ᵉ de Ligne		5 January 1808, the regiment possessed 454 *mousquetons*, of which 9 were issued to the staff, 15 to the *sous-officiers* of *voltigeurs*, 27 to corporals of *voltigeur* companies and 403 to the *voltigeurs* themselves. Some 369 had been issued on 11 November 1806 taken from Prussian stocks. More Prussian weapons were issued in new year 1807, when some 40 *mousquetons* were issued on 6 February 1807, taken from captured Prussian stocks. On 3 June 1807 39 *carabines rayé* were issued to the *sous-officiers* of *voltigeurs* taken from the Versailles arsenal.[88]
59ᵉ de Ligne	4 April 1808, 31m 44 chamois broadcloth had been used making *voltigeur* clothing.	Following the inspection, the *voltigeurs* were ordered to hand in their sabres and *baudriers*.[89]
60ᵉ de Ligne		27 January 1808, *voltigeur* companies were armed with 537 An XI light cavalry *mousquetons*.[90]
61ᵉ de Ligne		15 *carabines rayé*.
63ᵉ de Ligne	January 1808, the regiment had employed 14m 40 of chamois cloth making *voltigeurs'* distinctions.[91]	27 *carabine rayé*.
64ᵉ de Ligne	9 November 1807, 9m 90 of chamois broadcloth for the collars of *voltigeur habits*.[92]	
66ᵉ de Ligne		18 *carabines rayé*.
67ᵉ de Ligne	7 December 1807, stores had used 21m 30 of chamois broadcloth to make *voltigeurs'* clothing.	412 *voltigeurs* armed with An XI light cavalry carbines. 27 *carabines rayé*.[93]
70ᵉ de Ligne	26 December 1807, 14m 40 of chamois broadcloth to make *voltigeurs'* clothing.	291 An XI light cavalry carbines.[94]
72ᵉ de Ligne	20 November 1807, 10m 96 of chamois broadcloth had been used to make *voltigeurs'* distinctions.	Armed with 352 dragoon muskets and 92 An XI light cavalry carbines were in use and 27 *carabines rayé* with the officers and senior *sous-officiers* of *voltigeur* companies. As expected from the regulations, the *voltigeurs* had no sabres.[95]

Regiment	Clothing	Armament
75ᵉ de Ligne	6 January 1808, 19m 80 of chamois broadcloth had been used to make *voltigeurs'* distinctions.[96]	
79ᵉ de Ligne	20 January 1808, 19m 20 of chamois broadcloth had been used to make *voltigeur* clothing.	The *voltigeurs* had four *cornets*, who were armed with 519 dragoon muskets and had no sabres, as the regulations dictated.[97]
82ᵉ de Ligne	8 March 1808, chamois broadcloth of an unknown amount had been used to make *voltigeurs'* clothing.	205 An XI light cavalry *mousquetons* were issued to the regimental band, 28 to *voltigeur sous-officiers* and 171 to *voltigeurs* themselves. We also note 12 *carabines rayé* were issued to *voltigeur sous-officiers*. A further 77 *mousquetons* were issued to the staff, band, *sapeurs*, drummers and *cornets*.[98]
84ᵉ de Ligne	4 January 1808, 21m 27 of chamois broadcloth had been used to make *voltigeurs'* clothing.[99]	
85ᵉ de Ligne	16 November 1807, 14m 40 of chamois broadcloth used in the production of *voltigeurs'* distinctions.[100]	34 *carabines rayé*.
86ᵉ de Ligne	25 January 1808, 19m 20 chamois broadcloth used.	*Voltigeurs* were armed with 339 dragoon muskets and 27 *voltigeur* officers and *sous-officiers* were issued *carabines rayé*.[101]
88ᵉ de Ligne	16 November 1807, 14m 40 chamois broadcloth used.[102]	
93ᵉ de Ligne	6m yellow broadcloth obtained along with 411 yellow *houpettes*.[103]	
96ᵉ de Ligne		The *voltigeurs* carried sabres, with only the officers and *sous-officiers* being armed with An XI light cavalry carbines.[104]
100ᵉ de Ligne	Purchased in 1809, 200 *voltigeur* pompoms, 40 sets of *voltigeur schako* cords, 2 *voltigeur cornets*.[105]	
101ᵉ de Ligne	6 March 1808, 14m 35 chamois broadcloth used.[106]	
102ᵉ de Ligne	7 March 1808, 14m 40 chamois broadcloth used.[107]	
103ᵉ de Ligne	7 November 1807, 14m 80 yellow broadcloth used.[108]	
105ᵉ de Ligne	58 January 1808, 14m 40 chamois broadcloth used.[109]	
111ᵉ de Ligne		The *voltigeurs* were armed with 336 sabres and the same number of An XI light cavalry carbines.[110]

It is abundantly clear that no *voltigeurs* with distinctive facings were present at Austerlitz, and very few – if any – present at Jena, Eylau or Friedland. Given nearly every regiment clung on to *chapeaux* into 1808 due to the logistical challenge of shipping *schakos* to Germany from France, I doubt any sensible regimental colonel would ship hundreds of *voltigeur habits* to Germany, not knowing if they would arrive safe and sound. Ambiguities of the March 1806 decree also perhaps explains the absence of *voltigeur* clothing: the regulation makes no mention of chamois collars and other features for *voltigeurs*. Given collar colour was an integral part of the regulation for unit identification, the War Ministry sensibly enough sought to abolish chamois collars and other distinctives for *voltigeurs* and grenadiers – no bearskins are mentioned we recall – and such distinctives only returned with the re-adoption of blue *habits* at the end of 1807. The data set also proves categorically that chamois was the predominant colour used and not yellow – used by just three regiments – and moreover it is wrong to assume that every *voltigeur* had a pair of epaulettes or a distinctive collar. The data sets show – at least officially – that these items were few and far between. The data shows that *carabines rayé* were used far more commonly than heretofore accepted, and that the most common firearm for the *voltigeurs* after the infantry musket was a light cavalry firearm, again contradicting supposed facts that dragoon muskets were the most common firearm. We also see that a large number of regiments, never – at least officially – differentiated their *voltigeurs* from the fusilier companies, other than firearms, in some cases. It is wrong to assume that every regiment dressed its *voltigeurs* with epaulettes, chamois collars and other distinctives.

Schakos and *Chapeaux*

The felt *chapeau* remained the main item of headdress as the table below shows from inspection returns made November 1807 to June 1808:

Regiment	Chapeau	Schako	Notes
1ᵉ *de Ligne*[111]	90 with 3ᵉ battalion	1504 in use 28 June 1808 with War battalions, 108 needing replacement.	
2ᵉ *de Ligne*	A report dated 28 November 1807 tells us that the regiment was in the process of re-equipping with *schakos*. The *dépôt* held 266 brand-new *schakos*, which had been issued to the 3ᵉ battalion in the course of the year, and 706 additional *schakos* had been ordered to complete the equipment of the battalion.[112]		
3ᵉ *de Ligne*[113]	1765 in service, all to be replaced.	1800 in service 1 November 1807	
4ᵉ *de Ligne*[114]	1479 in good condition, 479 needing repairs, 821 to be written off 1 November 1807.	547 *schako* in use with 3e battalion, 78 in stores.	
5ᵉ *de Ligne*[115]	3,162 in use 18 January 1808.	None	

Regiment	Chapeau	Schako	Notes
6ᵉ de Ligne[116]	3ᵉ battalion 93 *chapeaux* in use, 260 with war battalions	1,757 *schakos* in use with the war battalions.	
7ᵉ de Ligne[117]	1,256 *chapeaux* in use 10 November 1807.	1,077 *schakos* in use.	
8ᵉ de Ligne[118]	1,687 in use November 1807.	548 in use with 3ᵉ battalion.	
9ᵉ de Ligne[119]		2,346 *schakos*, all brand new.	
10ᵉ de Ligne[120]	2,305 *chapeaux* in use 30 June 1808.	320 *schakos* with 3ᵉ battalion.	
11ᵉ de Ligne			
12ᵉ de Ligne[121]		1,193 in good condition, 307 needing repairs 21 March 1808.	
13ᵉ de Ligne[122]		Reviewed 7 January 1808, 2,177 *schakos* and 144 *chapeaux*.	
14ᵉ de Ligne	No Data		
15ᵉ de Ligne[123]	3,268 in use 13 February 1808.	2,750 in use	
16e de Ligne[124]	2,089 in use 22 November 1807.	1,456 in use.	
17ᵉ de Ligne[125]	1,554 in use 1 January 1808.	583 in use with 3ᵉ battalion, 1,554 in stores waiting to be issued	
18ᵉ de Ligne[126]	2,520 made since July 1805, 1,482 in service 4 November 1807.	857 in use with 3ᵉ battalion.	
19ᵉ de Ligne[127]		1,081 in use 1 January 1808.	
20ᵉ de Ligne[128]	2,147 in service 13 March 1808.	358 in use with 3ᵉ battalion.	
21ᵉ de Ligne[129]	4,595 in use 1 December 1807.	None	
22ᵉ de Ligne[130]	1,677 in use 21 December 1807, all to be replaced.	3,183 in service.	
23ᵉ de Ligne[131]	937 in service 19 January 1808.	2,834 in service, 367 needing replacement.	
24ᵉ de Ligne[132]	1,398 in service 29 January 1808.	2,701 in service with 3ᵉ and 4ᵉ battalion.	
25e de Ligne[133]	2,568 in service 28 December 1807.	2,000 in use with 3ᵉ and 4ᵉ battalion.	
26ᵉ de Ligne[134]	1,626 in service with 1ᵉ and 2ᵉ battalions 27 February 1808.	None	
27ᵉ de Ligne[135]	1,902 in use with 1ᵉ and 2ᵉ battalion 30 November 1807.	1,902 in service with 3ᵉ battalion.	

Conclusions

Regiment	Chapeau	Schako	Notes
28ᵉ de Ligne[136]	1,484 in use with 1ᵉ and 2ᵉ battalions 21 December 1807.	1,310 in use with 3ᵉ battalion.	
29ᵉ de Ligne	Inspected at Chieti on 9 November 1804, the inspecting officer was incredulous that every man of the regiment was wearing a *schako*.[137] The regiment was next inspected at Mantoue on 25 November 1805. The inspecting officers reported that the regiment was wearing 'a kind of helmet with an enormous front plate'.[138] 532 *schakos* in use 22 March 1808 and 99 *chapeaux*.[139]		
30ᵉ de Ligne[140]	3,522 in service	None	
32ᵉ de Ligne	War battalions wearing *chapeaux*.	300 in service with 3ᵉ battalion.[141]	Purchased in 1808 were 1,000 *schakos* and 100 set of *schako* cords for fusiliers and 185 *schakos* for grenadiers to replace the existing *chapeaux*.[142]
33ᵉ de Ligne[143]	1,752 examples all needing to be replaced.	None	
34ᵉ de Ligne[144]	3,611 in service 7 November 1807.	1,073 in use with 3ᵉ battalion and in stores.	
35ᵉ de Ligne[145]	1,886 in service November 1807	2,000 *schakos* in use January 1808.	
36ᵉ de Ligne[146]	2,977 in use 27 December 1807	300 in use with 3ᵉ battalion.	
37ᵉ de Ligne	In 1807 the regiment bought 270 *chapeaux* costing 5fr 75 each as well as 400 *schako* costing 11fr 50 each, including cords, plate and chinscales. A further 216 *schakos* were obtained in 1808, and finally replaced all its *chapeaux* in 1809 when 1,050 *schakos* were purchased for the 4ᵉ battalion and 300 for the other battalions as replacements.[147]		
39ᵉ de Ligne[148]	3,424 in use 15 December 1807.		
40ᵉ de Ligne[149]	3,279 in service 9 December 1807.	256 in service with 3ᵉ battalion, 3,535 to be made.	
42ᵉ de Ligne[150]		2,645 in service 8 February 1808	
43ᵉ de Ligne[151]	1942 in service, 300 needing repairs, remainder replacing, 31 December 1807.	1,012 in service, 38 in stores. 2,207 new examples ordered.	
45ᵉ de Ligne[152]	4,000 in service 29 November 1807, 1,023 issued since 1805, 29 in stores.	1,044 ordered.	
46ᵉ de Ligne[153]	The report dated 20 December 1807 states 600 *schakos* had been delivered from the government magazine and 961 *chapeaux* in good condition were in use, with 1,689 needing total replacement.		
47ᵉ de Ligne[154]	306 in use with 3ᵉ battalion	3,063 in use with 1ᵉ and 2ᵉ battalions 1 February 1808.	
48ᵉ de Ligne[155]	2,100 in use with 1ᵉ and 2ᵉ battalion 1 Decembre 1807.	1,278 in service with 3ᵉ battalion and *dépôt*.	

Regiment	Chapeau	Schako	Notes
50ᵉ de Ligne[156]	3,200 in use with 1ᵉ and 2ᵉ battalions 20 December 1807.	465 with 3ᵉ battalion, 335 brand-new examples in stores, 164 examples to be ordered.	
51ᵉ de Ligne[157]	2,448 *chapeaux* in use.	1,150 *schakos* and a stockpile of 150 *schakos* waiting to be issued.	
52ᵉ de Ligne	435 *chapeaux* to be written off 20 April 1808.	1,632 *schakos* with 1ᵉ and 2ᵉ battalions, 523 *schakos* ordered to be made.[158] 441 *schakos* in use with 3ᵉ battalion 6 March 1808.[159]	
53ᵉ de Ligne[160]	1,800 *chapeaux* with war battalions.	1,409 *schakos* with 3ᵉ battalion and in stores.	
54ᵉ de Ligne	None	1,547 examples in use 30 November 1807.[161]	
55ᵉ de Ligne[162]	15 December 1807, the regiment had 3,504 *chapeaux* in use, half of which needed replacement.	None	
56ᵉ de Ligne[163]	1,849 with war battalions.	1,309 with 3ᵉ battalion and stores.	
57ᵉ de Ligne[164]	2,441 examples.	None	
58ᵉ de Ligne[165]	None	2,897 examples in service 5 January 1808.	
59ᵉ de Ligne[166]	1,571 examples in use all to be written off 4 April 1808.	2,927 examples in use, 3,100 made since 1806.	
60ᵉ de Ligne[167]	None	3,273 *schakos* in all four battalions.	
61ᵉ de Ligne[168]	2,141 with war battalions.	1,892 with 3ᵉ and 4ᵉ battalions.	
62ᵉ de Ligne[169]	1,892 in war battalions 8 June 1808.	None	
63ᵉ de Ligne[170]	1,775 examples with war battalions.	None	
64ᵉ de Ligne[171]	9 November 1807 the regiment had 2,699 *chapeaux*,	864 *schakos* issued to the 3ᵉ battalion.	
65ᵉ de Ligne[172]	2,420 *chapeaux* with war battalions.	1,034 *schakos* with 3e battalion and *dépôt*.	
66ᵉ de Ligne[173]	1,441 *chapeaux* or *schakos* with war battalions.		
67ᵉ de Ligne	1,317 in use 7 December 1,807 with 852 to be replaced, 100 new examples in store.[174]	1,660 in use 7 December 1807.	September 1809 the regiment had 1,660 *schakos* in use alongside 1,307 *chapeaux*.[175]
69ᵉ de Ligne		2,261 in use.[176]	

Conclusions

Regiment	Chapeau	Schako	Notes
70ᵉ de Ligne	365 *chapeaux* in use 10 February 1808 with *dépôt* company.	3,000 in use with the three war battalions.[177]	11 February 1808 600 *schakos* purchased for 6,450fr, plates cost 4,958fr.[178]
72ᵉ de Ligne	2,693 in use 30 November 1807, of which 45 were in good condition, 383 needed repairs and the remainder to be written off. 606 brand-new examples in store.[179]	769 examples in use with 3ᵉ battalion. 932 examples ordered 30 November 1807.	
75ᵉ de Ligne	1,754 examples made since 1805, of which 1,083 remained in service 6 January 1808.[180]	2,187 examples in service of which 1,630 examples needed immediate replacement. 104 brand-new examples were in store. 1,083 new examples ordered.	
76ᵉ de Ligne	2,495 examples in use 15 December 1807, 82 in good condition the remainder to be written off.[181]	None	
79ᵉ de Ligne	None	3,524 examples in use 20 January 1808, with 881 ordered to be purchased.[182]	
81ᵉ de Ligne	None	Needed 68 *schakos* in 2ᵉ battalion, 120 in 3ᵉ.[183]	
82ᵉ de Ligne	1,592 *chapeaux* in service 8 March 1808. Unknown number of *schakos*.[184]	None	
84ᵉ de Ligne	2,073 *chapeaux* in use with 1ᵉ and 2ᵉ battalions, 519 brand-new examples in store.	2,030 *schakos* issued to 3ᵉ battalion and *dépôt*, 900 needed immediate replacement.[185]	
85ᵉ de Ligne	The report of 1 December 1807 merely says 4,203 *chapeaux* and *schakos* in use, 642 being ordered to replace *chapeaux*.[186]		
86ᵉ de Ligne[187]		2061 *schakos* in good condition, 1151 needing repairs.	
88ᵉ de Ligne[188]	2,664 *chapeaux* in service, with 2,819 made since 1805.	647 *schakos* with 3ᵉ battalion 10 November 1807, 53 brand-new examples in store.	
92ᵉ de Ligne	No Data		
93ᵉ de Ligne	No Data		
94ᵉ de Ligne[189]	3,196 in service 3 December 1807.	None	

Regiment	Chapeau	Schako	Notes
95ᵉ de Ligne[190]	3,549 *chapeaux* in service, 269 new *chapeaux* in stores.	None	
96ᵉ de Ligne[191]	2,339 in service, 385 good condition, 296 needing repairs, 1,658 immediate replacement.	1,067 in use 15 December 1807, with 33 brand-new examples in stores.	
100ᵉ de Ligne[192]	3,712 in service 31 October 1807, 712 in good condition, 1,000 needing repairs, remainder to be replaced.	175 in use with 3ᵉ battalion, 1,527 in stores waiting to be issued, the regiment was authorised to purchase 1,857 examples.	
101ᵉ de Ligne	1,173 *chapeaux* with war battalions in March 1808.[193]	2,145 new *schakos* in use by June 1808.[194]	
102ᵉ de Ligne[195]	932 with war battalions.	580 *schakos* with 3ᵉ battalion.	
103ᵉ de Ligne[196]	3,636 in service 7 November 1807.	3,626 *schakos* authorised for purchase at 11fr 50.	
105ᵉ de Ligne[197]	1,111 in use.	2,108 *schakos*, of which 1,311 needed replacing and 605 repairing.	
106ᵉ de Ligne[198]	None	2,557 in use.	
108ᵉ de Ligne[199]	2,899 *chapeaux* in use, 384 brand-new examples in store.	None	
111ᵉ de Ligne[200]	1,372 *chapeaux* in service	2,383 examples in use with 393 brand-new examples in store. 939 examples ordered to be purchased.	

From this resume of the data, it is overwhelmingly clear that the felt *chapeau* was the predominant headdress of the French Army in winter 1807 through to spring 1808. The decree introducing the *schako* was not fully implemented into 1809, almost four years after the decree was passed. Phasing in new items of equipment with an army at war was never going to be quick or simple. The absence or presence of *schakos* also means we can date the Otto MS to spring and summer 1808. In many cases the artist shows the use of *schakos* in regiments we know did not have them until spring 1808, meaning the artwork cannot have been produced in 1806–07 as many believe.

Greatcoats

An innovation on a scale never before witnessed was the supply of these garments in winter 1806. An analysis of regimental inspection returns reveals a mix of grey and beige broadcloth and also grey tricot. The process was overseen by the Commissioners for War, headed by Comte Daru. From Daru's correspondence, we learn that the Division of General Dupont in the 1806 had no *capotes*, and in order to enact the formal introduction of these, on 12 October 1806, he issued orders to requisition cloth, and in 8 days had produced 3,800 *capotes*.²⁰¹ A week or so later Daru was taxed to find 150,000 pairs of shoes and the cloth and materials necessary to make 8,000 officers' *habits*, 8,000 *redingotes* for officers, 8,000 of broadcloth or tricot *pantalons* for officers and 150,000 *capotes*.²⁰² To meet this demand, 32,000 aunes (1 aune = 119cm) of superfine broadcloth, 92,000 aunes of common broadcloth and 86,000 pairs of shoes were obtained within a few days from Prussian stocks. From Berlin Daru obtained 13,165 aunes of common broadcloth, from which he ordered the local production of 5,400 *capotes* and 2,000 pairs of broadcloth overalls for the heavy cavalry.²⁰³ A few days later Daru was able to report he had supplied Davout's 3ᵉ Corps with 6,000 *capotes* and 12,000 pairs of shoes and had obtained sufficient broadcloth to make 100,000 *capotes*, 100,000 pairs of *pantalons*, and 100,000 pairs of shoes. Daru notes that he was able to have made 1,500 pairs of shoes or infantry *chapeaux* a day. He further notes that Berlin had 28 clothiers, from which he obtained 17,142 aunes of common broadcloth to make a further 8,500 *capotes*.²⁰⁴ A report dated 28 October 1806 reveals the Army in Germany needed as a matter of urgency 58,250 *capotes*. Daru instructed that cloth was to be distributed to each regiment, who were then to oversee production of *capotes*.²⁰⁵

To try and make up for the lack of clothing, the Emperor gave to 3ᵉ Corps 12,000 *capotes* – 6,000 requisitioned from Frankfurt-sur-l'Oder, 4,000 captured from Prussian military stocks in Berlin, and 2,000 captured from magazines in Leipzig. To 7ᵉ Corps he gave 6,000 *capotes*, of which 4,000 were captured from Prussian magazines in Berlin and Leipzig; 12,000 to 4ᵉ Corps, of which 10,000 were captured; 10,000 were given to 3ᵉ Corps, some 9,000 of which came from Prussian stores in Leipzig; 9,000 went to 1ᵉ Corps, 8,000 to 6ᵉ Corps, and 1,200 to the 28ᵉ Legere.²⁰⁶ This measure was necessary as 3ᵉ Corps had 22,000 men but only had received cloth for 786 *capotes*! The 7ᵉ Corps had 13,000 infantry and just 2,000 *capotes*.²⁰⁷ One gains the feeling that the Grande Armée was dressed in virtually every single scrap of Prussian cloth that could be found.

On 14 November Daru reported that his agents had obtained in Magdeburg sufficient cloth to make 20,000 *capotes*, from Hambourg cloth to make 50,000 and from Lubeck sufficient to make 15,000 *capotes*.²⁰⁸ In Magdeburg Daru passed an order to make the cloth into *capotes*, each to cost 2fr each.²⁰⁹ On 23 November Daru ordered that 3,000 *capotes* were to be taken from the magazines in Berlin to be issued to the *Grenadiers Réunis*.²¹⁰ As the Grande Armée moved into Poland it captured huge stock piles of shoes and clothing. Between 16 and 22 January, 2,370 *capotes* were issued to 3ᵉ Corps, which had produced 9,162 *capotes* at regimental; 4,300 to 4ᵉ Corps, which had produced at regimental level a staggering 13,208 *capotes*; the 5ᵉ Corps had made 14,158; 1,500 *capotes* were issued to 7ᵉ Corps, which had been able to produce just 3,867; and just 423 *capotes* were passed to 1ᵉ Corps, but we note it had been able to produce at regimental level some 10,525.²¹¹ On 18 January 1807, the Emperor ordered that the workshops of Poland were to produce 16,000 *habits*, 32,000 *vestes manches* and 32,000 pairs of *culottes*. Each infantry regiment was to receive as a gratification 1,000 *habits*, 2,000 *vestes* and pairs of *culottes*.²¹² Initially, just 16 regiments therefore gained new clothing: the *habits* beyond any shadow of a doubt were made according to the white uniform regulations, and indeed we have found some regiments that benefited from this decree.

By 25 May it was reported that 36,136 *habits*, 62,601 *vestes manches* and 59,443 pairs of *culottes* had been made.[213] By the end of the campaign 100,616 *habits* had been distributed, along with 166,304 *vestes manches*, 159,514 pairs of *culottes*, 186,981 *capotes* issued ready-made, 95,694 issued as 'kits' to be sewn up by the regiments receiving them, 534,763 pairs of shoes, 239,638 shirts, 12,166 pairs of boots for the cavalry and 7,312 cavalry *manteaux*: a huge effort on Daru's part to cloth the army.[214] Each army corps had furthermore produced 27,000 *habits* since the campaign began from supplies they had locally obtained.[215]

Daru reported that from 1806 to 1807, in order to make the clothing some 1,058,146 aunes of broadcloth had been requisitioned by his agents solely to make *capotes*. We get the feeling not an inch of broadcloth remained in the theatre of operations of the Grande Armée, which had robbed or requisitioned whatever cloth could be found both in civilian homes and business as well as from the stocks of the defeated enemy. Without overrunning the Prussian army, the Grande Armée would have frozen to death and been wearing rags by spring 1807. The clothing *dépôts* in Germany were wound down in July 1808.[216]

As part of the preparation for the Austerlitz campaign, Daru was authorised to produce a reserve of 60,000 *capotes*, which were to be issued over winter 1804 to the troops at Boulogne, but we are ignorant of their destination.[217] The following tables shows the distribution and production of greatcoats in 1803–08:

Regiment	1803–05 regimental production	Campaign 1806–07 issued by Daru		1808	
		Ready Made	Kit Form	Broadcloth	Tricot
1e *de Ligne*	None	3		None	
2e *de Ligne*	None	1,813			Grey tricot
3e *de Ligne*	None	2,237		None	
4e *de Ligne*	None	1,960	312	Grey broadcloth *redingotes*	
5e *de Ligne*	None	4		None	
6e *de Ligne*	None	13			35 *capotes* were with the battalion and 252 in total with the regiment made from grey tricot.
7e *de Ligne*	None	None			Grey tricot
8e *de Ligne*	None	1,682	94	Beige broadcloth *redingotes*	Grey tricot *capotes*

Conclusions

Regiment	1803–05 regimental production	Campaign 1806–07 issued by Daru		1808	
		Ready Made	Kit Form	Broadcloth	Tricot
10ᵉ de Ligne	None				Grey tricot
11ᵉ de Ligne	None				Grey *tricot capotes*
12ᵉ de Ligne	None			Beige broadcloth *redingotes*	Grey tricot *capotes*
13ᵉ de Ligne				Grey broadcloth *redingotes*	Grey tricot *capotes*
14ᵉ de Ligne	1,599 in use	1,765	229	No Data	
15ᵉ de Ligne	None	244		None	
16ᵉ de Ligne	None	2,158		None	
17ᵉ de Ligne	Green broadcloth	4,138	250	Beige broadcloth *redingotes*	Grey tricot *capotes*
18ᵉ de Ligne	1,600 in use	1,212	1,407	Beige broadcloth *redingotes*	Grey tricot *capotes*
19ᵉ de Ligne		175		Beige broadcloth *redingotes*	Grey tricot *capotes*
20ᵉ de Ligne	None	3			Grey tricot *capotes*
21ᵉ de Ligne	None	3,726	197	Beige broadcloth *redingotes*	Grey tricot *capotes*
22ᵉ de Ligne	9,600fr spent on *capotes*, 33,900fr spent on *redingotes*, *pantalons de route*, smocks and shoes.	1,579			Grey tricot *redingotes*
23ᵉ de Ligne	None				Beige tricot *capotes*
24ᵉ de Ligne	regimental accounts report in the year to 1 September 1804, 45,600fr had been spent on *capotes*, smocks and *pantalons de route*, with a further 55,,497fr 20 spent on the same items.	1,490	1,075	Beige broadcloth *redingotes*	Grey tricot *capotes*
25ᵉ de Ligne	None	2,421	186	Beige broadcloth *capotes*	
26ᵉ de Ligne	1,600 *capotes*, smocks and pairs of *pantalons de route* made for 38,000fr.	14		Beige broadcloth *redingotes*	Beige tricot *capotes*
27ᵉ de Ligne	45,600fr spent on 1,600 *capotes*, smocks and pairs of *pantalons de route*.	868	47	Beige broadcloth *redingotes*	Beige tricot *redingotes*

Regiment	1803–05 regimental production	Campaign 1806–07 issued by Daru		1808	
		Ready Made	Kit Form	Broadcloth	Tricot
29ᵉ de Ligne	None	1		Grey broadcloth redingotes	
30ᵉ de Ligne	1,600	2,556	364	None	
32ᵉ de Ligne		1,722	32	None	
33ᵉ de Ligne	None	1,357	330	None	
34ᵉ de Ligne	None	1,966	17,68	Beige broadcloth redingotes	Grey tricot capotes
35ᵉ de Ligne	None				Grey tricot capotes
36ᵉ de Ligne	None	2,063	326		Grey tricot redingotes
37ᵉ de Ligne	1,600	2,093			
39ᵉ de Ligne	None				
40ᵉ de Ligne	None	1,801	1,700	Grey broadcloth redingotes	Grey tricot capotes
42ᵉ de Ligne	None				
43ᵉ de Ligne	1,600 capotes, smocks and pantalons de route	1,775	72		Grey tricot capotes
44ᵉ de Ligne	None	274	572	None	
45ᵉ de Ligne	None	2,188	103	None	
46ᵉ de Ligne	1,600 capotes, smocks and pantalons de route	1,563	352	None	
47ᵉ de Ligne	None				
48ᵉ de Ligne	None	965	234	None	
50ᵉ de Ligne	None	453	25		Grey tricot capotes
51ᵉ de Ligne	1,600 capotes, smocks and pantalons de route	2,022	370	Beige broadcloth redingotes	Grey tricot capotes
52e de Ligne	None				Grey tricot capotes
53ᵉ de Ligne	None	2,622	370		Grey tricot capotes
54ᵉ de Ligne	None	2,218	103	Beige broadcloth redingotes	Grey tricot capotes
55ᵉ de Ligne	None	1,990	322	None	
56ᵉ de Ligne	None	2,739		Beige broadcloth redingotes	Grey tricot capotes
57ᵉ de Ligne	None	1,553	248	None	
58ᵉ de Ligne	None	20		None	
59ᵉ de Ligne	1,600 capotes, smocks and pantalons de route	368		Beige broadcloth redingotes	Grey tricot capotes

Conclusions

Regiment	1803–05 regimental production	Campaign 1806–07 issued by Daru		1808	
		Ready Made	Kit Form	Broadcloth	Tricot
61ᵉ de Ligne	None				
62ᵉ de Ligne	1,600 Beige tricot *capotes*	None			Beige tricot *capotes*
63ᵉ de Ligne	None	1,102	619		Grey tricot *capotes*
64ᵉ de Ligne	1,600 *capotes*, smocks and *pantalons de route*	1,085	1,036		*Capotes* in use, unknown colour
65ᵉ de Ligne	None	3,180		None	
66ᵉ de Ligne	None				
67ᵉ de Ligne	None			Grey broadcloth *capotes*	
69ᵉ de Ligne	1,600 *capotes*, smocks and *pantalons de route*	733		None	
70ᵉ de Ligne	None			Beige broadcloth *capotes*	
72ᵉ de Ligne	None	1,600		None	
75ᵉ de Ligne	None	699	1,216	Beige broadcloth *redingotes*	Grey tricot *capotes*
76ᵉ de Ligne	None	519	6	None	
79ᵉ de Ligne	1,600 *capotes*, smocks and *pantalons de route*	None		Grey broadcloth *redingotes*	Grey tricot *capotes*
81ᵉ de Ligne	No Data				
82ᵉ de Ligne	None			Beige broadcloth *redingotes*	Grey tricot *capotes*
84ᵉ de Ligne	None				Grey tricot *capotes*
85ᵉ de Ligne	None	2,973	269	None	
86ᵉ de Ligne	None				Beige tricot *capotes*
88ᵉ de Ligne	None	894	1,812	None	
92ᵉ de Ligne	No Data				
93ᵉ de Ligne	1,600 *capotes*, smocks and *pantalons de route*	None		No data	
94ᵉ de Ligne	1,600 *capotes*, smocks and *pantalons de route*	1,357	94	None	
95ᵉ de Ligne	None	1,367	123	None	
96ᵉ de Ligne	None	1,305		None	
100ᵉ de Ligne	None	595	1,634	None	
101ᵉ de Ligne	None	595	1,934	None	

Regiment	1803–05 regimental production	Campaign 1806–07 issued by Daru		1808	
		Ready Made	Kit Form	Broadcloth	Tricot
103ᵉ de Ligne	None				Beige tricot *capotes*
105ᵉ de Ligne	None	193	717	Beige broadcloth *redingotes*	Grey tricot *capotes*
106ᵉ de Ligne	None				
108ᵉ de Ligne	None	1,109	489		Grey tricot *redingotes*
111ᵉ de Ligne	None	2,113	140	None	

Not every regiment had *capotes*, and most *sous-officiers* wore *redingotes* made in broadcloth.

The supply of these garments into the Peninsular theatre was problematical. For the Peninsular War the primary *dépôt* was at Bayonne. Indeed, throughout the French Empire, the army established large *dépôts* to house arms and clothing. As the Peninsular War progressed, ad hoc formations of men formed into temporary regiments would arrive at Bayonne having been superficially trained at their regimental *dépôt* and given a basic set of clothing and equipment. Once at the *dépôt*, they received, *if* the *dépôt* had the items, a full set of uniform. However, the system never really worked. Rather understandably, there was a huge backlog of getting men and clothing on time to the same place. With thousands of items of clothing and equipment being ordered, a lack of resources meant items were made from low-quality materials, often quickly and badly.

At the start of the Peninsular War, the dépôts at Bayonne and Bordeaux were to act as the principal supply *dépôts*. Huge stockpiles of clothing were sent there: 12,000 pairs of shoes, 23,000 new *habits*, 52,000 greatcoats, 64,000 pairs of shoes and 70,000 shirts were to be sent to the *dépôts* by January 1808.

In order to get clothing into the campaign theatre, a forward *dépôt* was established at Burgos and additional *dépôts* were set up at Toulouse, Nîmes and Montpellier for the army of Catalonia. By the end of January 1808, 12,400 pairs of shoes had arrived at Bayonne, and a further 20,000 had been authorised to be purchased locally. Every single pair was to be sent forward to Burgos. Furthermore, an additional 6,000 pairs were to be made each month. By these means, by the middle of April, the Administration of War had sent 47,000 pairs of shoes to Burgos, for the 70,000 men stationed there. As well as the supply of shoes, 10,000 *gibernes* and belts were to be prepared at Bayonne and 2,500 at Perpignan. In addition, 6,000 *marmites*, 6,000 *grand bidons* and 30,000 water canteens to contain 1½ pints were to be produced for the troops in Spain, along with 1,000 saddles and bridles for the cavalry. The canteens were to be made from white metal and to contain a water-vinegar mix. Cavalry troopers and mounted officers were to remove one of their pistol holsters from their saddle and to replace it with a canteen, made from a goat skin, to contain 1¼ litres of wine. Each company of artillery was to be issued with entrenching tools; the first squad was to be issued with axes, the second with shovels, the third with pickaxes, the fourth spare tools.

In August 1808, Napoleon ordered that the Army of the Centre was to receive a convoy of 3,000 pairs of shoes, 1,300 pairs of overalls and 1,700 shirts. Napoleon favoured taking the *capotes* from the men as he deemed them not necessary; this would represent a considerable saving in time and cost in making these items. According to General Dejean at the Ministry of War, this move was sheer folly as the mountains of Spain were capped with snow and as cold as Poland in the winter. Clearly, Napoleon failed to understand the campaign theatre's terrain and was more concerned with making war pay for itself than with the comfort of his soldiers. Indeed, on 17 August 1808, the army commissariat was ordered to send to Spain via Bayonne 10,000 pairs of gaiters, the same number of *schakos*, as well as 60,000 *capotes* and pairs of shoes. These items were to be taken from the magazines at Perpignan. A few days later, on 22 August, each regiment with men in Spain was ordered to send items of clothing and equipment for these men via Metz and Orlêans to Bayonne, to arrive there by 3 December 1808. The dépôts at Vauban, Strasbourg and Dunkirk were to send three quarters of their contents to Bayonne as well. Each regiment passing from Germany to Spain belonging to the 1e and 6e Corps was to be given 1,000 pairs of shoes when they passed through Mayence. The dépôt at Mayence was to have a stockpile of 70,000 pairs of shoes by 15 October 1808, and 100,000 by December 1808. Each man marching from Germany to Spain was to have five pairs of shoes. Each man was to wear a pair, and carry two pairs in his pack, the remaining two pairs being kept in the company baggage wagon. By December, Bayonne was to hold 15,000 line infantry *habits* and 5,000 light infantry *habits*, for the troops marching to Spain via Sedan as well as to equip the division of Polish troops. Over winter 1808 Marshall Soult was able to distribute 3,000 captured English greatcoats, which were part of the stores he had captured at Corunna, along with wool trousers and 3,400 pairs of shoes.

The Peninsular War was the graveyard for thousands of French soldiers. To provide reinforcements, 20,000 men from the recent conscription levy were assembled at Bayonne, of whom 17,000 had arrived; they were to be formed into three battalions of four companies. Soe 1,100 men were to be sent to the 1^e, 4^e and 6^e Corps, while the 3^e and 5^e Corps were each to receive 800 to 1,000 men. The 2^e and 8^e Corps were each to receive 800 men as reinforcements. The remaining conscripts were to be formed into five provisional line infantry regiments, to be numbered 114^e to 120^e *de Ligne*, each regiment to comprise 1,696 men, each company to have 120 men. The new regiments were to be ready to enter Spain on 1 February 1809. For these new regiments, on 31 October 1808 Napoleon wrote to Marshal Berthier, noting that he wished the new conscripts to be equipped with a waistcoat, a pair of overalls and a greatcoat at their *dépôts*, and when reaching Bayonne receive a uniform coat. For these 20,000 men, only 1,400 uniform coats and 7,000 greatcoats in lieu of 50,000, and 15,000 pairs of shoes in lieu of 229,000 pairs were held at Bayonne. Clearly the rate of demand of these items was outstripping their supply and manufacture. To make up some of this shortfall, the cloth workers at Bordeaux were ordered to supply 44,000 greatcoats and 20,000 uniform coats. However, these businesses objected to the amount of work they had to undertake in too short a period of time and demanded better pay and more money to buy better-quality cloth, otherwise the items produced would be of poor quality and defective. Napoleon ordered a tribunal be assembled to oversee these complaints.

At the same time, Napoleon ordered Intendant General Denniée on 31 October to send to Spain, by 1 January 1809, 50,000 greatcoats to the army, and a similar number of *habits*, *veste manches* and *culottes* for the infantry and similar numbers of *culottes de peau* and *habits* for the cavalry. Furthermore, 3,000 *schakos* were also to be delivered to the armies in Spain. General Clarke noted that a great many men serving in Spain either had a greatcoat or cloak, and no *habit*, or conversely a *habit* and no greatcoat. Many lacked shoes, primarily due to the lack of good leather in Spain, and protected their feet with rags or espadrilles. What cloth was available was often brown or grey. Due to the acute shortage of cloth, General Clarke, the minister for war, proposed changing the cloth colour for the armies in Spain to cornflower blue rather than indigo blue as was then in use. Napoleon favoured brown as the cloth was readily available in Spain and did not need to be dyed. Henceforth *capotes* and *pantalons* became brown.

By January 1809, 120,000 men had marched from Germany into Spain, and were at Bayonne ready for entry into Spain. These men were in theory re-equipped at Bayonne, where there were some 83,000 pairs of shoes, 140,000 shirts, 23,000 *havresacs*, 39,000 *schakos*, and 39,000 *capotes*. Clearly therefore, not all the men entering Spain in the new year of 1809 had been able to replace their equipment, which was last issued, in most cases, in 1807. From their entry into Spain, these men would have been in need of new items of clothing and equipment. The support network was not able to produce these items in sufficient number to keep the men well dressed. Nor were the logistical systems in use capable of getting the items to where they were needed. In addition, the state could not afford the burden of clothing and equipping two armies. Major cracks were beginning to show in Napoleon's military machine. Already by 1809 the army was lacking experienced officers and *sous-officiers*, and the means logistically and economically to support itself on two fronts, at great distances from France. The state had been overstretched by Napoleon.

Even with the political situation deteriorating in Germany, Napoleon still sent men into Germany, and the men in Spain still needed clothing and equipment. Writing from Madrid, Napoleon ordered a convoy of 16,000 pairs of shoes and 19,000 *capotes* to be sent from Berlin to Spain. He noted that men were in hospital due to lack of shoes and *capotes*. However, to save money, the *capotes* were to be only issued from August to March when the weather was cold, since during the summer these items were useless as the heat made the men burn, assuming they were not stationed in the north or mountainous regions of Spain. The cloth workers of Bordeaux were to start work to produce *capotes* for the August 1809 issue.

By 15 January 1809, 68,000 *capotes* had been assembled at Bayonne and 10,000 at Perpignan, with 48,000 still yet to be supplied, to arrive there by the first week of August 1809. This made a total order of 134,000 *capotes*. Napoleon ordered a levy of an additional 80,000 men for service in Spain to replace the 20,000 men in hospital, these men to be equipped by April 1809. The army administration was to prepare clothing for 140,000 conscripts.[218] From this all too brief resume, it is clear more research needs to be undertaken to fully understand the situation around supply of clothing to the Peninsular War and other theatres of operations.

Comment

This text has outlined the processes whereby men were cloth and equipped, and given some conclusions about how they were actually dressed in reality compared to the regulations. In most cases the dress regulations for grenadiers and *voltigeurs* were ignored until 1808 or later. About orders of dress, we can offer the following comment:

1. At no stage does archive research or regulations give credence to the idea of *etui d'habit* (covers for the *habit*) as used by the Garde Impériale. These never existed and were not part of the any regulation during the course of the Empire.
2. *Schako* covers were – at least officially – an innovation of Bardin regulation. They were unofficially adopted by some regiments. More research is needed to identify how prevalent the practice was.
3. *Schakos*. Overwhelming archive evidence informs us that that the 1806 *schako* was not in universal use until as late as 1809, and was issued with chinscales. The Otto MS and archive sources are mutually supporting on this. The 1810 decree introducing *schako* chinscales was merely confirming what was already unofficially happening. We can say that no *schako* were worn at the battles of Jena or Eylau, and likely none at Friedland. They were issued first to the *dépôt* battalions in France, and only those men marched out as reinforcements had them, as was the case with the *capote*.
4. The *capote* was issued first for troops at the camp of Boulogne, and was under the terms of the 1806 decree restricted initially to regiments in white uniforms. It then became, in theory, used universally. Yet we know from archive sources that these were not in universal use until 1808 or later. Of note, both *redingotes*, i.e., double-breasted garments, and *capotes*, i.e., single-breasted garments, were use. The majority were '*fait en capote*' i.e., single-breasted. These garments were worn over the cross belts in bad weather on the march, and under the cross belts in winter and guard mounting. They were worn over the *veste manche*, and only in cold weather was the *habit* worn under the *habit*. The *capote* was worn in most orders of dress, with the *veste manche*, reserving the *habit* for parades and formal occasions in good weather. Re-enactors like to think that a special cover existed for the *capote* – yes these indeed exist but for the Garde Impériale alone and were not sanctioned for the line until 1822.
5. *Giberne* covers. These were never part of the 1802 regulations. They may have been used unofficially. More research is needed to identify how prevalent the practice was.
6. Gaiter straps. Re-enactors and artists like to show soldiers wearing long gaiters using garters or gaiter straps to hold the gaiters up. As the gaiter buttoned to the *culottes* to hold them in place, no items were ever needed.

7. Black gaiters. Re-enactors and artists like to show soldiers wearing black gaiters as habitual dress. This is wrong. Soldiers habitually wore their long, grey, linen gaiters, both worn with the tricot *culottes*. Black gaiters were saved for very formal full-dress parades. Overwhelming evidence from the period shows that grey gaiters were worn in parade – meaning that the black gaiters were hardly ever worn. The plates by Martinet and the drawings by Otto and Vernet all present soldiers as if they were on parade in front of the Emperor. In everyday life, the black gaiters were hardly ever worn. We cannot rely on these images to tell us how soldiers were actually dressed. Black gaiters, like grey gaiters had prior to 1812, horn or leather buttons, never copper. Martinet, in a print of a grenadier of the 32ᵉ *de Ligne*, despite incorrectly showing bearskins for the grenadiers does show grey gaiters used for parade, as supported by the order books of the 3ᵉ and 64ᵉ *de Ligne*.
8. White gaiters. These existed before 1805, and some regiments did indeed have them. The only recorded instance is for the 64ᵉ *de Ligne*, and yet we do not know if the ordered gaiters ever arrived with the regiment. White gaiters certainly existed with many regiments in 1814, a mere half dozen out of 137 regiments. Despite what Martinet prints show, regiments simply never had white parade gaiters. Black gaiters were for full dress parades.
9. Linen *pantalons*. From period documentation, they were made so as to be worn over the *culottes*, literally as overalls. Soldiers never wore these tucked into the black parade gaiters as artists and re-enactors like to imagine. This is a modern re-enactorism and totally wrong. They were made from ecru (i.e., light brown) course linen and were not brilliant white, again contrary to what artists and re-enactors have one believe. Only in exceptional circumstances was white linen used.
10. Tight-fitting *culottes en tricot* were worn by soldiers, even on the march, in most orders of dress. The linen *pantalons* were worn in wet weather and on fatigues. On the march the grey gaiters were worn with the knee *culottes* as we noted earlier.
11. Hairstyles. Soldiers did not wear beards, nor did many *sapeurs*. Until Wagram, many regiments still wore the queue. Artists and re-enactors take note.
12. Bread bags. Many re-enactors and artists like to give Napoleonic soldiers a bread bag like the British *havresac*. They never existed.
13. Full dress. This was never worn in battle. In nearly all orders of dress a soldier wore his *capote*. *Habits* were seldom worn on campaign. Plumes and other adornments seem to be a legacy of 'peace and plenty' in 1808, leading to the campaign of Germany in 1809.
14. Do research. This scheme of work has shown beyond reasonable doubt that you cannot rely on the pretty pictures of Aaron Martinet and other artists to inform us how a particular regiment was dressed. Nor can we assume that the official dress regulations were in use. Grenadiers on the whole never had bearskins,

while *voltigeurs* in some cases never had distinctions whatsoever. Therefore, before one embarks on painting a regiment of war game figures, painting a book illustration of a particular regiment or indeed recreating a regiment, it is of vital importance that one visits the French Army archive and find out what exactly your chosen regiment actually wore.

What Does all this Mean?

Primarily it means that is a re-enactor, artist, model maker, wargamer wants to recreate or depict a particular regiment at a particular time, then they must do archive research to find out what their chosen regiment actually wore. Until now, no one had ever studied in the required level of detail until this book appeared to give real, empirical facts about how the army was dressed rather than relying on guesswork, supposition, the work of others and pretty pictures. Military history, especially uniformology, suffers from a lack of academic, re-evaluative research as it tends to be dominated by amateur historians who look solely at pretty pictures with no academic framework or theory to their work. A vast array of archive documents still await analysis in archives in France. What I have presented here is the tip of the iceberg of archive holdings, and it has taken decades of work to copy 1,000 archive boxes, less than 20 per cent of the total. My work is a springboard for others to build on, and indeed to correct my assumptions. One of the big issues with reconstructing what soldiers of the past wore is the reliance on a minimal data set of extant items. By their very nature, items that exist made from degradable materials such as cloth and leather, or where the materials can be recycled, metal, leather, fabric etc, means that what exists are 'freaks', the items that fell through the gaps. Museum collections contain an imbalance to officers' items – being private purchase and often kept in a wardrobe or drawer for decades in a private home, means that these items had less chance of being recycled or worn until they disintegrated. The clothing of the common soldier is largely missing, with very few items surviving. Therefore, why do they survive? What processes have enabled them to come down to us to the present day? Perhaps a half a million or more 1812 *habits* were made for common soldiers, but less than 20 can be found today, representing 1 per cent at most. Are they typical of what was worn? Of course not, and we cannot take them to be representative of the material culture of the army. These items are all atypical. However, by an analysis of these garments we can gain an understanding of how things were in terms of cut, and construction, which can be scaled up to represent the totality of material culture. Yet at the same time, we need to be cautious of museums. The Musée de l'Armée in Paris until recent years had many mannequins on display of complete sets of uniform. However, in most cases the mannequins had one or two original items, displayed on reconstructions, yet no museum guide ever mentioned this, that the bulk of the displays were from the 1960s and not the period of the First Empire. We need to understand what we are looking at rather than believing what we are told it is we are being shown in a museum display case. Indeed, many items in the Musée de l'Armée have been heavily restored since accession and are thus no longer in their historical form, and are thus totally useless to use in reconstructing the material culture of the period.

Despite the analysis of thousands of archive documents, we have to admit that we cannot present the detail that wargamers, re-enactors and artists demand about the dress of every regiment of ligne. After February 1808 virtually no archive paperwork exists until summer 1814. Into this vacuum of data, we have trust contemporary iconography such as Otto, who was working in spring and summer of that year and no earlier. Yet, what Otto and others like Martinet show may not be representative of the army as a whole: what is shown maybe the atypical and not the typical. We can say that drummers, other than in exceptional circumstances, were dressed as their parent company, ditto *cornets*. They lost their *gibernes* and firearms sometime after 1808. The dress of *sapeurs* is again largely unknown.

This body of work has hopefully moved on the debate about the dress of the French soldier in 1802 to 1812.

Notes

Acknowledgements
1. Aron Guverich, 'The French Historical Revolution: The Annales School', in Hodder et al (1995), *Interpreting Archaeology*, Routledge, London and New York, pp.158–161. This short paper offers a good introduction to the notion and concept of the Annales school for those unfamiliar with the theory of history.

Chapter 1
1. Service Historique de la Défense Armée de Térre (hereafter SHDDT) Xs 525 PROJET D'ARRÊTÉ Relatif à l'Habillement des troupes pour l'an X.
2. Malibran *Guide a l'Usage des Artistes et des Costumiers Contenant la Description Des Uniformes de l Armée Française de 1780 à 1848*. Combet & Cie: Paris. 1904, pp.195–202.
3. Ibid., p.66.
4. SHDDT Xs 525 circulaire 29 Frimaire An 14.
5. Ibid., p.48.
6. Crowdy (2015), p.79.
7. Archives Nationales de France (hereafter AN)/AF/IV/ 1600B plaquette 2 État des effets de campemins nécessaires pour l'armée des Côtes.
8. SHDDT GR 2C 275 Habillement.

Chapter 2
1. Etienne Alexandre Bardin, *Manuel d'infanterie, ou Résumé de tous les règlements, décrets, usages, renseignements concernant l'infanterie, dans lequel se trouve renfermé tout ce que doivent savoir les sergents et caporaux.* Paris: Chez Magimel, 1808, p.335.
2. Bibliothèque Musée de l'Armée, Manuscripts and printed books, Volume 1 du projet de règlement sur l'Habillement du major Bardin, pp.27–31.
3. SHDDT Xb 499 84e *de Ligne*. Dossier 1808. Rapport 14 Janvier 1808.
4. Crowdy (2015), p.127.
5. SHDDT Xb 499 84e *de Ligne*. Dossier 1808. Rapport 14 Janvier 1808.
6. Crowdy (2015), pp.121–127.
7. Bardin (1808), p.335.
8. SHDDT GR 21 YC 332 37e *régiment d'infanterie de Ligne*, 15 Janvier 1809–20 Février 1812 (matricules 7 801 à 9 600).
9. Livret in the author's collection.
10. Ibid.
11. Ibid.

Chapter 3
1. Anon (1779), p.5.
2. Paul Lindsay Dawson *Napoleon's Imperial Guard Uniforms and Equipment: The Infantry*. Frontline: Barnsley, 2019, pp.37–38.
3. Ibid., p.45.
4. Ibid.
5. Ibid., p.49.

6. Ibid., p.50.
7. Ibid.
8. Ibid., pp.50–51.
9. Ibid., p.51.
10. AN/AF/IV/1179. Relatifs à une nouvelle fixation de la Masse d'habillement. 25 Mars 1811.
11. SHDDT Xd 11 3ᵉ *régiment d'Artillerie à Pied* An XII a 1815. Dossier 1807.
12. AN/AFIV/1172.
13. SHDDT Xb 348 3ᵉ *régiment de Ligne* 1813 à 1815. Historique du Corps.

Chapter 4
1. Anon, *Les Guides des Sous-officiers de L'infanterie Francaise*, 2ᵉ Edition Leroy-Berge, Paris, 1809, pp.268–272.
2. SHDDT GR 2C 412 Registre d'Ordres du 64ᵉ *de Ligne*.
3. Bibliothèque Musée de l'Armée. Fonds Rousselot. Infanterie de la Ligne. Extraits de Livre d'Ordres du Colonel Schobert.
4. Ibid.
5. SHDDT Xb 375 15ᵉ *de Ligne* An XII a 1811. Dossier 1805.
6. SHDDT GR 2C 412 Registre d'Ordres du 64ᵉ *de Ligne*.

Chapter 5
1. Malibran (1904), p.203.
2. Etienne Alexandre Bardin, *Mémorial de l'officier d'infanterie*. Chez Magimel: Paris, 1813. 2 Volumes. 2 tome, p.689.
3. Crowdy (2015), pp.35–36.
4. SHDDT Xs 525 Projet de décret portant création d'une compagnie de voltigeurs dans chaque bataillon des régiments d'infanterie *de Ligne*.
5. SHDDT Xb 349 4ᵉ *régiment d'infanterie de la Ligne*. Lettre au Colonel 2 Janvier 1806.
6. SHDDT Xs 525. Circulaire 2 Sansculottides An 14.
7. SHDDT Xs 526 Circulaire 27 Xbre 1807.
8. SHDDT Xs 526 Circulaire 15 Xbre 1811.
9. SHDDT Xs 525 Circulaire 7 8bre 1807.
10. SHDDT Xb 477 65ᵉ *de Ligne* 1812 a 1815, Dossier 1815. Rapport 13 Avril 1819.

Chapter 6
1. Bibliothèque Musée de l'Armée. Fonds Rousselot. Infanterie de la Ligne. Extraits Journal Militaire.
2. SHDDT Xs 525 Circulaire 11 Fructidor An XII.
3. SHDDT Xs 525 Rapport 14 Prairial An XII.
4. SHDDT GR 2C 223 Correspondance et Ordres Marechal Soult, Ordre 23 Messidor An XII.
5. Ibid. Ordre 28 Messidor AN XII.
6. SHDDT Xs 526 Circulaire 25 February 1806.
7. Bibliothèque Musée de l'Armée. Fonds Rousselot. Infanterie de la Ligne. Extraits Journal Militaire.
8. Crowdy (2015,) p.47.
9. Anon (1779), p.7.
10. Crowdy (2015), p.39.
11. SHDDT Xb 380 12ᵉ *de Ligne*. Dossier An 13. Rapport 23 Thermidor 13.
12. SHDDT GR 1M 1962 Fonds Preval.
13. Ibid.
14. SHDDT Xb 367 12ᵉ *régiment de Ligne* An XII a 1808. Dossier 1808. Rapport 21 March 1808.
15. SHDDT Xb 597 17ᵉ *Légère*. Dossier An 13. Rapport 28 Thermidor An 13.
16. SHDDT Xb 395 23ᵉ *de Ligne*. Dossier An 13 Rapport 21 Thermidor An 13.
17. SHDDT GR 2C 412 Registre d'Ordres du 64ᵉ *de Ligne*.

18. SHDDT GR 1M 1962 Fonds Preval.
19. Bibliothèque Musée de l'Armée. Fonds Rousselot. Infanterie de la Ligne. Extraits Journal Militaire.
20. Bibliothèque Musée de l'Armée. Fonds Rousselot. Infanterie de la Ligne. Extraits de Livre d'Ordres du Colonel Schobert.
21. SHDDT Xb 348 3e *de Ligne*. Dossier 1814.
22. SHDDT GR 21 YC 31 3e *régiment* d'infanterie *de Ligne* dit régiment du Dauphin, 16 Juillet 1814–17 Décembre 1814 (matricules 1 à 1 800).

Chapter 7

1. Correspondance de Napoléon.
2. AN/AF/IV/1116 Baraguay de Hilliers au Napoléon 110 Nivôse An 13. See also Ibid. Napoleon au Baraguay de Hilliers 8 Ventose An 13, Baraguay de Hilliers au Napoléon 16 Fructidor An 13.
3. SHDDT Xs 525 PROJET DE DÉCRET Sur l'Habillement des Troupes. Art. 1.er A dater du 18 Mars 1806.
4. Ibid.
5. SHDDT GR C2 275 Habillement.
6. Crowdy (2015), p.59.
7. SHDDT Xs 525 Armée du Rhine. Situation 1 Nivôse An 8.
8. AN/AF/IV /600B plaquette 2. Mémoire sur les approvisionnements et l'organisation administrative de l'armée de Saint-Omer adressé au ministre de la Guerre Berthier par Pierre Daru, intendant général, le 9 prairial an XI.
9. SHDDT Xb 349 4e *régiment d'infanterie de la Ligne*. Rapport 28 Messidor An XIII.
10. Correspondance de Napoléon.
11. Bibliothèque Musée de l'Armée. Fonds Rousselot. Infanterie de la Ligne. Extraits Journal Militaire, p.77.
12. AN/AF/IV/1600 Registre Correspondance Comte Daru. Rapport 21 Décembre 1808.
13. SHDDT GR 1M 275 Habillement.
14. SHDDT GR 2C 412 Registre d'Ordres du 64e *de Ligne*.
15. Bardin (1808) pp.41–42.
16. Bibliothèque Musée de l'Armée. Fonds Rousselot. Infanterie de la Ligne. Extraits de Livre d'Ordres du Colonel Schobert.
17. Bibliothèque Musee de l'Armée. Fonds Rousselot. Infanterie de la Ligne. Habillement Infanterie de a Ligne. 30 Novembre 1807.
18. SHDDT Xs525 Décret 12 Juillet 1808.
19. SHDDT Xs 525 Rapport 18 Juillet 1808, read by the Emperor 26 Juillet 1808.

Chapter 8

1. SHDDT Xb 353 6e *de Ligne*. Dossier 1807. Designation des Etoffe.
2. Bibliothèque Musée de l'Armée. Fonds Rousselot. Infanterie de la Ligne.
3. SHDT Xs 525 Arête 11 Thermidor An 7.
4. SHDDT Xs 525 Devis des étoffes et doublures nécessaires pour la confection de l'Habillement complet d'un volontaire d'infanterie *de Ligne* et d'un volontaire d'infanterie légère, avec les dimensions de chaque partie de l'Habillement, et des effets de grand et petit équipement communs à chacun d'eux.
5. Bibliothèque Musée de l'Armée. Fonds Rousselot. Journal Militaire 1791, p.749.
6. SHDDT Xb 353 6e *de Ligne*. Dossier 1807. Designation des Etoffe.
7. SHDDT Xb 395 23e *de Ligne*. Dossier An 13 Rapport 21 Thermidor An 13.
8. Anon *Instruction pour servir a expliquer les principes d'après lesquels on ete executes les différends modeles de coiffure, Habillement & equipment envoys a chacun des Regiments d'infanterie*. Imprimerie Royale: Paris 1787, p.7.
9. SHDDT Xb 353 6e *de Ligne*. Dossier 1807. Designation des Etoffe.

10. SHDDT Xs 525 Décret 18 Fevrier 1808.
11. Honoré Hugues Berriat, *Législation militaire* A Alexandrie: Paris, 1812, 3 volumes. Vol 3, pp.235–236.
12. AN/AF/IV/4837.
13. Anon, *Ordonnance du 12 août 1788*, Ordonnances militaires (1788–1789), Paris, pp.1–2.
14. Bibliothèque Musée de l'Armée. Fonds Rousselot. Infanterie de la Ligne. Extraits Journal Militaire.
15. Ibid.
16. SHDDT Xb 346 2e *de Ligne* 1814–1815. Dossier 1815.
17. SHDDT Xb 391 9e *de Ligne* 1812 a 1815. Dossier 1815. Rapport 26 Avril 1819.
18. SHDDT Xb 392 21e *de Ligne*. Dossier 1811. Rapport 4 Juillet 1811.
19. SHDDT Xb 398 24e *de Ligne* 1809 a 1812. Dossier 1815. Rapport 21 Janvier 1817.
20. SHDDT Xb 442 48e *de Ligne*. Dossier 1815. Rapport 1 Décembre 1815.
21. Les Gupil *Administrations du Masses*, Chez Magimel: Paris, 1812, p.122.
22. Les Gupil, p.219.
23. Bardin (1813) *tome* 2, p.695.
24. Les Gupil, pp.219–220.
25. Bardin (1813) tome 2. p.703.
26. Ibid., p.695.
27. SHDDT Xs 525 Décret 21 Fevrier 1811.
28. SHDDT Xs 525 circulaire No. 149.
29. AN/AF/IV/1179. Relatifs à une nouvelle fixation de la Masse d'habillement, 25 Mars 1811.
30. SHDDT Xs 525–526.

Chapter 9
1. Amy Miller, *Dressed to Kill*, London: National Maritime Museum, 2021.
2. David, Alison Matthews. 2003. 'Decorated Men: Fashioning the French Soldier, 1852–1914', In *Fashion Theory*, Volume 7, pp.3–38.
3. SHDDT Xb 342 1e *régiment d'infanterie de la Ligne*. Rapport 2 Juillet 1808.
4. Ibid.
5. SHDDT Xb 342 1e *régiment d'infanterie de la Ligne*. Rapport 13 Mars 1808.
6. SHDDT Xb 342 1e *régiment d'infanterie de la Ligne*. Rapport 1 Juin 1809.
7. SHDDT Xb 344 2e *de Ligne*. Dossier An 13. Rapport 1 Vend An 13.
8. SHDDT Xb 344 2e *de Ligne*. Dossier An 13. Rapport 6 Thermidor An 13.
9. SHDDT Xb 344 2e *de Ligne*. Dossier An 14. Proces verbal formation des compagnies de *Voltigeur*s, 1 Brumaire An 14.
10. SHDDT GR 2C 275 Habillement.
11. SHDDT Xb 344 2^e *de Ligne*. Dossier 1808. Rapport 26 9bre 1807.
12. SHDDT Xb 345 2^e *de Ligne* 1808 a 1814. Dossier 1808. Lettre 28 9bre 1807.
13. SHDDT Xb 345 2e *de Ligne* An XII a 1812. Dossier 1808. Rapport 28 9bre 1807.
14. SHDDT Xb 347 3e *de Ligne* An XII a 1810. Dossier An XII. Rapport 3 Brumaire An XIII.
15. SHDDT Xb 347 3e *de Ligne* An XII a 1810. Dossier An XII. Rapport 18 Thermidor An XIII.
16. Bibliothèque Musée de l'Armée. Fonds Rousselot. Infanterie de la Ligne. Extraits de Livre d'Ordres du Colonel Schobert.
17. SHDDT GR 2C 275 Habillement.
18. SHDDT Xb 347 3e *de Ligne* An XII a 1810. Dossier 1807. Rapport 1 9bre 1807.
19. SHDDT Xb 349 4e *régiment d'infanterie de la Ligne*. Rapport 1 Vendémiaire An XIII.
20. SHDDT Xb 349 4e *régiment d'infanterie de la Ligne*. Rapport 28 Messidor An XIII.
21. SHDDT Xb 349 4e *régiment d'infanterie de la Ligne*. Lettre 10 Nivôse An XIV.
22. SHDDT Xb 349 4e *régiment d'infanterie de la Ligne*. Rapport 1 Brumaire An XIV.
23. SHDDT GR 2C 275 Habillement.
24. SHDDT Xb 349 4e *de Ligne*. Dossier 1807. Rapport 1 Novembre 1807.

25. SHDDT Xb 349 4ᵉ *de Ligne.*
26. SHDDT Xb 352 5ᵉ *régiment d'infanterie de la Ligne.* Dossier 1807 Rapport 23 Fevrier 1807.
27. Ibid. Rapport 18 Janvier 1808.
28. SHDDT Xb 353 6ᵉ *de Ligne* Dossier 1808. Rapport 5 Mars 1808.
29. SHDDT Xb 355 6ᵉ *de Ligne* 1812 à 1815. Dossier 1815. Rapport 5 Fevrier 1821.
30. SHDDT Xb 356 7ᵉ *de Ligne.* An 12 à 1810. Dossier 1806. Lettre 26 Frimaire An XIV.
31. SHDDT Xb 356 7ᵉ *de Ligne.* An 12 à 1810. Dossier 1806. Rapport 12 Mars 1806.
32. SHDDT Xb 356 7ᵉ *de Ligne.* An 12 à 1810. Dossier 1808. Rapport 10 Novembre 1807.
33. SHDDT Xb 358 8ᵉ *de Ligne* 1792 à 1811. Dossier An 13. Rapport 5 Vend An 13.
34. SHDDT GR 2C 275 Habillement.
35. SHDDT Xb 358 8ᵉ *de Ligne* 1792 a 1811. Dossier 1807. Rapport 3 Décembre 1807.
36. SHDDT Xb 358 8ᵉ *de Ligne* 1792 a 1811. Dossier 1807. Etat de Prix 3 Décembre 1807.
37. SHDDT Xb 360 9ᵉ *de Ligne.* Dossier An 13. Rapport 25 Fructidor An 13.
38. SHDDT Xb 360 9ᵉ *de Ligne.* Dossier An 13. Rapport 1 Juin 1807.
39. SHDDT Xb 360 9ᵉ *de Ligne.* Dossier 1808. Rapport 11 Janvier 1808.
40. SHDDT Xb 360 9ᵉ *de Ligne.* Dossier 1809. Rapport 7 Juin 1809.
41. SHDDT Xb 361 9ᵉ *de Ligne.* Dossier 1815. Proces verbal 25 9bre 1815.
42. SHDDT Xb 362 10ᵉ *de Ligne.* Dossier 1808. Rapport 30 Juin 1808.
43. SHDDT Xb 362 10ᵉ *de Ligne.* Dossier 1808. Rapport 5 Mai 1808.
44. SHDDT Xb 365 11ᵉ *de Ligne.* Dossier An 12. Rapport 1 Brum An 12.
45. SHDDT Xb 365 11ᵉ *de Ligne.* Dossier An 13. Rapport 1 Vend An 13.
46. SHDDT Xb 365 11ᵉ *de Ligne.* Dossier 1808. Rapport 21 Janvier 1808.
47. SHDDT GR 2C 275 Habillement.
48. SHDDT Xb 367 12ᵉ *de Ligne* 1792 à 1808, Dossier 1807. Rapport 21 Mars 1808.
49. SHDDT Xb 367 12ᵉ *de Ligne* 1792 à 1808 Dossier 1807. Rapport 21 Mars 1808.
50. SHDDT Xb 367 12ᵉ *de Ligne* 1792 à 1808. Dossier 1807. Rapport 21 Mars 1808.
51. SHDDT Xb 369 12ᵉ *de Ligne.* Dossier 1815. Rapport 21 Mars 1821.
52. SHDDT GR 2C 275 Habillement.
53. Bibliothèque Nationales de France, Paris. Uniformes des régiments d'infanterie et *de Ligne* sous le Consulat et lᵉ 1er Empire / aquarelles par E. Fort.
54. SHDDT GR 2C 518 Résumé d'revue 1 Mai 1811.
55. SHDDT Xb 370 13e *de Ligne.* Dossier An 13. Rapport 23 Vend An 13.
56. SHDDT Xb 370 13ᵉ *de Ligne.* Dossier An 13. Rapport 5 Thermidor An 13.
57. SHDDT Xb370 13ᵉ *de Ligne.* Dossier 1807. Rapport 3 Décembre 1807.
58. SHDDT Xb370 13ᵉ *de Ligne.* Dossier 1808. Rapport 7 Janvier 1808.
59. SHDDDT Xb 373 14ᵉ *de Ligne.* An XII a 1811. Dossier An 13. Rapport 15 Vend An 13.
60. SHDDT Xb 373 14ᵉ *de Ligne.* Dossier An 13. Rapport 2 Thermidor An 13.
61. SHDDT GR 2C 275 Habillement.
62. SHDDT Xb 373 14ᵉ *de Ligne* Dossier 1807. Rapport 26 Mars 1808.
63. Luis Sorando Muzas pers comm citing AHN, Estado 8612, exp. 350, rapport 27 Janvier 1809.
64. SHDDT Xb 375 15ᵉ *de Ligne.* Dossier An 13. Rapport 18 Thermidor An 13.
65. SHDDT Xb 375 15ᵉ *de Ligne* Dossier 1808. Rapport 13 Fevrier 1808.
66. SHDDT GR 2C 275 Habillement.
67. Boucquet de Beauval 'Les Souvenirs du lieutenant-colonel Boucquet de Beauval 1804–1830' in *Carnets de la Sabretache* 1897, pp.298–310, p.301.
68. A.L. Dawson pers comm.
69. SHDDT Xb 376 15ᵉ *de Ligne.* Dossier 1811. Rapport 16 Mai 1811.
70. SHDDT Xb 378 16ᵉ *de Ligne.* Dossier An 13. Rapport 6 Ven An 13.
71. SHDDT Xb 378 16ᵉ *de Ligne.* Dossier An 13. Rapport 7 Thermidor An 13.
72. SHDDT Xb 378 16ᵉ *de Ligne.* Dossier 1808. Rapport 22 Novembre 1807.
73. SHDDT GR 2C 275 Habillement.

74. SHDDT Xb 380 17ᵉ *de Ligne*. Dossier An 12. Rapport 1 Brumaire An 12.
75. SHDDT Xb 380 12ᵉ *de Ligne*. Dossier An 13. Rapport 23 Thermidor 13.
76. SHDDT GR 2C 275 Habillement.
77. SHDDT Xb 381 17ᵉ *de Ligne*. Dossier 1808. Rapport 1 Janvier 1808.
78. SHDDT Xb 380 17ᵉ *de Ligne* An XII a 1807. Rapport 1 Janvier 1808.
79. SHDDT GR C2 518 Résume d'revue 1 Mai 1811.
80. SHDDT Xb 383 18ᵉ *de Ligne*. An XII a 1811. Dossier An 13. Rapport 26 Vend An 13.
81. SHDDT Xb 383 18ᵉ *de Ligne*. Dossier An 13. Rapport 1 Thermidor An 13.
82. SHDDT Xb 383 18ᵉ *de Ligne*. Dossier 1808. Rapport 4 Novembre 1807.
83. SHDDT GR 2C 275 Habillement.
84. SHDDT Xb 386 19ᵉ *régiment de Ligne*. An XII a 1812. Dossier 1807. Rapport 27 Décembre 1807.
85. SHDDT Xb 386 19ᵉ *régiment de Ligne*. An XII a 1812. Dossier 1807. Rapport 8 Janvier 1808.
86. SHDDT Xb 388 20ᵉ *de Ligne*. Dossier 1808. Rapport 13 Mars 1808.
87. SHDDT Xb 388 20ᵉ *de Ligne*. Dossier 1808. Rapport 29 Mai 1808.
88. SHDDT GR 2C 275 habillement.
89. SHDDT Xb 391 21ᵉ *de Ligne*. An XII a 1811. Dossier 1807. Rapport 1 Décembre 1807.
90. Ibid etat de prix 1 Décembre 1807.
91. SHDDT GR 2C 518 Résume d'revue 1 Mai 1811.
92. SHDDT Xb 392 21ᵉ *de Ligne*. 1811 à 1815 Dossier 1811. Rapport 1 Juillet 1811.
93. SHDDT Xb 392 21ᵉ *de Ligne*. Dossier 1811. Rapport 4 Juillet 1811.
94. SHDDT GR 2C 275 habillement.
95. SHDDT Xb 393 22ᵉ *de Ligne*. An XII a 1811. Dossier 1807. Rapport 21 Décembre 1807.
96. SHDDT Xb 395 23ᵉ *de Ligne*. Dossier An 13 Rapport 20 Vend An 13.
97. SHDDT Xb 395 23ᵉ *de Ligne*. Dossier An 13 Rapport 21 Thermidor An 13.
98. SHDDT Xb 395 23ᵉ *de Ligne*. Dossier 1808. Rapport 29 Janvier 1808.
99. SHDDT XB 397 24ᵉ *de Ligne*. An XII a 1809. Dossier An XIII. Rapport 9 Thermidor An XII.
100. SHDDT GR 2C 275 habillement.
101. SHDDT XB 397 24ᵉ *de Ligne* An XII a 1809. Dossier 1807. Rapport 29 Janvier 1808.
102. SHDDT XB 397 24ᵉ *de Ligne* An XII a 1809. Dossier 1807. Rapport 1 8bre 1808.
103. SHDDT XB 397 24ᵉ *de Ligne* An XII a 1809. Dossier 1807. Rapport 1 8bre 1808.
104. SHDDT Xb 398 24ᵉ *de Ligne* 1809 à 1812. Dossier 1815. Rapport 21 Janvier 1817.
105. SHDDT Xb 399 25ᵉ *de Ligne*. An XII a 1808. Dossier An 13 Rapport 6 Brum An 13.
106. SHDDT GR 2C 275 habillement.
107. SHDDT Xb 399 25ᵉ *de Ligne* An XII a 1808. Dossier 1807. Rapport 27 Décembre 1807.
108. SHDDT GR 2C 518 Résume d'revue 1 Mai 1811.
109. SHDDT Xb 399 25ᵉ *de Ligne* An XII a 1808. Dossier 1811. Rapport 14 Mai 1811.
110. Ibid.
111. SHDDT Xb 401 26ᵉ *de Ligne*. Dossier An 12. Rapport 5 jour complémentaire An 12.
112. SHDDT Xb 401 26ᵉ *de Ligne*. Dossier 1808. Rapport 27 Fevrier 1808.
113. SHDDT Xb 403 27ᵉ *de Ligne*. An 12 à 1811. Dossier 1811. Rapport 21 Juin 1811.
114. Bibliothèque Musée de l'Armée. Fonds Rousselot. Infanterie de la Ligne.
115. SHDDT GR 2C 275 habillement.
116. SHDDT Xb 405 28ᵉ *de Ligne*. An 12 à 1810. Dossier 1807. Inspection 26 Décembre 1807.
117. SHDDT Xb 407 29ᵉ *de Ligne*. Dossier An 13. Rapport 18 Brumaire An 13.
118. SHDDT Xb 407 29ᵉ *de Ligne*. Dossier An 13. Rapport Fructidor An 13.
119. SHDDT Xb 407 29ᵉ *de Ligne*. Dossier 1808. Rapport 22 Mars 1808.
120. SHDDT Xb 407 29ᵉ *de Ligne*. Dossier 1808. Rapport 17 Avril 1808.
121. SHDDT Xb 409 30ᵉ *de Ligne*. Dossier An 13. Rapport 20 Vend An 13.
122. SHDDT Xb 409 30ᵉ *de Ligne*. Dossier An 13. Rapport 8 Thermidor An 13.
123. SHDDT Gr 2C 275 Habillement.
124. SHDDT Xb 409 30ᵉ *de Ligne*. Dossier 1808. Rapport 26 Novembre 1807.

125. SHDDT Xb 410 30ᵉ *de Ligne* 1808 à 1815. Dossier 1811. Rapport 1 Juillet 1811.
126. Ibid.
127. SHDDT GR 2C 518 Résume d'revue 1 Mai 1811.
128. SHDDT Xb 411 32ᵉ *de Ligne*. Dossier An 13. Rapport 25 Fructidor An 13.
129. SHDDT GR 2C 275 habillement.
130. SHDDT Xb 411 32ᵉ *de Ligne*. Dossier 1807. Rapport 31 Décembre 1807.
131. SHDDT Xb 412 32ᵉ *de Ligne*. Dossier 1814. Rapport 1 Aout 1814.
132. Ibid.
133. SHDDT GR 2C 275 habillement.
134. SHDDT Xb 413 33ᵉ *de Ligne*. An 12 à 1808. Dossier 1808. Rapport 22 Novembre 1807.
135. SHDDT GR 2C 518 Résume d'revue 1 Mai 1811.
136. SHDDT Xb 414 33ᵉ *de Ligne* 1808 à 1813. Dossier 1811. Rapport 1 Juillet 1811.
137. SHDDT Xb 416 34ᵉ *de Ligne*. Dossier An 13. Rapport 7 Brumaire An 13.
138. SHDDT Xb 416 34ᵉ *de Ligne*. Dossier An 13. Rapport 24 Thermidor An 13.
139. SHDDT Xb 416 34ᵉ *de Ligne*. Dossier 1808. Rapport 7 Novembre 1807.
140. SHDDT Xb 417 34ᵉ de *de Ligne* 1812 à 1815. Dossier 1814. Rapport 29 Juillet 1814.
141. SHDDT GR 2C 275 habillement.
142. SHDDT Xb 418 35ᵉ *de Ligne*. Dossier An 12. Rapport 1 Brumaire An 12.
143. SHDDT Xb 418 35ᵉ *de Ligne*. Dossier 1808. Rapport 8 Janvier 1808.
144. SHDDT Xb 418 35ᵉ *de Ligne*. Dossier 1809. Rapport 1 Juin 1809.
145. SHDDT Xb 420 36ᵉ *de Ligne*. An XII a 1811. Dossier 1807. Rapport 27 Décembre 1807.
146. SHDDT Xb 421 36ᵉ *de Ligne*. 1811 à 1815. Dossier 1815. Rapport 1 Décembre 1815.
147. SHDDT GR 2C 275 habillement.
148. SHDDT Xb 422 37ᵉ *de Ligne*. Dossier An 13. Rapport 1 Messidor An 13.
149. SHDDT Xb 424 37ᵉ *de Ligne* 1812 à 1815. Dossier 1815. Rapport 24 Mai 1821.
150. SHDDT GR 2C 518 Résume d'revue 1 Mai 1811.
151. SHDDT Xb 425 39ᵉ *de Ligne*. Dossier 1807. Rapport 15 Décembre 1807.
152. SHJDDT GR 2C 275 Habillement.
153. SHDDT Xb 427 40ᵉ *de Ligne*. An 12 à 1811. Dossier 1807. Inspection 9 Décembre 1807.
154. SHDDT Xb 429 42ᵉ *de Ligne*. An XII à 1811. Dossier 1807. Rapport 8 Fevrier 1808.
155. SHDDT Xb 429 42ᵉ *de Ligne*. Dossier 1807. Rapport 29 Mars 1808.
156. SHDDT GR 2C 275 habillement.
157. SHDDT Xb 431 43ᵉ *de Ligne*. Dossier 1808. Rapport 31 Xbre 1807.
158. SHDDT Xb 433 44ᵉ *de Ligne*. Dossier An 12. Rapport 25 Fructidor An 12.
159. SHDDT GR 2C 275 Habillement. Rapport 8 Avril 1808.
160. SHDDT Xb 433 44ᵉ *de Ligne*. Dossier 1808. Rapport 28 Janvier 1808.
161. Luis Sorando Muzas pers comm citing AHN, Estado 8612, exp. 350, rapport 27 Janvier 1809.
162. SHDDT Xb 435 45ᵉ *de Ligne*. An XII a 1811. Dossier An XIII. Rapport 18 Fructidor An XIII.
163. SHDDT GR 2C 275 habillement.
164. SHDDT Xb 435 45ᵉ *de Ligne*. Dossier 1808. Rapport 29 Novembre 1807.
165. Pierre Juhel pers comm.
166. SHDDT Xb 436 45ᵉ *de Ligne*. Dossier 1815.
167. SHDDT Xb 436 45ᵉ *de Ligne*. Dossier 1815. Rapport 30 Mars 1819.
168. SHDDT Xb 437 46ᵉ *de Ligne*. An XII a 1811. Dossier An XII Rapport 5 Sansculottides An XII.
169. SHDDT Xb 437 46ᵉ *de Ligne*. Dossier An XII Rapport 5 Sansculottides An XII.
170. SHDDT GR 2C 275 habillement.
171. SHDDT Xb 437 46ᵉ *de Ligne*. Dossier 1807. Rapport 20 Xbre 1807.
172. SHDDT Xb 437 46ᵉ *de Ligne*. Dossier An XII Rapport 5 Sansculottides An XII.
173. SHDDT Xb 437 46ᵉ *de Ligne*. Dossier An XIII. Rapport 27 Thermidor An XIII.
174. SHDDT Xb 438 46ᵉ *de Ligne* 1812 à 1815. Dossier 1815. Rapport 20 Mars 1820.
175. SHDDT Xb 438 46ᵉ *de Ligne*. Dossier 1811. Rapport 15 Mai 1811.

176. SHDDT Xb 467 60ᵉ *de Ligne*. 1812 à 1815. Dossier 1811. Rapport 24 Juillet 1811.
177. SHDDT Xb 438 46ᵉ *de Ligne*. Dossier 1815. Rapport 20 Mars 1820.
178. SHDDT Xb 438 46ᵉ *de Ligne*. Dossier 1812. Rapport 2 Mai 1812.
179. SHDDT Xb 439 47ᵉ *de Ligne*. Dossier An 13. Rapport 4 Vend An 13.
180. SHDDT Xb 439 47ᵉ *de Ligne*. Dossier An 13. Rapport 10 Thermidor An 13.
181. SHDDT Xb 439 47ᵉ *de Ligne*. Dossier 1808. Rapport 2 Fevrier 1808 .
182. SHDDT Xb 441 48ᵉ *de Ligne*. Dossier An 13. Rapport 5 Brumaire An 13.
183. SHDDT Xb 441 48ᵉ *de Ligne*. Dossier An 13. Rapport 10 Thermidor An 13.
184. SHDDT Xb 441 48ᵉ *de Ligne*. Dossier 1806. Lettre 5 Mai 1806.
185. SHDDT Xb 441 48ᵉ *de Ligne*. Dossier 1808. Rapport 1 Xbre 1807.
186. SHDDT GR 2C 275 Habillement.
187. SHDDT Xb 443 50ᵉ *de Ligne*. An 12 a 1811. Dossier 1808. Rapport 20 Décembre 1807.
188. SHDDT Xb 444 50ᵉ *de Ligne*. 1811 à 1815. Dossier 1815. Rapport 8 8bre 1821.
189. SHDDT Xb 445 51ᵉ *de Ligne*. Dossier 1808. Rapport 29 9bre 1807.
190. SHDDT Xb 448 52ᵉ *de Ligne*. Dossier 1808. Rapport 20 Avril 1808.
191. SHDDT Xb 448 52ᵉ *de Ligne*. Dossier 1808. Rapport 6 Mars 1808.
192. SHDDT Xb 450 53ᵉ *de Ligne*. Dossier 1808. Rapport 14 Janvier 1808.
193. SHDDT Xb 450 53ᵉ *de Ligne*. Dossier 1808. Rapport 31 Juillet.
194. SHDDT GR 2C 275 Habillement.
195. Pierre Juhel pers comm.
196. SHDDT GR 2C 275 Habillement.
197. SHDDT Xb 452 54ᵉ *de Ligne*. An XII à 1811. Dossier 1807. Rapport 30 9bre 1807.
198. SHDDT Gr 2C 275 Habillement.
199. SHDDT Xb 454 55ᵉ *régiment de Ligne*. An XII à 1809. Dossier 1807. Rapport 15 Xbre 1807.
200. SHDDT Xb 454 55ᵉ *régiment de Ligne*. Dossier 1807. Rapport 3 février 1808.
201. SHDDT Xb 457 56ᵉ *de Ligne*. 1808 à 1813. Dossier 1813. Rapport 27 9bre 1807.
202. Bibliothèque Musée de l'Armée. Fonds Rousselot. Infanterie de la Ligne. Descriptions des régiments d'infanterie, p.5.
203. SHDDT Xb 457 56ᵉ *de Ligne* 1808 à 1813. Dossier 1809. Rapport 5 août 1809.
204. SHDDT Xb 459 57ᵉ *de Ligne*. An XII à 1811. Dossier An XIII. Rapport 6 Fructidor An XIII.
205. SHDDT GR C2 275 Habillement.
206. SHDDT Xb 459 57ᵉ *de Ligne*. An XII a 1811. Dossier 1807. Rapport 10 9bre 1807.
207. Bibliothèque Musée de l'Armée. Fonds Rousselot. Infanterie de la Ligne.
208. SHDDT Xb 459 57ᵉ *de Ligne*. Dossier AN XII. Rapport par General Muller 19 Prairial An XI.
209. SHDDT Xb 459 57ᵉ *de Ligne*. Dossier 1808. Lettre au ministre de guerre 12 Janvier 1808.
210. SHDDT Xb 461 58ᵉ *régiment de Ligne*. Dossier 1808. Rapport 4 Avril 1808.
211. SHDDT Xb 463 59ᵉ *de Ligne*. Dossier An 13. Rapport 20 Vend An 13.
212. SHDDT Xb 463 59ᵉ *de Ligne*. Dossier An 13. Rapport 20 Thermidor An 13.
213. SHDDT Xb 463 59ᵉ *de Ligne*. Dossier 1808. Rapport 4 Avril 1808.
214. SHDDT Xb 465 59ᵉ *de Ligne* 1812 à 1815. Dossier 1815. Rapport 29 7bre 1815.
215. SHDDT Xb 465 59ᵉ *de Ligne*. Dossier 1815. Rapport 29 7bre 1815.
216. SHDDT Xb 465 59ᵉ *de Ligne*. Dossier 1815. Rapport 29 7bre 1815.
217. SHDDT Xb 466 60ᵉ *de Ligne*. Dossier 1808. Rapport 27 Janvier 1808.
218. AN/AF/IV1632/2 Dossier 6, folder 5.
219. SHDDT GR 2C 275 habillement.
220. SHDDT Xb 468 61ᵉ *de Ligne*. Dossier 1808. Rapport 29 9bre 1807.
221. SHDDT GR 2C 518 Résume d'revue 1 Mai 1811.
222. SHDDT Xb 471 62ᵉ *de Ligne* 1810 a 1815. Dossier 1814. Rapport 8 Mai 1821.
223. SHDDT Xb 470 62ᵉ *de Ligne*, Dossier 1808. Rapport 20 Mars 1808.
224. SHDDT Xb 470 62ᵉ *de Ligne*, Dossier 1808. Rapport 8 Juin 1808.
225. SHDDT Xb 471 62ᵉ *de Ligne* 1810 a 1815. Dossier 1814. Rapport 8 Mai 1821.

226. Boucquet de Beauval 'Les Souvenirs du lieutenant-colonel Boucquet de Beauval 1804–1830', in *Carnets de la Sabretache* 1897, pp.298–310. p.301.
227. SHDDT GR 2C 275 habillement.
228. SHDDT Xb 472 63ᵉ *de Ligne*. An XII a 1811. Dossier 1807. Rapport 31 Janvier 1808.
229. SHDDT Xb 474 64ᵉ *de Ligne*. An XII a 1809. Dossier An XIII.
230. SHDDT GR 2C 275 Habillement.
231. SHDDT Xb 474 64ᵉ *de Ligne*. An XII a 1808. Dossier 1807. Rapport 9 Novembre 1807.
232. SHDDT GR 2C 275 Habillement.
233. SHDDT Xb 476 65ᵉ *de Ligne*. Dossier 1808. Rapport 25 9bre 14807.
234. SHDDT Xb 477 65ᵉ *de Ligne* 1812 à 1815, Dossier 1815. Rapport 13 Avril 1819 a.
235. SHDDT Xb 478 66ᵉ *de Ligne*. Dossier 1808. Rapport 28 Fevrier 1808.
236. SHDDT Xb 480 67ᵉ *de Ligne*. Dossier 1808. Rapport 7 Décembre 1807.
237. SHDDT Xb 482 69ᵉ *de Ligne*. Dossier An 13. Rapport 25 Therm An 13.
238. SHDDT Xb 482 69ᵉ *de Ligne*. Dossier 1808. Rapport 30 Mars 1808.
239. SHDDT Xb 485 70ᵉ *de Ligne*. Dossier 1808. Rapport 10 Fevrier 1808.
240. Luis Sorando Muzas pers comm citing AHN, Estado 8612, exp. 350, rapport 27 Janvier 1809.
241. SHDDT Xb 487 72ᵉ *de Ligne*. Dossier 1808. Rapport 30 Novembre 1807.
242. SHDDT Xb 489 75ᵉ *de Ligne* An XII à 1811. Dossier An XII. Lettre Pixier a son Colonel 30 Germinal An XII.
243. SHDDT Xb 489 75ᵉ *de Ligne*. Dossier An XIII.
244. SHDDT Xb 489 75ᵉ *de Ligne*. Dossier An XIII. Rapport 24 Fructidor An XIII.
245. SHDDT Xb 489 75ᵉ *de Ligne*. Dossier 1806.
246. SHDDT Xb 489 75ᵉ *de Ligne*. Dossier 1806. Lettre 3 Mars 1806.
247. SHDDT Xb 489 75ᵉ *de Ligne*. Dossier 1806.
248. SHDDT Xb 489 75ᵉ *de Ligne*. Dossier 1806. Rapport 25 7bre 1806.
249. SHDDT GR 2C 275 Habillement.
250. SHDDT Xb 489 75ᵉ *de Ligne*. Dossier 1807. Rapport 1 Juillet 1807.
251. SHDDT Xb 489 75ᵉ *de Ligne*. Dossier 1807. Rapport 25 7bre 1807.
252. SHDDT Xb 489 75ᵉ *de Ligne*. Dossier 1807. Rapport 15 aout 1807.
253. SHDDT Xb 489 75ᵉ *de Ligne*. Dossier 1807. Rapport 6 Janvier 1808.
254. SHDDT Xb 491 76ᵉ *de Ligne*. Dossier An 13. Rapport 24 Vend An 13.
255. SHDDT GR 2C 275 Habillement.
256. SHDDT Xb 491 76ᵉ *de Ligne*. Dossier 1808. Rapport 15 Xbre 1807.
257. SHDDT Xb 493 79ᵉ *de Ligne*. Dossier An 13. Rapport 20 Vend An 13.
258. SHDDT Xb 493 79ᵉ *de Ligne*. Dossier 1808. Rapport 20 Janvier 1808.
259. SHDDT Xb 496 81ᵉ *de Ligne* 1812 à 1815. Dossier 1815. Rapport 20 septembre 1819.
260. SHDDT Xb 497 82ᵉ *de Ligne*. Dossier Ab13. Rapport 6 Thermidor An 13.
261. SHDDT Xb 499 84ᵉ *de Ligne* Dossier 1808. Rapport 4 Janvier 1808.
262. SHDDT Xb 499 84ᵉ *de Ligne* Dossier 1808. Rapport 4 Janvier 1808.
263. SHDDT Xb 500 84ᵉ *de Ligne*. Dossier 1815. Historique du Corps a 1820.
264. SHDDT Xb 501 85ᵉ *de Ligne*. An XII a 1811. Dossier 1807. Rapport 16 9bre 1807.
265. SHDDT Xb 502 85ᵉ *de Ligne*. Dossier 1815. Rapport 1 Xbre 1815.
266. SHDDT Xb 503 86ᵉ *de Ligne*. Dossier 1808. Rapport 25 Janvier 1808.
267. SHDDT Xb 505 88ᵉ *de Ligne*. An X a 1811. Dossier 1807. Rapport 16 9bre 1807.
268. SHDDT Xb 507 92ᵉ *de Ligne*. Dossier An 12. Rapport 22 Brumaire An 12.
269. SHDDT Xb 507 92ᵉ *de Ligne*. Dossier An 13. Rapport 8 Thermidor An 13.
270. SHDDT Xb 509 93ᵉ *de Ligne*. Dossier An 13. Rapport 20 Thermidor An 13.
271. SHDDT Xb 511 93ᵉ *de Ligne*. Dossier 1815. Historique du Corps.
272. SHDDT Xb 512 94ᵉ *régiment de Ligne*. An XII a 1810. Rapport 16 Thermidor An XIII.
273. SHDDT Xb 512 94ᵉ *de Ligne*. Dossier An 14. Rapport 26 Vend An 14.
274. SHDDT Xb 512 94ᵉ *de Ligne*. Dossier 1808. Rapport 3 Xbre 1807.

275. SHDDT Xb 512 94ᵉ *de Ligne*. Dossier 1808. Rapport 29 Fevrier 1808.
276. SHDDT Xb 512 94ᵉ *de Ligne*. Dossier 1808. Etat de Prix 3 Xbre 1807.
277. SHDDT Xb 514 95ᵉ *de Ligne*. An XI a 1811. Dossier 1807. Rapport 27e 9re 1807.
278. SHDDT Xb 516 96ᵉ *de Ligne*. Dossier 1808. Rapport 15 Décembre 1807.
279. SHDDT Xb 518 100ᵉ *de Ligne*. An XII a 1812. Dossier An XIII. Rapport 20 Vend An XIII.
280. SHDDT Xb 518 100ᵉ *de Ligne*. Dossier 1807. Rapport 31 8bre 1807.
281. SHDDT Xb 519 100ᵉ *régiment d'infanterie de la Ligne*. 1812 à 1815. Dossier 1815. Historique du Corps.
282. SHDDT Xb 520 101ᵉ *de Ligne*. Dossier 1808. Rapport 15 Juillet.
283. SHDDT GR 2C 275 habillement.
284. SHDDT Xb 520 101ᵉ *de Ligne*. Dossier 1808. Rapport 6 Mars 1808.
285. SHDDT Xb 520 101ᵉ *de Ligne*. Dossier 1808. Rapport 15 Juin 1808.
286. SHDDT Xb 522 102ᵉ *de Ligne*. Dossier An 13. Rapport 8 Vend An 13.
287. SHDDT Xb 522 102ᵉ *de Ligne*. Dossier An 14. Rapport 18 Frimaire An 14.
288. SHDDT Xb 522 102ᵉ *de Ligne*. Dossier 1808. Rapport 7 Mars 1808.
289. SHDDT Xb 524 103ᵉ *de Ligne*. An XI a 1811. Dossier 1807. Rapport 7 9bre 1807.
290. SHDDT Xb 527 105ᵉ *de Ligne*. Dossier An 13. Rapport 17 Vend An 13.
291. SHDDT GR 2C 275 habillement.
292. SHDDT Xb 527 105ᵉ *de Ligne*. Dossier 1808. Rapport 28 Janvier 1808.
293. SHDDT Xb 529 106ᵉ *de Ligne*. Dossier An 13. Rapport 15 Fructidor An 13.
294. SHDDT Xb 529 106ᵉ *de Ligne*. Dossier 1807. Rapport an 1807.
295. SHDDT Xb 529 106ᵉ *de Ligne*. Dossier 1808. Rapport 4 Janvier 1808.
296. SHDDT Xb 529 106ᵉ *de Ligne*. Dossier 1808. Rapport 5 Janvier 1808.
297. SHDDT Xb 529 106ᵉ *de Ligne*. Dossier 1809. Rapport 1 Juin 1809.
298. SHDDT Xb 532 108ᵉ *de Ligne*. Dossier An 13. Rapport 18 Vend An 13.
299. SHDDT Xb 532 108ᵉ *de Ligne*. Dossier An 13. Rapport 25 Thermidor An 13.
300. SHDDT Xb 532 108ᵉ *de Ligne*. Dossier 1808. Rapport 30 Novembre 1807.
301. SHDDT Xb 534 111ᵉ *de Ligne*. Dossier 1808. Rapport 23 Novembre 1807.
302. SHDDT Xb 534 111ᵉ *de Ligne*. Dossier 1808. Etat de prix des effets 23 Novembre 1807.
303. SHDDT GR 2C 518 Résume d'revue 1 Mai 1811.
304. SHDDT Xb 536 112ᵉ *de Ligne*.
305. Luis Sorando Muzas pers comm citing AHN, Estado 8612, exp. 350, rapport 27 Janvier 1809.
306. Luis Sorando Muzas pers comm citing AHN, Estado 8612, exp. 350, rapport 27 Janvier 1809.
307. Luis Sorando Muzas pers comm citing AHN, Estado 8612, exp. 350, rapport 27 Janvier 1809.
308. Luis Sorando Muzas pers comm citing AHN, Estado 8612, exp. 350, rapport 27 Janvier 1809.
309. Luis Sorando Muzas pers comm citing AHN, Estado 8612, exp. 350, rapport 27 Janvier 1809.
310. SHDDT Xb 548 122ᵉ *de Ligne*. 1809 à 1814.
311. SHDDT Xb 354 6ᵉ *de Ligne*. Dossier 1811. Rapport 25 8bre 1811.

Chapter 10

1. SHDDT Xb 342 1e regiment d'infanterie de la Ligne. Rapport 1 Juin 1809
2. SHDDT Xb 347 3ᵉ *de Ligne* An XII a 1810. Dossier An XII. Rapport 3 Brumaire An XIII.
3. SHDDT Xb 347 3ᵉ *de Ligne* An XII a 1810. Dossier An XII. Rapport 18 Thermidor An XIII.
4. SHDDT Xb347 3ᵉ *de Ligne* An XII a 1810. Dossier 1807. Rapport 1 9bre 1807.
5. Bibliothèque Musée de l'Armée. Fonds Rousselot. Infanterie de la Ligne. Extraits de Livre d'Ordres du Colonel Schobert.
6. SHDDT Xb 355 6ᵉ *de Ligne* 1812 a 1815. Dossier 1815. Rapport 5 Fevrier 1821.
7. SHDDT Xb 356 7ᵉ *de Ligne*. An 12 a 1810. Dossier 1807. Rapport 11 Novembre 1807.
8. SHDDT Xb 356 7ᵉ *de Ligne*. An 12 a 1810. Dossier 1807.
9. SHJDDT Xb 356. An 12 a 1810. Dossier 1807. Rapport 11 Novembre 1807.
10. SHDDT Xb 358 8ᵉ *de Ligne* 1792 a 1811. Dossier An 13. Rapport 5 Vend AN 13.

11. SHDDT Xb 360 9ᵉ *de Ligne*. Dossier 1809. Rapport 7 Juin 1809.
12. SHDDT Xb 367 12 *de Ligne* 1792 a 1808. Dossier 1807.
13. SHDDT Xb 378 16ᵉ *de Ligne*. Dossier An 13. Rapport 6 Ven An 13.
14. SHDDT Xb 378 16ᵉ *de Ligne*. Dossier 1808. Rapport 22 Novembre 1807.
15. SHDDT GR 2C 518.
16. SHDDT Xb 383 18ᵉ *de Ligne*. Dossier An 13. Rapport 3 Therm An 13.
17. SHDDT Xb 383 18ᵉ *de Ligne*. Dossier 1807. Rapport 4 Novembre 1807.
18. SHDDT Xb 387 19e régiment *de Ligne*. Dossier 1815. Rapport 16 Janvier 1821.
19. SHDDT Xb 391 21ᵉ *de Ligne*. Dossier 1808. Rapport 1 Décembre 1807.
20. SHDDT XB 397 24e *de Ligne* An XII a 1809. Dossier 1807. Rapport 1 8bre 1808.
21. SHDDT Xb 401 26ᵉ *de Ligne*. Dossier 1808. Rapport 27 Fevrier 1808
22. SHDDT Xb 412 32e *de Ligne*. Dossier 1814. Rapport 1 Aout 1814.
23. SHDDT Xb 418 35ᵉ *de Ligne*. Dossier 1809. Rapport 1 Juin 1809.
24. SHDDT Xb 420 36ᵉ *de Ligne*. Dossier 1808. Rapport 27 Décembre 1807.
25. SHDDT Xb 421 36ᵉ *de Ligne* 1812 a 1815. Dossier 1814. Rapport 1 7bre 1814.
26. SHDDT Xb 422 37ᵉ *de Ligne*. Dossier An 13. Rapport 1 Messidor An 13.
27. SHDDT Xb 435 45ᵉ *de Ligne* An XII a 1811. Dossier An XIII. Rapport 18 Fructidor An XIII.
28. SHDDT Xb 436 45ᵉ *de Ligne*. Dossier 1815.
29. SHDDT Xb 437 46ᵉ *de Ligne* An XII a 1811. Dossier 1807. Rapport 20 Xbre 1807.
30. SHDDT Xb 438 46ᵉ *de Ligne* 1812 a 1815. Dossier 1814. Rapport 1 Aout 1814.
31. SHDDT Xb 443 50ᵉ *de Ligne*. Dossier 1808. Rapport 20 Décembre 1807.
32. SHDDT Xb 454 55ᵉ *regiment de Ligne*. An XII a 1809. Dossier 1807. Rapport 15 Xbre 1807.
33. SHDDT Xb 459 57ᵉ *de Ligne* An XII a 1811. Dossier An XIII. Rapprt 6 Fructidor AN XIII.
34. SHDDT Xb 465 59ᵉ *de Ligne* 1812 a 1815. Dossier 1815. Rapport 29 7bre 1815.
35. SHDDT XB 397 24ᵉ *de Ligne* An XII a 1809. Dossier 1807. Rapport 1 8bre 1808.
36. SHDDT Xb 477 65ᵉ *de Ligne* 1812 a 1815, Dossier 1815. Rapport 13 Avril 1819.
37. Prints, drawings, and watercolours from the Anne S.K. Brown Military Collection. Port-Aigle du 75ᵉ *de Ligne* bdr: 225232.
38. SHDDT Xb 489 75ᵉ *de Ligne* An XII a 1811. Dossier 1806.
39. SHDDT Xb 489 75ᵉ *de Ligne* An XII a 1811. Dossier 1806. Rapport 25 7bre 1806.
40. SHDDT Xb 493 79ᵉ *régiment de Ligne*. Dossier An 13. Rapport 16 Vend An 13.
41. SHDDT Xb 493 79ᵉ *de Ligne*. Dossier 1808. Rapport 20 Janvier 1808.
42. SHDDT Xb 496 81ᵉ *de Ligne* 1812 a 1815. Dossier 1815. Rapport 29 Septembre 1819.
43. SHDDT Xb 496 81ᵉ *de Ligne* 1812 a 1815. Dossier 1815. Rapport 20 Septembre 1819.
44. SHDDT Xb 518 100ᵉ *de Ligne* An XII a 1812. Dossier An XIII. Rapport 20 Vend An XIII.
45. SHDDT Xb 519 100ᵉ *régiment d'infanterie de la Ligne* 1813 a 1815. Historique du Corps.
46. SHDDT Xb 523 103ᵉ *de Ligne*. Dossier An 13. Rapport 8 Vend An 13.
47. SHDDT XB 397 24ᵉ *de Ligne* An XII a 1809. Dossier 1807. Rapport 1 8bre 1808.
48. SHDDT Xb 529 106ᵉ *de Ligne*. Dossier 1809. Rapport 1 Juine 1809.
49. SHDDT Xb 364 10ᵉ *de Ligne* 1813 a 1815. Dossier 1814.
50. SHDDT Xb 546 121ᵉ *de Ligne* 1808 a 1814. Dossier 1814. Rapport 15 Janvier 1816.
51. Bibliothèque Musee de l'Armée. Fonds Rousselot. Infanterie de la Ligne. Extraits de Livre d'Ordres du 64ᵉ *de Ligne*, pp.3–4. See Also, Ibid. Order book of Colonel Schobert p.10. SHDDT C2 222 Ordre du Jour 6 Messidor An 13.
52. SHDDT Xb 342 1e régiment d'infanterie de la Ligne. Rapport 17 Juin 1808
53. SHDDT Xb 342 1e régiment d'infanterie de la Ligne. Rapport 13 Mars 1808
54. SHDDT Xb 344 2ᵉ *de Ligne*. Dossier 1808. Rapport 26 9bre 1807
55. SHDDT Xb 344 2ᵉ *de Ligne*. Dossier 1808. Rapport 26 9bre 1807
56. Bibliothèque Musée de l'Armée. Fonds Rousselot. Infanterie de la Ligne. Extraits de Livre d'Ordres du Colonel Schobert.
57. SHDDT Xb 348 3ᵉ *régiment de Ligne* 1813 a 1815. Historique du Corps.

58. SHDDT Xb 349 4ᵉ *de Ligne*. Dossier 1808. Rapport 1 Novembre 1807.
59. SHDDT Xb 355 6ᵉ *de Ligne* 1812 a 1815. Dossier 1815. Rapport 5 Fevrier 1821.
60. SHDDT Xb 356 7ᵉ *de Ligne*. An 12 a 1810. Dossier 1807.
61. SHDDT Xb 362 10ᵉ *de Ligne*. Dossier 1808. Rapport 30 Juin 1808.
62. SHDDT Xb 367 12ᵉ *de Ligne*. Dossier 1808. Rapport 21 Mars 1808.
63. SHDDT Xb370 13ᵉ *de Ligne*. Dossier 1808. Rapport 7 Janvier 1808.
64. SHDDT Xb 375 15ᵉ *de Ligne* An XII a 1811. Dossier 1808. Rapport 13 Fevrier 1808.
65. SHDDT Xb 375 15ᵉ *de Ligne* An XII a 1811. Dossier 1806. Lettre Ministre de Guerre 27 Janvier 1806.
66. SHDDT Xb 375 15ᵉ *de Ligne* An XII a 1811. Dossier 1808. Rapport 13 Fevrier 1808.
67. SHDDT Xb 378 16ᵉ *de Ligne*. Dossier 1808. Rapport 22 Novembre 1807.
68. SHDDT Xb 380 17ᵉ *de Ligne* An XII a 1807. Dossier 1808. Rapport 1 Janvier 1808.
69. SHDDT Xb 383 18ᵉ *de Ligne* An XII a 1809. Dossier 1808. Rapport 4 Novembre 1807.
70. SHDDT Xb 386 19ᵉ *regiment de Ligne*. An XII a 1812. Dossier 1807. Rapport 27 Décembre 1807.
71. SHDDT Xb 387 19ᵉ *regiment de Ligne*. Dossier 1815. Rapport 16 Janvier 1821.
72. SHDDT Xb 388 20ᵉ *de Ligne*. Dossier 1808. Rapport 29 Mai 1808.
73. SHDDT Xb 401 26ᵉ *de Ligne*. Dossier 1808. Rapport 27 Fevrier 1808.
74. SHDDT Xb 403 27ᵉ *de Ligne*. An 12 a 1811. Dossier 1807. Inspection 30 Novembre 1807.
75. SHDDT Xb 407 29ᵉ *de Ligne*. Dossier 1808. Rapport 17 Avril 1808.
76. SHDDT Xb 411 32ᵉ *de Ligne*. Dossier 1807. Rapport 31 Décembre 1807.
77. SHDDT Xb 412 32ᵉ *de Ligne*. Dossier 1814. Rapport 1 Aout 1814.
78. SHDDT Xb 416 34ᵉ *de Ligne*. Dossier 1808. Rapport 7 November 1807.
79. SHDDT Xb 418 35ᵉ *de Ligne*. Dossier 1808. Rapport 8 Janvier 1808.
80. SHDDT Xb 427 40ᵉ *de Ligne* An 12 a 1811. Dossier 1807. Inspection 9 Décembre 1807.
81. SHDDT Xb 431 43ᵉ *de Ligne*. Dossier 1808. Rapport 31 Xbre 1807.
82. SHDDT Xb 443 50ᵉ *de Ligne*. Dossier 1808. Rapport 20 Décembre 1807.
83. SHDDT Xb 445 51ᵉ *de Ligne*. Dossier 1808. Rapport 29 9bre 1807.
84. SHDDT Xb 450 53ᵉ *de Ligne*. Dossier 1808. Rapport 31 Juillet.
85. SHDDT Xb 452 54ᵉ *de Ligne*. An XII a 1811. Dossier 1807. Rapport 30 9bre 1807.
86. SHDDT Xb 454 55ᵉ *régiment de Ligne*.
87. SHDDT Xb 457 56ᵉ *de Ligne* 1808 a 1813. Dossier 1813. Rapport 27 9bre 1807.
88. SHDDT Xb 461 58ᵉ *régiment de Ligne*.
89. SHDDT Xb 463 59ᵉ *de Ligne*. Dossier 1808. Rapport 4 Avril 1808.
90. SHDDT Xb 466 60ᵉ *de Ligne*. Dossier 1808. Rapport 27 Janvier 1808.
91. SHDDT Xb 472 63ᵉ *de Ligne* An XII a 1811. Dossier 1807. Rapport 31 Janvier 1808.
92. SHDDT Xb 474 64ᵉ *de Ligne*. An XII a 1808. Dossier 1807. Rapport 9 Novembre 1807.
93. SHDDT Xb 480 67ᵉ *de Ligne*. Dossier 1808. Rapport 7 Décembre 1807.
94. SHDDT Xb 485 70ᵉ *de Ligne*. Dossier 1808. Rapport 10 Fevrier 1808.
95. SHDDT Xb 487 72ᵉ *de Ligne*. Dossier 1808. Rapport 30 Novembre 1807.
96. SHDDT Xb 489 75ᵉ *de Ligne* An XII a 1811. Dossier 1807. Rapport 6 Janvier 1808.
97. SHDDT Xb 493 79ᵉ *de Ligne*. Dossier 1808. Rapport 20 Janvier 1808.
98. SHDDT Xb 497 82ᵉ *de Ligne*. Dossier 1808. Rapport 8 Mars 1808.
99. SHDDT Xb 500 84ᵉ *de Ligne*. Dossier 1815. Historique du Corps a 1820.
100. SHDDT Xb 501 85ᵉ *de Ligne* An XII a 1811. Dossier 1807. Rapport 1 Xbre 1815.
101. SHDDT Xb 503 86ᵉ *de Ligne*. Dossier 1808. Rapport 25 Janvier 1808.
102. SHDDT Xb 505 88ᵉ *de Ligne* An X a 1811. Dossier 1807. Rapport 16 9bre 1807.
103. SHDDT Xb 511 93ᵉ *régiment d'infanterie de la Ligne* 1815. Historique du Corps.
104. SHDDT Xb 516 96ᵉ *de Ligne*. Dossier 1808. Rapport 15 Décembre 1807.
105. SHDDT Xb 519 100ᵉ *régiment d'infanterie de la Ligne*. Dossier 1815. Historique du Corps.
106. SHDDT Xb 520 101ᵉ *de Ligne*. Dossier 1808. Rapport 15 Juin 1808.
107. SHDDT Xb 522 102ᵉ *de Ligne*. Dossier 1808. Rapport 7 Mars 1808.

108. SHDDT Xb 524 103ᵉ *de Ligne* An XI a 1811. Dossier 1807. Rapport 7 9bre 1807.
109. SHDDT Xb 527 105ᵉ *de Ligne*. Dossier 1808. Rapport 28 Janvier 1808.
110. SHDDT Xb 534 111ᵉ *de Ligne*. Dossier 1808. Rapport 23 Novembre 1807.
111. SHDDT 342 1ᵉ *de Ligne*. Dossier 1808. Rapport 28 Juin 1808.
112. SHDDT Xb 345 2ᵉ *de Ligne* 1808 a 1814. Dossier 1808. Lettre 28 9bre 1807.
113. SHDDT Xb 347 3ᵉ *de Ligne*. Dossier 1808. Rapport 3 Novembre 1807.
114. SHDDT Xb 349 4ᵉ *régiment d'infanterie de la Ligne*. Rapport 1 Novembre 1807.
115. SHDDT Xb 352 5ᵉ *régiment d'infanterie de la Ligne*. Rapport 18 Janvier 1808.
116. SHDDT Xb 353 6ᵉ *de Ligne* Dossier 1808. Rapport 5 Mars 1808.
117. SHDDT Xb 356 7ᵉ *de Ligne*. An 12 a 1810. Dossier 1807.
118. SHDDT Xb 358 8ᵉ *de Ligne*. Dossier 1807.
119. SHDDT Xb 360 9ᵉ *de Ligne*. Dossier 1808. Rapport 11 Janvier 1808.
120. SHDDT Xb 362 10ᵉ *de Ligne*. Dossier 1808. Rapport 30 Juin 1808.
121. SHDDT Xb 367 12ᵉ *de Ligne*. Dossier 1808. Rapport 21 Mars 1808.
122. SHDDT Xb370 13ᵉ *de Ligne*. Dossier 1808. Rapport 7 Janvier 1808.
123. SHDDT Xb 375 15ᵉ *de Ligne*. Dossier 1808. Rapport 13 Fevrier 1808.
124. SHDDT Xb 378 16ᵉ *de Ligne*. Dossier 1808. Rapport 22 Novembre 1807.
125. SHDDT Xb 381 17ᵉ *de Ligne*. Dossier 1808. Rapport 1 Janvier 1808.
126. SHDDT Xb 383 18ᵉ *de Ligne*. Dossier 1808. Rapport 4 Novembre 1807.
127. SHDDT Xb 385 19ᵉ *de Ligne*. Dossier 1808. Rapport 1 Janvier 1808.
128. SHDDT Xb 388 20ᵉ *de Ligne*. Dossier 1808. Rapport 13 Mars 1808.
129. SHDDT Xb 391 21ᵉ *de Ligne*. Dossier 1807. Rapport 1 Décembre 1807.
130. SHDDT Xb 393 22ᵉ *de Ligne*. Dossier 1808. Rapport 21 Décembre 1807.
131. SHDDT Xb 395 23ᵉ *de Ligne*. Dossier 1808. Rapport 19 Janvier 1808.
132. SHDDT Xb 397 24ᵉ *de Ligne*. Dossier 1808. Rapport 29 Janvier 1808.
133. SHDDT Xb 399 25ᵉ *de Ligne*. Dossier 1808. Rapport 27 Décembre 1807.
134. SHDDT Xb 401 26ᵉ *de Ligne*. Dossier 1808. Rapport 27 Fevrier 1808.
135. SHDDT Xb 403 27ᵉ *de Ligne*. Dossier 1808. Rapport 30 Novembre 1807.
136. SHDDT Xb 405 28ᵉ *de Ligne*. Dossier 1808. Rapport 21 Décembre 1807.
137. SHDDT Xb 407 29ᵉ *de Ligne* An XII a 1808. Dossier An XIII. Rapport 18 Brumaire An XIII.
138. Ibid. Rapport 4 Frimaire An XIV.
139. Ibid. Rapport 22 Mars 1808.
140. SHDDT Xb 409 30ᵉ *de Ligne*. Dossier 1808. Rapport 26 Novembre 1807.
141. SHDDT Xb 411 32ᵉ *de Ligne*. Dossier 1807. Rapport 31 Décembre 1807.
142. SHDDT Xb 412 32ᵉ *de Ligne*. Dossier 1814. Rapport 1 Aout 1814.
143. SHDDT Xb 413 33ᵉ *de Ligne*. Dossier 1808. Rapport 22 Novembre 1807.
144. SHDDT Xb 416 34ᵉ *de Ligne*. Dossier 1808. Rapport 7 Novembre 1807.
145. SHDDT Xb 418 35ᵉ *de Ligne*. Dossier 1808. Rapport 8 Janvier 1808.
146. SHDDT Xb 420 36ᵉ *de Ligne*. Dossier 1808. Rapport 27 Décembre 1807.
147. SHDDT Xb 424 37ᵉ *de Ligne* 1812 a 1815. Dossier 1815. Rapport 24 Mai 1821.
148. SHDDT Xb 425 39ᵉ *de Ligne*. Dossier 1808. Rapport 15 Décembre 1807.
149. SHDDT Xb 427 40ᵉ *de Ligne*. Dossier 1808. Rapport 9 Décembre 1807.
150. SHDDT Xb 429 42ᵉ *de Ligne*. Dossier 1808. Rapport 8 Fevrier 1808.
151. SHDDT Xb 421 43ᵉ *de Ligne*. Dossier 1808. Rapport 31 Décembre 1808.
152. SHDDT Xb 435 45ᵉ *de Ligne* An XII a 1811. Dossier 1807. Rapport 29 9bre 1807.
153. SHDDT Xb 437 46ᵉ *de Ligne* An XII a 1811. Dossier 1807. Rapport 20 Xbre 1807.
154. SHDDT Xb 439 47ᵉ *de Ligne*. Dossier 1808. Rapport 1 Fevrier 1808.
155. SHDDT Xb 441 48ᵉ *de Ligne*. Dossier 1808. Rapport 1 Décembre 1807.
156. SHDDT Xb 443 50ᵉ *de Ligne*. Dossier 1808. Rapport 20 Décembre 1807.
157. SHDDT Xb 445 51ᵉ *régiment de Ligne*. Dossier 1807. Rapport 23 9bre 1807.
158. SHDDT Xb 448 52ᵉ *de Ligne*. Dossier 1808. Rapport 20 April 1808.

159. SHDDT Xb 448 52ᵉ *de Ligne*. Dossier 1808. Rapport 6 Mars 1808.
160. SHDDT Xb 450 53ᵉ *de Ligne*. Dossier 1808. Rapport 31 Juillet.
161. SHDDT Xb452 54ᵉ *de Ligne*. Dossier 1808. Rapport 30 Novembre 1807.
162. SHDDT Xb 454 55ᵉ *régiment de Ligne*. Dossier 1808. Rapport 15 Décembre 1807.
163. SHDDT Xb 458 56ᵉ *de Ligne* 1810 a 1815. Dossier 1813. Rapport 27 9bre 1807.
164. SHDDT Xb 459 57ᵉ *de Ligne*. Dossier 1808. Rapport 10 9bre 1807.
165. SHDDT Xb 461 58ᵉ *de Ligne*. Dossier 1808. Rapport 5 Janvier 1808.
166. SHDDT Xb463 59ᵉ *de Ligne*. Dossier 1808. Rapport 4 Avril 1808.
167. SHDDT Xb 466 60ᵉ *de Ligne*. Dossier 1808. Rapport 27 Janvier 1808.
168. SHDDT Xb 468 61ᵉ *de Ligne*. Dossier 1808. Rapport 29 9bre 1807.
169. SHDDT Xb 470 62ᵉ *de Ligne*. Dossier 1808. Rapport 8 Juin 1808.
170. SHDDT Xb 472 63e *de Ligne* An XII a 1811. Dossier 1808.
171. SHDDT Xb 474 64e *de Ligne*. An XII a 1808. Dossier 1807. Rapport 9 Novembre 1807.
172. SHDDT Xb 476 65ᵉ *de Ligne*. Dossier 1808. Rapport 25 9bre 14807.
173. SHDDT Xb 478 66ᵉ *de Ligne*, Dossier 1808. Rapport 28 Fevrier 1808.
174. SHDDT Xb 480 67ᵉ *de Ligne*. Dossier 1808. Rapport 7 Xbre 1807.
175. SHDDT Xb 481 67ᵉ *de Ligne*. Dossier 1809. Rapport 23 7bre 1809.
176. SHDDT Xb 482 69ᵉ *de Ligne*. Dossier 1808. Rapport 30 Mars 1808.
177. SHDDT 485 70ᵉ *de Ligne*. Dossier 1808. Rapport 10 Fevrier 1808.
178. SHDDT 485 70ᵉ *de Ligne*. Dossier 1808. Rapport 14 Fevrier 1808.
179. SHDDT Xb 487 72ᵉ *de Ligne*. Dossier 1808. Rapport 30 9bre 1807.
180. SHDDT Xb 489 75ᵉ *de Ligne*. Dossier 1808. Rapport 6 Janvier 1808.
181. SHDDT Xb 491 76ᵉ *de Ligne*. Dossier 1808. Rapport 15 Xbre 1807.
182. SHDDT Xb 493 79ᵉ *de Ligne*. Dossier 1808. Rapport 20 Janvier 1808.
183. SHDDT XB 495 81ᵉ *de Ligne*. Dossier 1808 Lettre, 24 Janvier 1808.
184. SHDDT Xb 497 82ᵉ *de Ligne*. Dossier 1808. Rapport 8 Mars 1808.
185. SHDDT Xb 499 84ᵉ *de Ligne*. Dossier 1808. Rapport 14 Janvier 1808.
186. SHDDT Xb 501 85ᵉ *de Ligne*. Dossier 1808. Rapport 1 Xbre 1807.
187. SHDDT Xb 503 86ᵉ *de Ligne*. Dossier 1808. Rapport 25 Janvier 1808.
188. SHDDT Xb 505 88ᵉ *de Ligne*. Dossier 1808. Rapport 10 Novembre 1807.
189. SHDDT Xb 512 94ᵉ *de Ligne*. Dossier 1808. Rapport 3 Décembre 1807.
190. SHDDT Xb 514 95ᵉ *de Ligne*. Dossier 1808. Rapport 27 Novembre 1807.
191. SHDDT Xb516 96ᵉ *de Ligne*. Dossier 1808. Rapport 15 Décembre 1807.
192. SHDDT Xb 518 100ᵉ *de Ligne*. Dossier 1808. Rapport 31 Octobre 1807.
193. SHDDT Xb 520 101ᵉ *de Ligne*. Dossier 1808. Rapport 6 Mars 1808.
194. SHDDT Xb 520 101ᵉ *de Ligne*. Dossier 1808. Rapport 15 Juin 1808.
195. SHDDT Xb 522 102ᵉ *de Ligne*. Dossier 1808. Rapport 7 Mars 1808.
196. SHDDT Xb524 103ᵉ *de Ligne*. Dossier 1808. Rapport 9 9bre 1807.
197. SHDDT Xb 527 105ᵉ *de Ligne*. Dossier 1808. Rapport 28 Janvier 1808.
198. SHDDT Xb 529 106ᵉ *de Ligne*. Dossier 1808. Rapport 4 Janvier 1808.
199. SHDDT Xb 532 108ᵉ *de Ligne*. Dossier 1808. Rapport 30 Novembre 1807.
200. SHDDT Xb 534 111ᵉ *de Ligne*. Dossier 1808. Rapport 23 Novembre 1807.
201. AN AF IV 283-297 Registre Correspondance Comte Daru. Rapport de Daru sur les distributions de drap et *capotes* faites au Troupes, 14 Mars 1807.
202. Ibid. Berthier to Daru 21 Octobre 1806.
203. AN AF IV Registre Correspondance Comte Daru. Daru to Napoleon 25 Octobre 1806.
204. AN AF IV 283–297 Registre Correspondance Comte Daru. Daru to Napoléon 28 Octobre 1806.
205. Ibid. Rapport 25 Décembre 1806.
206. Ibid. Ordre du Jour 1 Novembre 1806.
207. Ibid. Rapport 16 Novembre 1806.
208. Ibid. Rapport 14 Novembre 1806.

209. SHDDT GR 2C 275 Habillement. Marche 25 Décembre 1806.
210. AN AF IV 283-297 Registre Correspondance Comte Daru. Ordre 23 Novembre 1806.
211. Ibid. Rapport de Daru sur les distributions de drap et *capotes* faites au Troupes, 14 Mars 1807.
212. SHDDT GR 2C 275 Habillement. Décret 18 Janvier 1807.
213. Ibi Rapport de Daru sur les distributions d'habillement faites au Troupes, 29 Mai 1807.
214. Ibid. Rapport 8 Avril 1808.
215. AN AF IV 283-297 Registre Correspondance Comte Daru. Rapport de Daru sur les distributions d'habillement faites au Troupes, 11 Juillet 1807.
216. AN AF IV Registre Correspondance Comte Daru. Rapport 21 Décembre 1808.
217. AN AF IV 1600B plaquette 2. Mémoire sur les approvisionnements et l'organisation administrative de l'armée de Saint-Omer adressé au ministre de la Guerre Berthier par Pierre Daru, intendant général, le 9 prairial an XI.
218. AN/AF/IV/1628.

Bibliography

Printed Sources

Anon *Reglement Arête pour le Roi pour l'habillement et l'equipment des ses troupes* Imprimerie Royale: Paris, 1779

Anon *Instruction pour servir à expliquer les principes d'après lesquels on ete executes les différends modeles de coiffure, Habillement & equipment envoys a chacun des Regiments d'infanterie.* Imprimerie Royale: Paris, 1787

Anon, *Ordonnance du 12 août 1788*, Ordonnances militaires (1788–1789), Paris

Anon *Les Guides des Sous-officiers de L'infanterie Francaise.* 2e Edition Leroy-Berge: Paris, 1809

Etienne Alexandre Bardin *Manuel d'infanterie, ou Résumé de tous les règlements, décrets, usages, renseignements concernant l'infanterie, dans lequel se trouve renfermé tout ce que doivent savoir les sergents et caporaux.* Chez Magimel: Paris, 1808

Etienne Alexandre Bardin *Manuel d'infanterie, ou Résumé de tous les règlements, décrets, usages, renseignements concernant l'infanterie, dans lequel se trouve renfermé tout ce que doivent savoir les sergents et caporaux.* Chez Magimel: Paris, 1813

Etienne Alexandre Bardin *Mémorial de l'officier d'infanterie.* Chez Magimel: Paris, 1813

Honoré Hugues Berriat, *Législation militaire* A. Alexandrie: Paris, 1812, 3 volumes

Boucquet de Beauval 'Les Souvenirs du lieutenant-colonel Boucquet de Beauval 1804–1830' in *Carnets de la Sabretache* 1897, pp.298–310

Alison Matthews David, 2003. *Decorated Men: Fashioning the French Soldier, 1852–1914.* In *Fashion Theory* Volume 7, pp.3–38.

Paul Lindsay Dawson *Napoleon's Imperial Guard Uniforms and Equipment: The Infantry.* Frontline: Barnsley, 2019

Aron Guverich, 'The French Historical Revolution: The Annales School', in Hodder et al (1995), *Interpreting Archaeology*, Routledge, London and New York, pp.158–161.

Les Gupil *Adminstrations du Masses,* Chez Magimel: Paris, 1812

Malibran *Guide a l'Usage des Artistes et des Costumiers Contenant la Description Des Uniformes de l Armée Française de 1780 à 1848.* Combet & Cie: Paris. 1904,

Amy Miller, *Dressed to Kill* London: National Maritime Museum, 2021

Archive Sources

Bibliothèque Musée de l'Armée
Manuscripts and printed books, Volume 1 du projet de règlement sur l'habillement du major Bardin
Fonds Rousselot

Archives Nationales
AN/AF/IV/1116
AN/AF/IV/1179
AN/AF/IV/1600B plaquette 2 État des effets de campements nécessaires pour l'armée des Côtes
AN/AF/IV1632/2
AN/AF/IV/4837

Service Historique de la Armée de Terre
SHDDT GR 1M 275 Habillement
SHDDT GR 1M 1962 Fonds Preval
SHDDT GR 2C 223 Correspondance et Ordres Marechal Soult
SHDDT GR 2C 412 Registre d'Ordres du 64e *de Ligne*
SHDDT GR 2C 518
SHDDT GR 2C 275 Habillement
SHDDT GR 21 YC 31 3e *régiment d'infanterie de Ligne* dit *régiment du Dauphin*, 16 Juillet 1814–17 Décembre 1814 (matricules 1 à 1 800)
SHDDT GR 21 YC 332 37e *régiment d'infanterie de Ligne*, 15 Janvier 1809–20 Février 1812 (matricules 7 801 à 9 600)
SHDDT Xb 342 1e *régiment d'infanterie de la Ligne*
SHDDT Xb 344 2e *de Ligne*
SHDDT Xb 345 2e *de Ligne*
SHDDT Xb 346 2e *de Ligne*. 1814–1815
SHDDT Xb 347 3e *de Ligne*. An XII a 1810
SHDDT Xb 348 3e *régiment de Ligne*. 1813 à 1815
SHDDT Xb 349 4e *régiment d'infanterie de la Ligne*
SHDDT Xb 352 5e *régiment d'Infanterie de la Ligne*
SHDDT Xb 353 6e *de Ligne*
SHDDT Xb 356 7e *de Ligne*. An 12 à 1810
SHDDT Xb 358 8e *de Ligne* 1792 à 1811
SHDDT Xb 360 9e *de Ligne*
SHDDT Xb 361 9e *de Ligne*
SHDDT Xb 362 10e *de Ligne*
SHDDT Xb 365 11e *de Ligne*
SHDDT Xb 367 12e *de Ligne*. 1792 à 1808
SHDDT Xb 368 12e *de Ligne*. 1808 à 1812
SHDDT Xb 369 12e *de Ligne*. 1812 à 1815
SHDDT Xb 370 13e *de Ligne*
SHDDDT Xb 373 14e *de Ligne*. An XII à 1811
SHDDT Xb 375 15e *de Ligne*. An XII à 1811
SHDDT Xb 378 16e *de Ligne*
SHDDT Xb 380 17e *de Ligne*
SHDDT Xb 381 17e *de Ligne*
SHDDT Xb 383 18e *de Ligne*. An XII a 1811
SHDDT Xb 386 19e *régiment de Ligne*. An XII a 1812
SHDDT Xb 387 19e *de Ligne*. 1812 à 1815
SHDDT Xb 388 20e *de Ligne*
SHDDT Xb 391 21e *de Ligne*. An XII a 1811
SHDDT Xb 392 21e *de Ligne*.1811 à 1815
SHDDT Xb 393 22e *de Ligne*. An XII a 1811
SHDDT Xb 395 23e *de Ligne*
SHDDT XB 397 24e *de Ligne*. An XII a 1809
SHDDT Xb 398 24e *de Ligne*. 1809 à 1812
SHDDT Xb 399 25e *de Ligne*. An XII a 1808
SHDDT Xb 401 26e *de Ligne*
SHDDT Xb 403 27e *de Ligne*. An 12 à 1811
SHDDT Xb 405 28e *de Ligne*. An 12 à 1810
SHDDT Xb 407 29e *de Ligne*
SHDDT Xb 409 30e *de Ligne*. An 12 à 1808

SHDDT Xb 410 30ᵉ *de Ligne*. 1808 à 1815
SHDDT Xb 411 32ᵉ *de Ligne*
SHDDT Xb 412 32ᵉ *de Ligne*
SHDDT Xb 413 33ᵉ *de Ligne*. An 12 à 1808
SHDDT Xb 414 33ᵉ *de Ligne* 1808 à 1813
SHDDT Xb 415 33ᵉ *de Ligne* 1813 à 1815
SHDDT Xb 416 34ᵉ *de Ligne*. An 12 à 1811
SHDDT Xb 417 34ᵉ *de Ligne*. 1812 à 1815
SHDDT Xb 418 35ᵉ *de Ligne*
SHDDT Xb 420 36ᵉ *de Ligne*. An XII à 1811
SHDDT Xb 421 36ᵉ *de Ligne*. 1811 à 1815
SHDDT Xb 422 37ᵉ *de Ligne*
SHDDT Xb 424 37ᵉ *de Ligne*. 1812 à 1815
SHDDT Xb 425 39ᵉ *de Ligne*
SHDDT Xb 427 40ᵉ *de Ligne*. An 12 à 1811
SHDDT Xb 429 42ᵉ *de Ligne*. An XII à 1811
SHDDT Xb 431 43ᵉ *de Ligne*
SHDDT Xb 435 45ᵉ *de Ligne*. An XII à 1811
SHDDT Xb 436 45ᵉ *de Ligne*. 1811 à 1815
SHDDT Xb 437 46ᵉ *de Ligne*. An XII à 1811
SHDDT Xb 438 46ᵉ *de Ligne* 1812 à 1815
SHDDT Xb 439 47ᵉ *de Ligne*
SHDDT Xb 444 48ᵉ *de Ligne*
SHDDT Xb 442 48ᵉ *de Ligne*
SHDDT Xb 443 50ᵉ *de Ligne*. An12 à 1811
SHDDT Xb 444 50ᵉ *de Ligne*. 1811 à 1815
SHDDT Xb 445 51ᵉ *de Ligne*
SHDDT Xb 448 52ᵉ *de Ligne*
SHDDT Xb 450 53ᵉ *de Ligne*
SHDDT Xb 452 54ᵉ *de Ligne*. An XII à 1811
SHDDT Xb 454 55ᵉ *régiment de Ligne*. An XII à 1809
SHDDT Xb 455 55ᵉ *de Ligne*. 1809 à 1815
SHDDT Xb 456 56ᵉ *de Ligne*. An XII à 1809
SHDDT Xb 457 56ᵉ *de Ligne*. 1808 à 1813
SHDDT Xb 459 57ᵉ *de Ligne*. An XII à 1811
SHDDT Xb 461 58ᵉ *régiment de Ligne*
SHDDT Xb 463 59ᵉ *de Ligne*. An XII à 1809
SHDDT Xb 464 59ᵉ *de Ligne*. 1809 à 1812
SHDDT Xb 465 59ᵉ *de Ligne* 1812 à 1815
SHDDT Xb 466 60ᵉ *de Ligne*. An XII à 1811
SHDDT Xb 467 60ᵉ *de Ligne*. 1812 à 1815
SHDDT Xb 468 61ᵉ *de Ligne*
SHDDT Xb 469 62ᵉ *de Ligne*. An 12 à 1808
SHDDT Xb 470 62ᵉ *de Ligne*. 1808 à 1810
SHDDT Xb 471 62ᵉ *de Ligne*. 1810 à 1815
SHDDT Xb 472 63ᵉ *de Ligne*. An XII à 1811
SHDDT Xb 473 63ᵉ *de Ligne*. 1811 à 1815
SHDDT Xb 474 64ᵉ *de Ligne*. An XII a 1809
SHDDT Xb 475 64ᵉ *de Ligne*. 1810 à 1815
SHDDT Xb 476 65ᵉ *de Ligne*
SHDDT Xb 477 65ᵉ *de Ligne*. 1812 à 1815

SHDDT Xb 478 66ᵉ *de Ligne*
SHDDT Xb 480 67ᵉ *de Ligne*
SHDDT Xb 482 69ᵉ *de Ligne*
SHDDT Xb 485 70ᵉ *de Ligne*
SHDDT Xb 487 72ᵉ *de Ligne*
SHDDT Xb 489 75ᵉ *de Ligne* An XII à 1811
SHDDT Xb 491 76ᵉ *de Ligne*
SHDDT Xb 493 79ᵉ *de Ligne*
SHDDT Xb 495 81ᵉ *de Ligne*. An 12 à 1812
SHDDT Xb 496 81ᵉ *de Ligne*. 1812 à 1815
SHDDT Xb 497 82ᵉ *de Ligne*
SHDDT Xb 499 84ᵉ *de Ligne*
SHDDT Xb 500 84ᵉ *de Ligne*
SHDDT Xb 501 85ᵉ *de Ligne*. An XII à 1811
SHDDT Xb 502 85ᵉ *de Ligne*. 1812 à 1815
SHDDT Xb 503 86ᵉ *de Ligne*
SHDDT Xb 505 88ᵉ *de Ligne*. An X à 1811
SHDDT Xb 507 92ᵉ *de Ligne*
SHDDT Xb 509 93ᵉ *de Ligne*
SHDDT Xb 510 93ᵉ *de Ligne*
SHDDT Xb 511 93ᵉ *de Ligne*
SHDDT Xb 512 94ᵉ *régiment de Ligne*. An XII à 1810
SHDDT Xb 514 95ᵉ *de Ligne*. An XI à 1811
SHDDT Xb 516 96ᵉ *de Ligne*
SHDDT Xb 518 100ᵉ *de Ligne*
SHDDT Xb 519 100ᵉ *régiment d'Infanterie de la Ligne*. 1812 à 1815
SHDDT Xb 520 101ᵉ *de Ligne*
SHDDT Xb 522 102ᵉ *de Ligne*
SHDDT Xb 524 103ᵉ *de Ligne*. An XI à 1811
SHDDT Xb 527 105ᵉ *de Ligne*
SHDDT Xb 529 106ᵉ *de Ligne*
SHDDT Xb 532 108ᵉ *de Ligne*
SHDDT Xb 534 111ᵉ *de Ligne*
SHDDT Xb 536 112ᵉ *de Ligne*
SHDDT Xb 548 122ᵉ *de Ligne*. 1809 à 1814
SHDDT Xd 11 3ᵉ *régiment d'Artillerie à Pied*
SHDDT Xs 525
SHDDT Xs 526
SHDDT Xs 528

Dear Reader,

We hope you have enjoyed this book, but why not share your views on social media? You can also follow our pages to see more about our other products: facebook.com/penandswordbooks or follow us on X @penswordbooks

You can also view our products at www.pen-and-sword.co.uk (UK and ROW) or www.penandswordbooks.com (North America).

To keep up to date with our latest releases and online catalogues, please sign up to our newsletter at: www.pen-and-sword.co.uk/newsletter

If you would like a printed catalogue with our latest books, then please email: enquiries@pen-and-sword.co.uk or telephone: 01226 734555 (UK and ROW) or email: uspen-and-sword@casematepublishers.com or telephone: (610) 853-9131 (North America).

We respect your privacy and we will only use personal information to send you information about our products.

Thank you!